T0248343

# HIGHER GROUND

an imprint of Amplify | Publishing Group

# www.amplifypublishinggroup.com

**Photo credits:**
» Page 110: Courtesy UC Davis.
» Page 148: Courtesy the U.S. Green Building Council
» Page 170: Photo by Max Whittaker/Reuters
» Page 228: Photo by Tanya Perez/*Davis Enterprise*
» Page 256: Photo by John Nikolau
» All other photos courtesy of the author.

**For more information, please contact:**
Amplify Publishing, an imprint of Amplify Publishing Group
620 Herndon Parkway, Suite 320
Herndon, VA 20170
info@amplifypublishing.com

Library of Congress Control Number: 2021917263

CPSIA Code: PRV0223A

ISBN-13: 978-1-68401-723-2

Printed in the United States

To my mom and my husband.

# HIGHER GROUND

*My American Dreams and Nightmares
in the Hidden Halls of Academia*

**LINDA KATEHI**, PHD

*Chancellor Emerita, University of California, Davis*

an imprint of Amplify Publishing Group

# CONTENTS

Salamis, the island my family lived on for almost seven centuries. Its solemn name and hard-minded and hard-working people have survived through 3,500 years of history.

## CHAPTER ONE

# BACK TO MY ROOTS

**August 25, 2016**

WE WERE DRIVING STOP-AND-GO ON the Bay Bridge to the San Francisco International Airport. Spyros was quiet, his left hand resting on the steering wheel and the other holding the side of his leather seat, a habit acquired from days spent driving a manual car. I put my hand over his. I felt relaxed as he firmly cupped his warm hand around mine. I looked at him and remembered again why I had loved him at first sight forty-three years ago.

It had been at a party a college friend of mine had put together at the last minute, when he had found out his parents were going to be traveling for the weekend and the house would be his to enjoy. I reluctantly decided to go, worried that most of my friends would come with their dates and I would be the oddball waiting around, alone and watching everyone else dancing and having fun.

It was December 15, 1973; a clear, warm evening in Athens that was comfortable with just a light jacket. I put my new jeans on, a plaid shirt, and a red knit jacket that I left unbuttoned in case I felt hot and wanted to take it off and tie it around my waist.

I pulled my thick and unruly brown hair back with a hairpin and put makeup around my eyes just for the party. I looked at the mirror inside the closet door and scoffed at the image I saw hanging there, with clothes too big for a thin body, looking back uncertainly and intensely with eyes too big for a small face.

I hesitated. "Well, who cares?" I grumbled as I shut the mirror door. I slipped on my boots, picked up my handbag, and ran out of the tiny flat I shared with my parents. I heard the door shut behind me as I started running down two flights of stairs.

I found myself outside of the building, breathing hard. The days were getting shorter, and this December evening, lit by a few streetlights and dressed up in many shadows, felt heavy.

It was almost an hour away from the onset of the curfew imposed a few weeks earlier on the people of Athens by the military junta that was desperately trying to avoid political gatherings and demonstrations. It was only three weeks after the events at the Polytechnic, and I had not seen or heard from many of my friends since. I wondered whether they were alive and safe. This was the first day I had planned to stay out late, just to make the point to my mother that I was too old to be told when to come back. "They will arrest you," she had screamed at me, trying to block the door.

"I'd rather have that than stay at home," I hissed at her as I ran out.

I walked quickly for a while and tried to calm down. I could hear my heavy breathing as I walked up the steep road toward the bus stop. I arrived at the bus shelter sweating from my fast pace. An old man was sitting on the bench smoking a cigarette. Deep lines showing his age covered his tired face. His eyes were almost shut as he puffed the smoke in short intervals, holding it in his lungs long enough till the nicotine filled every neuron of his brain.

"Going home?" he asked plainly, without looking at me. And then, as if he knew my answer, he added, "Me neither." He laughed strangely. "What are they gonna do to me? Arrest me? Ha! I was years in the joint after the war for killing one of the motherfuckers. I am not afraid of them."

I shrugged my shoulders and looked away. The night was beautiful under the full moon just beginning to rise behind Mount Penteli. I could see the Acropolis from where I was, still glorious, dressed in its shadowy gown, dark and serious; a true protector of the city in both war and peace and a living contradiction between a beautiful past, a horrible present, and an uncertain future, the three coexisting for centuries.

The bus screeched to a halt, and I got on, leaving the old man behind still talking to himself. I showed the driver my student ID and walked to the back of the bus. The bus was almost empty, and those few passengers occupying some of the seats were silent and avoided eye contact. Nobody talked while the bus took us from stop to stop, finally arriving at my friend's street. I was happy to get off and leave my sullen fellow passengers behind. The silence of fear was deafening. I rushed to get off the bus, sending the bus driver a nod of thanks for his whispered advice of "Stay safe."

I ran around the corner to my friend's house: a two-story building in good shape for its age. I found the front door open with a note taped to it: "Friends welcome—come in, drink, and dance—John." Standing there, unsure for a moment, I felt as if I were about to enter a different universe.

I walked into a dark room that I assumed was John's parents' living room. The furniture had been moved to the side; the rugs were rolled up and placed by the walls; and yellow, red, and blue lights were strung all around, changing colors to the music.

The air was dense with the smell of sweat, smoke, and alcohol. It took some time for my eyes to adjust to the shadowy faces, some of which gradually became familiar. I knew most of the men from my sophomore classes, but I could only guess that the young women dancing, laughing, and kissing with them were their girlfriends. I already regretted accepting John's invitation. I felt out of place, and the whole scene reminded me I was alone.

"Linda, you are here!" John shouted at me from the other side of the room as he rushed to my side. He was my height, thin with long hair down to his shoulders, glasses, and a big smile. I liked him because he was so different. Born in Congo, he understood a world that fascinated me. We both loved chess and always sat next to each other in our freshman chemistry class in the Polytechnic's big auditorium. Our hatred for chemistry was another thing that bonded us. He had a little chess set that he kept in his pocket. When the two of us got bored, he would pull it out, and we would play until the end of the lecture, sometimes a little longer.

"I will get you a drink. What do you want?" he asked.

"Gin and tonic," I said. I looked around.

"Aha, is this new? I thought you hated gin," he remarked.

"Yes, until I tried it in a bar last summer. This young Brit girl made the best gin and tonic I ever had," I responded, still looking around.

He laughed. "Do not expect that from me! You will get what you pay for." He walked off, still laughing.

The room seemed to grow bigger as my eyes adjusted, and I could see more people blending with the colorful lights as they danced to the music. *This is weird*, I thought. *Being alone at such a party says something about me. Well, what is the plan?*

I looked around the space a few times as I walked slowly across the dance floor to the other side of the room. I stopped and sensed eyes staring at me. I became aware of the source of the stare off to the side, just as I heard John's voice behind me.

"This is Spyros," I heard my friend say. I turned and took my gin and tonic. "He is my best friend from high school. A very good guy . . . he is total fun!"

Then, more quietly and suggestively, "Maybe talking to him will make my drink better than the Brit's." John then walked away.

Spyros was sitting on a rolled-up rug, wearing jeans like mine and a worn-out brown leather jacket. He did not move; he just kept looking. I sat next to him.

His Hermes profile was framed by long, brown, curly hair, and his olive-green eyes stared out at me intensely. He had a straight Greek nose over a strong, red-bearded chin supported by a broad neck and wide shoulders; his body looked thin but masculine.

"I am Linda," I heard myself say. I thought I sounded awkward.

"Do you know John?" he asked in a voice that hid a smile.

"We are friends from the Polytechnic. I study electrical engineering. You?" I responded, trying to control the high pitch in my voice.

"I'm in chemical engineering, and John's friend from high school."

"I hope you are not as boring as chemistry," I said, not believing these words that came out of my mouth.

"Probably less so than those who hate it," he replied as he pulled a pipe from his pocket and started stuffing it with tobacco from a green, square, metal box that he rested on his knee. His unpretentious style was utterly disarming and his humor unmatched—without the distasteful sexual undertones I could detect in the comments of some of my classmates when they pretended to be cool and smart. I fell for him right then.

Forty-three years later, driving and deep in thought, Spyros looked the same but older, the brightness of his olive green eyes a little hazier, the red of his beard now totally white, and the brown curls of his hair now gray. Yet he was still very attractive. His smile was sweet, his face unchanged save a few lines of wisdom etched by the years, or perhaps from always smiling in my company.

The weather that evening was warm and clear—very comfortable for summer in San Francisco. The slight breeze kept the water in the bay smooth, while gently carrying along many sailing boats, small and large, toward the mouth of the bay, where the Golden Gate Bridge, glorious in size and shape, holds the line between East and West. Red and powerful like a Chinese dragon, it stretches between the northern tip of the San Francisco Peninsula to the southern tip of Marin County, as if trying to keep the mouth of the bay from opening up to the relentless force of the Pacific, never slipping from its original purpose to keep the bay safe. The bridge stands tall: an engineering marvel that reminds us that human creativity is unbound by technology and uncompromised by resources when the mind is free to reach for the stars. This suspension bridge was imagined by Joseph Strauss in 1917 and designed ten years later by Charles Alton Ellis and Leon Moisseiff. The Golden Gate Bridge was the first structure to utilize Moisseiff's innovative "deflection theory," by which a thin, flexible roadway would bend with the wind, greatly reducing the stress transmitted via the suspension cables to the bridge towers. At 4,200 ft. (1,280m) long, the Golden Gate Bridge held the title as the longest suspension bridge in the world until 1964, when the Verrazano-Narrows Bridge was built in New York City and stole that title. Yet, the Golden Gate Bridge is still famed for being the most beautiful bridge in the United States, if not the world. Her slick body, hanging beautifully between two suspension towers, appears as a road to the stars, her narrow red path disappearing into the fog that regularly covers the bridge's two abutments. The Golden Gate Bridge is considered one of the modern marvels of the world, created during one of those rare moments in history when people felt empowered to make miracles. There are not many of these points in our history, as human nature always finds ways to constrict the imagination with a simple tool: fear.

We drove onto one of the new sections of the Bay Bridge that connects San Francisco to Oakland. The old bridge, a magnificent engineering puzzle like its more famous sister bridge, had been taken away piece by piece during the previous four years as a penalty for its failure to withstand the last big earthquake of 1989. We rarely gave any attention to this bridge, our passage always consumed by the problems of the day and the anxiety of the chronic traffic.

Nobody felt any pride in the renovation, even if construction of the new section and the dismantling of the old one had utilized the most sophisticated pieces of design software, the most modern materials, and the most inexpensive labor. It had been sad to read in the media all the criticism of this project. It felt like few cared to celebrate this amazing product of globalization; it was conceived in California, designed and manufactured in China, and constructed in San Francisco. Experts were confident that the new bridge could withstand earthquakes up to 8.0.

This project, living and breathing under our eyes, day after day, for the previous eight years, will probably be recognized eventually as one of the biggest engineering achievements in Northern California in the twenty-first century.

We were nervous, stuck in traffic on the bridge, and anxious to catch our night flight to Greece. The evening sun took a final dive into a red and purple mist, signaling the coming of a warm dusk. The city looked as if it had been born out of the earth's scorching depths, with its tall buildings of steel and glass lit up by a million lights, from small lamps under the bridges to the great chandeliers in its finest hotels and mansions.

We were ready for our trip, though we had decided to take it in a hurry. It was to be a pilgrimage back to the old country, back to the familiar islands of our childhoods and to the people who cared for us. I kept looking nervously at my iPhone as we drove, a habit I had acquired in the past few months: a fidgety play of my fingers on the shiny black surface of the device, a mental game rather than a genuine effort to learn anything new.

A Sacramento newspaper had been busy printing stories. There had been thirty-four in the past six months—thirty-four variations on the same theme.

"What are you looking at?" Spyros asked me with some hesitation in his voice.

"Nothing!" I said quietly as I pushed the phone into my bag next to my feet.

"We are going on vacation! Remember?" he said in a playful tone.

I nodded.

I knew he was not in the mood to be playful, but he was trying to calm me down.

*He worries about me*, I thought.

"Yes, the moment we get on the plane, I will turn the phone off and will keep it off for the rest of the time. I promise," I said. I took his hand and slowly raised it to my lips.

Two weeks before, I had resigned from my position as a chancellor at the University of California, Davis, after a six-month ordeal. We'd felt the need then to fly away as far as we could, to live for a few weeks in a place where we could feel safe, loved, and welcome. Those six months had placed a tremendous weight on our hearts and minds. For both of us, it had felt like living in a nightmare we could not wake up from.

Between May 15, 2009, when Spyros and I visited UC Davis for the first time, the day I was announced as the new chancellor for the campus, and August 10, 2016, the day I resigned in disgust at the actions of the University of California President Janet Napolitano, our seven-year experience became the antithesis of what I could have predicted.

The experience left me with many painful, unanswered questions. What made a university leader crush a subordinate publicly without evidence of wrongdoing? What clouded her judgment and led her to falsely accuse me and publicly threaten me with such foolishness? What made my closest collaborator, whom I had helped the most, compromise me and betray me instead of supporting me? What made a local newspaper call me "incompetent and greedy" at every opportunity they found and insist that I resign on the basis of their own made-up accusations? What made a local legislator support and mentor a small activist group called "Fire Katehi" and rally around others to join them? What could cause this behavior? There were a lot of theories offered as explanations, but most of them left me wondering. Some called it politics; others called it self-interest. I call it hatred. In the end, every explanation seemed incomplete.

I shook my head, trying to cast off these thoughts. I looked toward the Golden Gate Bridge, now totally covered by fog, and tried to fill my mind with the intense red of the Greek summer sun, hoping that it would melt my anxiety in its warmth.

The drive between the city and the airport was uneventful, as it almost always is. If you manage to escape from the traffic through the city, the rest of the way is an easy ride with very little to notice besides a group of homes built on the hill overlooking the bay. These houses have been built so close to each other that, from far away, they look like a colorful splash, something an artsy preschooler might paint on her first day in school: boxes made out of ticky-tacky, as the singer-songwriter Malvina Reynolds once characterized them.

We arrived at the airport and quietly moved through lines of busy people traveling to all places, speaking all languages, dressed in all possible ways: an explosion of colors and designs. Yet, what speaks about them is their faces, images of their identity, living time-maps of their lives where every line marks a year, every smile shows acceptance, every laugh signals happiness or contempt. Their lips speak the words, but the eyes tell the story. We have trained our brains to hide intentions behind words, but we know that our eyes are an undeniable path to our soul and tell the truth. Happiness, despair, arrogance, trust, love, hate, and, above all, fear: it is all there if we look carefully. I looked intensely at the faces of those around me. I found myself wanting to know the stories of the people who surrounded me, to learn about their pain, and be guided by their recovery.

"Do not stare at people, Mom," my daughter had once scolded me when we were traveling together. "It feels weird when someone looks at you like that."

"People fascinate me, and I cannot stop looking at them," I told her in a low voice, even though I knew that she was right.

"Yes, but they don't like it," she added in an equally low voice, looking around to see whether anyone was listening.

"Probably they are afraid they may reveal their secrets," I muttered. "Only children understand me, and they look back at me with equal curiosity!"

"Aha! So, you have found your equals," she answered with a laugh.

"You mean inquisitive?" I asked.

"No, I mean *silly*," she responded.

Two weeks earlier, I was standing in almost the same place at Oakland airport, hugging my cousin Eleni goodbye on her trip back to Greece. She had come for my daughter's wedding in July and had stayed to provide us with support during those dark days when Spyros and I needed someone to lean on. I had promised to see her soon, but I had no idea what that meant. She looked at me with a glimmer in her dark eyes showing anxiety, which she tried to hide under a faint smile that disappeared quickly.

Eleni was the older sister I never had. She made me a promise to protect me the day her toddler hands curiously touched mine under the watchful eyes of the two sisters, her mom and mine. Since then, I have very few memories without Eleni next to me. We spend all our summers together, with the exception of the year when she was in college and I was in the last year of high school. She met Spyros only a few days after he and I started dating, and since then, she has been a sister to both of us. She has been next to us in good and in challenging times, on every memorable occasion, and in every moment that has been lost in the fog of the past.

"I will see you in Tinos," she had yelled from behind the security gate at the airport on her way back to Greece. "I will open the house for you," she said through the kiss she blew at me.

Now, as I was waiting in line for the security agent to check my passport, the idea that I was going to see her again sent a warm feeling through my body.

Spyros and I moved along the lines like robots and quickly found our seats on the plane. I sat by the window and rested my handbag containing my laptop, books, and cell phone next to my legs. Strapped into my seat, I looked through the narrow window down at the ground crew, who were busy at the wing filling the plane with diesel fuel and checking the huge turbines, which had begun to slowly rotate. I could see inside these turbines from where I sat, and I was mesmerized by their forever-turning helix. The magnificent sight of the jet engine reminded me of my visit to the Rolls Royce plant in Indianapolis when I was the dean of engineering at Purdue. Almost as heavy as two Escalade SUVs, with an opening as tall as the average NBA player, this engine is made of thousands of pieces (among them a thousand single crystal blades) and about thirty miles of wiring.

This creation is put together by hand—a marvel of a human precision that refuses to give up control to a robot. Each blade is made with great accuracy, to less than the thickness of a human hair. This is done using a 6,000-year-old technique developed in Mesopotamia: casting. The turbine blades powering our planes are hidden away in the hottest part of the jet engine. They combine a Spartan, utilitarian appearance with complexity of form and function and a diamond-like internal perfection and strength. Weighing only 300g and small enough to fit in the palm of a hand, each of the hundreds or thousands of blades has a composition such that when the engine is in operation, they look like jewels hidden in the nine circles of Dante's *Inferno*; jewels that transform flames into an amazing force that lifts you to heights once thought impossible. *Could you imagine the world without aviation?* I heard the question in my head. I kept looking at the engine until it finally roared to life.

As I settled nervously back into my seat, my mind drifted. Both mine and Spyros's parents had passed away during the past five years. We had kept their homes in Athens, complete with their clothes and personal things, afraid to lose what felt so deeply familiar. This summer, however, after having gone through such a harrowing experience, we decided that it was time to go back and face our parents' passing so we could move forward.

*In about twenty hours,* I thought with a yearning in my heart, *I will be back home.*

In Thesion, near the Temple of Hephaestus—across from Acropolis and next to the Agora. The photo was taken by my cousin in September 2016.

# CHAPTER TWO

# IN ATHENS

**August 27, 2016**

SUNLIGHT CREPT THROUGH THE CRACKS of the window shutters, turning into streams of dust particles glittering weightlessly in the air. They made the darkness of the room more intense. It took me a moment to realize that we were in Holargos, a northern suburb of Athens, at the flat Spyros's parents had lived in for over forty years.

We had arrived the night before, after a twenty-hour trip that had included two flights and one of those layovers *just* long enough to give you hope that you may make it to the next flight. We were already delayed leaving San Francisco Airport, so our layover at Charles de Gaulle had been squeezed into a dangerously short time. We managed to get to the gate for Athens just in time for departure, wet from sweat and gasping for air after pushing our way through the lines of annoyed travelers who did not mind showing their disgust.

As I tried to adjust my eyes to the darkness of our bedroom, I felt the air, heavy and musty.

*This house needs cleaning and airing,* I thought, realizing that it had been almost two years since we last visited for the funeral of my parents, one after the other, five weeks apart.

Spyros was breathing quietly next to me in the bedroom his mother had decorated for us the summer we came for vacation in 1986. It was the first time we had come back since we had left for the United States in the summer of 1979, married and with our two-year-old son, Erik. Our bed, with its puffy headboard and mattress folding into a sofa, was decorated with large, comfortable pillows for those extended periods of time we were away. Along the long wall there was a large, wooden bookcase filled with all kinds of books, which we had read over the years, from children's books to translations of Homer, Plato, and Cicero, to Kazantzakis, Asimov, Eco and others—the leftovers of a long timeline marking the lifecycle of three generations.

Next to our bed, baskets full of toys reminded me of summer vacations when our children were very young. A plane with a TWA sign on its wings brought me a glimpse of two-year-old Erik, laughing and screaming with excitement as he watched it, powered by two type-A batteries, driving in circles on the marble floor of our living room with its lights blinking and a siren going off periodically.

A doll with frizzy blonde hair wearing a faded green dress and a broken shoe made me long for the three-year-old toddler, Helena, with her dirty-blonde hair in two pigtails and her wide, round, blue eyes hissing mischief when, during one of those tantrums, she threw her doll over the balcony onto the tiles of the entrance to our apartment building. Twenty-seven years later, I felt guilt for the moments that had passed almost unnoticed. More toys, in another basket in a corner, brought similar memories; old times remembered with an intense feeling of loss for a life that went by so fast.

Spyros's chest moved peacefully with a steady rhythm that matched his personality. I let my palm rest on his arm and felt the warmth of his body against my sweaty hands. He moved slightly, but his eyes remained shut, and his mouth made a grin, a sign that he was not ready to wake up.

I got out of bed quietly and walked toward the large living room, trying to adjust my eyes to the darkness. The apartment was exactly the way we left it nearly two years ago but dusty. Furnished with heavy antiques whose golden tones contrasted with the green marble floors and the dark-colored, silk-covered walls, the apartment felt old but alive.

Spyros's mom loved antiques of all kinds and used them as flamboyant decorations. From sofas to chandeliers to the smallest ornaments now sitting forgotten on dusty shelves, each object was selected to give the "sense of class" she craved her whole life. It was this class divide that raised a wall between Spyros's parents and mine and became a barrier in our relationship—a wall we fought hard to break down and were able to eliminate only after we left Greece in 1979.

This apartment had all aspects of his mom's personality, and standing proud with its glamorous appeal, it still reminded me of this divide. I crossed the living room toward the balcony door, pulled apart the heavy drapes, and pushed the door shutters wide open to reveal the veranda looking over a small park called Democracy Square.

A cool morning breeze flowed into the room, and the street noise reminded me of a life I had left behind many years ago. The view to the small park was familiar and welcoming. The few benches were occupied by older women, who found the opportunity to sit and catch up on the most recent gossip.

The park's paved paths that separated the green grass and trees heavy with fruit led to the center of the square, where I could see kids and dogs running and playing with each other, competing for a ball with laughter and happy barks.

A light scent of citrus, a mix of orange and lemon, filled the room and brought memories of those sunny Christmas days when our fruit basket at home was full of fresh oranges and mandarins our neighbors had shared with us. I missed those days so much, when Mom and I were preparing our home for the holidays, decorating our small tree and baking cookies that filled the house with the scent of cinnamon and orange. Those days gave me a pure and uninterrupted feeling of happiness.

One path of the Democracy Square ended at a playground full of swings. They all looked new, as if someone had recently replaced them, but they had remained in the same place I first saw them the evening I came to meet Spyros's parents forty years ago. For all these years, they kept busy swaying generations of young kids with hands clutching the ropes and feet flying in the air, moving their bodies in a relentless rhythm that made them giggle with thrill and excitement.

Our children had played in this park for countless hours on those laid-back summer days when they truly believed that Greece was a wonderland, where school did not exist and homework was a forbidden word.

"We should get going," I said, turning to Spyros, who was now up and entering the room.

He looked tired, his eyes almost closed, and his hands extended as if trying to feel his way around. It is not easy to wake up your first morning in a country ten hours ahead of your normal time. It feels as if your body is tight with invisible strings and your brain is numb. Everything happens in slow motion—your thoughts, your impressions, and even your reactions.

It took us an hour to get ready and to open all the windows and doors to let the air in. With the morning light filling the rooms, the dust became even more apparent.

*Who is going to clean it?* I wondered. *Not me, not today.*

"What are we going to do for breakfast?" I heard Spyros calling as he came out of the bathroom wrapped in a bath towel. "Should I invite my brother to join us?" he added. Before I found the time to respond, he was on his cell phone calling Elias. Spyros had missed his brother, and their relationship had become increasingly important to him as the years had gone by.

I first met Elias a few days after meeting Spyros in December of 1973. He was only sixteen years old at the time. A shy, thin, tall boy with dark brown hair and light brown eyes, he looked like his brother but was totally different in character: calmer, more serious, and much more introverted. Being next to him, it always felt as if he were hiding a secret.

Elias had always looked up to Spyros and me for friendship and guidance, and he became like my younger brother. As the younger of two boys in a family with a domineering father, Elias turned to Spyros for comfort. Spyros was too young to understand his brother's sensitivity and respond to his needs. He assumed that Elias would handle their father's aggression and authoritarian style the same way he did—by dismissing him. Instead, Elias responded by leaving home twice before his sixteenth birthday.

When Spyros left him behind to follow me to the United States, Elias felt deserted and hurt by the brother he loved so much and, over the years, slowly drifted away. As time passed, he fell deeper into his own isolation, finding refuge in his reading. Their mother became his only bridge to the world he had abandoned. When she passed away in 2012, hit by a young and careless driver, the relationship between the two brothers went through a crisis as they both moved through a long period of denial and anger. It was only those past few months when Elias, feeling that his older brother needed him more than he needed Spyros, stopped running away from us and came back to give us comfort.

That morning, I had no doubt he would come to see us. About twenty minutes after Spyros made his call, we heard someone at the front door trying to open it from the outside. I ran through the long hallway to the foyer and opened the wooden door before Elias was able to turn the key. A draft of air came through the door and pushed the heavy yellow drapes of the living room away, bringing light into the large space and exposing all its grandeur and the many sofas and coffee tables, all turned to face the long dining table in front of a walnut cabinet filled with china, crystal, silver, glassware, and platters.

"Hi, Elias," I said and, after a brief pause, hugged him and kissed him on his bearded cheek.

He still looked like Spyros, just younger, with long hair tied in a ponytail, worn-out jeans, sandals, and a fresh, clean shirt.

"You look good," he said with a smile. "How are you?"

Spyros came out from the kitchen wearing long shorts and a T-shirt bearing the University of Michigan logo. "Hey, brother," he said, grabbing Elias and kissing him on his cheeks with a broad smile on his face.

They looked at each other for some time without saying a word.

"That's how Greek men communicate," I muttered.

More loudly, I said, "Let's go. Time for breakfast!"

The three of us went to a café that served all kinds of tasty breads and sweets and Greek coffee that infused the air with an irresistible smell. This was a new hangout for the residents of the neighborhood, which I had seen for the first time a couple of years back when we came to Athens in August to spend time with my sick mother. It started as a bakery but had become a popular café. Starting at ten in the morning, people of all ages sat next to each other around tables that tightly filled the space, drinking coffee, smoking cigarettes, and munching on sweet treats. They spoke loudly with dramatic gestures about politics and the failed promises of the government. We found a table and sat with our coffees, croissants, and a thick piece of raisin bread the girl behind the bakery counter had generously cut for me.

"How long are you staying in Athens?" Elias asked, looking at both of us, his eyes asking more than his question.

"We are leaving tomorrow," I answered with a determination that sounded defensive. "I do not want to stay in Athens. It feels too heavy with memories and too crowded with people," I murmured, looking away.

Elias shifted in his seat.

Without hearing the unspoken question, I responded even more determinedly, "I want to go to Tinos."

They knew this island meant something special to me. It is a beautiful island in its own way: plain, mountainous, dry, and barren, with a unique charm and history.

I visited the island in the mid-nineties when Eleni, whose heart was falling in love with old ruins and was giving her tantalizing ideas of how to bring them to life, took a 400-year-old wine cellar in an old village on the top of the mountain and turned it into a small house with an amazing view of a castle.

I fell in love with Tinos at first sight in 1994 and, after multiple visits to Eleni's beautifully restored house, we started building our own summer home there in 2001. For the past fifteen years, our house in Tinos had become our sanctuary. This island has been the place of our rebirth; a place where our roots to the past are so delicately sculpted in the thousands of terraces; a place where our bridge to the future so clearly hangs overhead at night, where the countless stars knit a majestic net of hope.

"It's the only place I will be able to feel myself again," I said, examining the few crumbs of raisin bread left on my plate. I tried to avoid looking at Elias, afraid of the questions his eyes were asking.

"I would like you to come with us," I said. "Spyros and I need you."

"I will," I heard him say.

His willingness to join us was a pure gift of love. I looked at him and smiled with gratitude. But then, as if I had forgotten an important meeting, I stood up, grabbed a small bag that I had stuffed with my passport, driver's license, cards, cash, and a couple of lipsticks, and threw my blue and white shawl around my shoulders.

"I am going to visit my mom," I said with urgency in my voice. "I'll take the car. Could I have the keys?" I asked Spyros. He had already placed the keys in front of me on the small marble table.

I left them still as statues as I ran out of the café. I felt their gaze heavy on my back until my footsteps disappeared in the street noise. I found the car we had rented at the airport, a small white Hyundai, parked a few blocks away. We were lucky to find this parking spot the night before after circling around the neighborhood a few times. I got in the car, and after a number of clumsy maneuvers, I managed to get out, aware of the impatient smile of the driver who waited to occupy the spot. Gritting my teeth, I started the drive to the place where my mom was: Salamis, the island where countless generations of my mother's people lived and died. They were simple but proud people who made the island part of our family's identity and culture, a piece of my soul. This island is where I grew up, the place where my parents have been buried, and the only place that can truly claim me.

My mom and I in her apartment in Salamis during my
visit over the Christmas holiday in December 2013.

## CHAPTER THREE

# VISITING MY MOTHER

SALAMIS IS THE ISLAND CLOSEST to Athens in the Gulf of Saronikos. It is famed for a battle that defined Western civilization, but it has been sleeping quietly under the covers of a long and fairly foggy history. Over a period of 2,500 years, the island saw multiple masters, including the Romans, the Byzantines, the Venetians, and the waves of those who came from the northern mountains of the Greek peninsula in 1200 AD to make the island their new home. Among those were my ancestors, who continued the island's flame of life with the same zeal for protecting their freedom from Ottoman rule and continuing their proud history.

It took me only thirty minutes to get to the island's port, Paloukia, from Holargos, a journey that includes a drive through the busy streets of Athens and a fifteen-minute ferry ride from the mainland to the island, where I lived the first seventeen years of my life. As the ferry approached, I looked to the foothills for what the locals call "Vroki," the rocky, bare hill that separates the town from the naval base. My eyes scanned quickly, but I could hardly spot our house or what had become of it. The hillside next to our house, where once prairies decorated the land with an explosion of year-round wildflowers, was totally covered with two-story buildings tightly spaced.

This place had changed so much in the past sixty years! When I was born, the island had fewer than 10,000 people, and my little town could count no more than 500 people. In six decades, the island population grew to more than 100,000.

Saint Barbara's Church was next to the school. The bakery, general store, butcher shop, pharmacy, and outdoor movie theater were all surrounded by no more than a hundred homes at one time: a tiny splash of small, white buildings that lined the fishing port and the main road connecting our small town to the island's capital, Koulouri. Our pharmacy served as the ER for everyone, mostly kids who hit their heads, scratched their arms and legs, or came down with a virus. For anything else more serious, people had to be taken to a hospital in Athens, or otherwise manage to recover at home with a mix of medicine and old remedies administered by the pharmacist. He was the most popular person in town. He knew everyone's secrets and could keep them close to his chest, despite his often-flamboyant outbursts. Our streets did not have names, and our homes did not have numbers. They were all named after us because we all knew where each other lived, and the mailman knew where to bring the letters that we rarely received from family members who had moved away. Our house was known as the Katehis' house.

*Today, things are so different,* I thought with a sense of loss. *This past has been hidden behind today's progress. My old town has transformed into a nameless suburb of Athens.*

I barely recognized the road to our house—a narrow, steep, dirt path I once took multiple times a day to run errands and go to school. Our house was built in the early 1930s, and though it was old with few amenities, it had the warmth of my mom's cuddles, which I still feel engulfing my body whenever I remember her.

Our house, the one my parents moved into when they got married, was conveniently located near the docks, close to the naval base where my father served first as a sailor and then as a petty officer, and a short walk from where my grandmother lived. This house was old but solid. It had thick stone walls, a tiled roof, and doors opening to the front and back yards. The landowner had promised nothing to my father in terms of upkeep, but she had offered a very low rent in return.

Black-and-white tiles covered the floors of the bedroom and family room, whose cracks and holes told stories and tales of their own. They were scars from bombs during the Second World War that had exploded nearby and gunfire from when the Greek communist liberation army (EAM) had occupied the house for a few days during the Greek Civil War, right after the German occupation.

Those days when I was bored of helping Mom with chores, I would climb the hill to the top, ignoring her warnings and pretending that I did not hear the whistles the navy guards blew to deter me from trespassing onto the base. I knew how to stay a safe distance from their guard towers, being assured by my friends that the sentries would not leave their post to run after me.

"Get out of there, you little bastard, before we shoot you!" they would yell, agitated.

"No, you won't. My dad is in the navy, and he will punish you!" I would yell back.

"We are going to tell your dad, you little devil. Leave before we arrest you."

"My dad is gone with his ship, but when he comes back, *he* will arrest *you!*"

With that, I would turn my back to them, knowing that the rubble they were throwing to scare me away could not reach me.

Then, sitting on a rock and shielding my eyes with my hand, I would look intensely for my dad's ship, overtaken by a feeling of hope and anxiety. I wanted my father back home but not the way he was before he left for the trip. I wished so hard that he would come back happy, gentle, and loving toward us.

Those few times when I saw his ship docking, I would run home, eager to tell Mom that Dad might come home any time. Most of those times, however, Dad came home days later, angry and broke, only to have Mom clean and iron his uniform before he left again for another trip.

There were only a few times when my father was genuinely happy. I remember him once tenderly holding my hand as we were walking to the bakery, where he asked me to select one of the little, round cookies he knew I loved. He told me I could pick any one I liked.

Another time, I remember trying to force his hand open as he held one of those flat and round chewing gums wrapped in bright yellow foil that made them look like gold coins with the head of a king or queen embossed on each side. After I had nearly exhausted myself laughing and trying to get the coin by force, he finally smiled and let me have the treat.

These memories, few and precious, I have tried to preserve in hopes of remembering that there were moments when he truly loved me.

The best part of our house was its view to the sea, toward the eastern bay of the island, where Themistocles once led the Greeks to a witty win against the Persian army of Xerxes in the famous sea battle of 480 BC. This enchanting story, a mix of a fairy tale and legend that I had heard many times in my life, has stuck with me through the years.

One early summer afternoon, a few short days after my class graduation, Mom and I were in the backyard hanging our clothes out to dry when we heard the sound of a growing crowd—a commotion that meant trouble. We rushed to the narrow side door of our yard and saw people running toward the small hill behind our house. "What is happening?" Mom asked a young boy.

"They found dead people," he responded and kept following the crowd.

The whole neighborhood gathered around a pile of dirt, curious to see who the dead were. I could see the farmer from the neighboring farm standing close to the pile with his ax and shovel stuck prominently next to it. He was talking to the sheriff with large gestures that showed fear and excitement together.

"There are many dead people," a woman next to the sheriff yelled to the rest of us who stayed at a distance, afraid to face the dead and feel their wrath.

"Somebody call the priest," she yelled again, gesturing in the direction of the church. "Quickly!"

A group of kids ran toward the church. Everybody else remained in their place. The crowd was numb, and the initial commotion turned to a whispering noise until the priest showed up in his long black robe with his golden stole around his neck, the Bible in one hand and a cross in the other, signs of Christ's power over Death. He walked slowly and steadily through the crowd of people who parted for him and silently crossed themselves multiple times as he was passing by.

"These are old bodies," the priest yelled to the crowd after he inspected the pile of bones and dirt. "These are not our people," he repeated with a strong voice. "This is a tomb," he said, "a grave for ancient people." The silent crowd watched, breathless. "We have to close the hole and leave these people in peace."

"Bless them, Father," one voice said slowly. "Their souls will not rest until God receives them."

In the following days, the gossip in the neighborhood and at school was thriving, adding new twists to the story that now included ghosts and demons casting spells on the farmer. Trying to calm the community, our schoolteachers organized many lessons on the battle of Salamis and asked us to share these lessons with our parents. A few weeks later, we had all calmed down, but our fear for the wrath of the dead whose peace we had disturbed remained no less. We were told that thousands of men had died in a big battle between the Greeks and the Persians two and a half thousand years ago. The two navies, carrying heavily armed soldiers called *hoplites*, met in the bay of the island of Salamis the morning of September 27, 480 BC. The Athenian general, Themistocles, in charge of the Greek ships, knew the island's waters well and misled the Persians to a place where their big vessels (*triremes*) could not maneuver. Thousands died that day by iron and fire, and thousands more drowned, taken to the bottom of the sea by their own ships. Those whose bodies were recovered were buried on the island in tombs over a period of three days, as was the Greek custom. The dead, both Greek and Persian, had begun their journey to the underworld buried together in solemn graves, unrecognized and unnamed.

Despite this historic battle, there is nothing left on the island to elicit its old glory. Only the bay has remained, a wet tomb for the Greeks who died struggling to keep their freedom, and the Persians who were killed for viciously obeying their king.

During my childhood summers, the bay was the center of our excitement. All the kids of our neighborhood loved swimming, fishing, and sailing—much to the dismay of our mothers, who were continuously trying to keep us away from the fishing boats. This was difficult to do, as we all knew how to release the boats from the mooring bollards and go for a fun ride.

I do not know how old I was when I started taking these boat rides. As a young kid, I sat in the center of the boat observing the older ones who, after pushing the boat away from the docks, started rowing hard to take us as far away from the shore as possible. Among them was my other cousin, Eleni. Her mom was my mother's oldest sister. We used to call her (sometimes still do) "Eleni the Older" to differentiate her from our other younger cousin of the same name. Seven years older than I, she was the clan leader. Taller and more aggressive than most boys her age, she imposed her will with her thin and strong physique and unwavering determination. Most of the time, the boat we stole belonged to her dad's brother. I remember taking those boat rides despite the screams from our distressed mothers, who all lined the docks, afraid that the boat would sink under the weight of a dozen kids, and the horrific curses from Eleni's uncle.

To keep me away from swimming by myself in the bay, my grandmother told me the story of the battle, adding that the bottom of the sea was covered with the broken triremes and the swords and body armor of the Greek and Persian warriors, whose skeletons were asleep on the seabed, ready to be awakened and take anyone who swims alone down with them. Oftentimes while swimming, I tried to look through the clear water at the sandy bottom of the sea, thinking that the old warriors in their armor might just wake up and pull me under. The only thing I could see were the reflections of the wave ripples and my own shadow, causing a chill to run up my spine.

On my return many years later on that day in August 2016, the ferry came fast to the dock and the cars started their engines, creating a cacophony of people's voices surrounded by smoke. I drove straight from the ferry to the cemetery to visit my parents, who had lain there since the summer of 2014. My father was the first to go. My mother passed away five weeks later, on September 3, 2014.

She was buried in the same place as her three sisters, her brother, parents, and grandparents, in a family burial crypt that goes back hundreds of years. No one from our family knows how old this grave is. My father was buried in a different place; he was never considered part of that family.

People used to say that this cemetery was as old as the island. Throughout their history, Greeks respected their cemeteries more than their temples, and they feared the wrath of their dead more than the wrath of their gods.

With a small Greek Orthodox church in the middle and a series of closely planted cypress trees along the perimeter, this cemetery looks reclusive and remote, even if the sprawling town around it has brought it closer and closer to its center.

As you pass through the iron gate, you hear the silence of the dead. Their white marble graves, elevated off the ground, are decorated with stone crosses, pictures of the dead at a younger age, and inscriptions etched along with messages from their families—a cultural tradition that has survived for thousands of years. Tightly gripping the flowers I bought at the little store outside the gate, I walked fast until my steps brought me to her grave.

The two marble vases on each side of her picture were ready to receive the stems in their cool water. It was a hot afternoon, and sweat ran down my face as I stood there, hands clasped in front, silently waiting for a sign. I looked at her picture, realizing how young she was when the photo was taken. It showed her being charming but serious, the way I've remembered her since I was little.

Emotions overwhelmed me as I stood speechless in front of her picture, trying to calm my anxiety. It felt like the life I had with her as a little girl belonged to someone else, as if the girl who had grown up in that poor yet proud community was not me but the girl in a book I had read some time ago. It was hard to relate to that time, that community, and even that girl.

I looked at my mom's picture again. I focused on her face, hoping to notice a flicker in her eyes, to see a smile coming from her lips. She remained serious and silent. My hands moved nervously now and rose up to rest on my chest. I closed my eyes and heard the breeze through the cypress trees around the perimeter of the cemetery and in between the graves. The air became cooler and lighter.

For a moment I felt something move behind me.

I heard the ruffling of feathers.

*Maybe a cat running after a pigeon*, I thought. I turned around quickly to look behind me, but there was nothing.

Only the wheezing of a sleeping cat near a cup of water disturbed the silence. I focused on Mom again, but I had lost the urge to fight against her silence. I only wanted to talk to her, to tell her everything important that happened since her passing.

I told her of the two weddings: our son's the year before and our daughter's just a month ago. Mom had wanted to live to see her grandchildren married. This was her last wish that she had whispered to me bitterly from her deathbed in the hospital where she was treated for brain cancer. She did not hear me when I accused her in anger of lying when she told me that she would not abandon me—her last words to me. After that, she fell into a coma and remained in it until her heart gave up a few days later.

My feet then took me to my dad's grave, just a few steps away.

I looked at his picture, in which he is a young officer, standing straight and proud in his navy uniform, resting his hands on his ceremonial sword with all his medals from the two wars pinned on his jacket and covering half his chest. He looked remote, stiff, and uncompromising.

The two wars he fought for almost ten years, the Second World War and then the Greek Civil War, became his life and defined his character. He was nineteen years old when he enlisted, as the Germans were coming to his island of Corfu, and was almost thirty when he came out of war.

He grew up away from his family, believing them to be dead. He saw his friends die horrible deaths, others imprisoned, and many executed. He was captured and tortured twice—first by the Italians and then the Germans. The first time, he escaped; the second time, his SS torturers thought he was dead and threw his body onto the side of the road for the passersby to see it and learn a lesson. An old woman realized that he was alive and secretly moved him to her house, where he recovered and was able to escape for a second time from his island of Corfu and go to Alexandria in Egypt.

He grew up fighting a war that defeated him and imprisoned him for life. It captured his soul and made him find escape in things that took him away from us. This was the war he was fighting every day until he died. Years later, in his nineties, he could not remember anyone but his war comrades. He could not remember me.

"Dad, I love you," I said. I touched his hand as he lay in his hospice bed, days before he passed away in the summer of 2014.

His eyes were intense as they looked toward me, but they did not see me. They were fixed on a point in the distance. "Do you know that I want to love you?" I kept repeating, afraid to ask him whether he remembered me.

"Yes," he said finally, and his face flinched. I ran out of the room and cried hard. I had lied to him, and he had lied back.

Two days later, he died alone in the company of his ghosts.

The war had made him fear love. I wanted to love him, but he did not let me. He made me fear him, and he drove me away as if he were afraid that my love would hurt him.

"Why did you not let me love you?" I could hear my hoarse voice asking him, as I looked at his gravestone picture, his youthful face forever frozen in time. "I wish I could hate you forever."

He looked remote and uninterested, caught up in his own thoughts, ready to recite another war story.

I ran back to my mom, as I did whenever he pushed me away. It was getting late, and the shadows of the trees from the setting sun had now covered the cemetery. My mom's picture and her worried eyes filled my mind.

"Be careful," a voice told me. I looked around to check if someone was watching me. I saw no movement. Maybe it was her voice, maybe mine.

"It is getting late, and I need to go," I said, as if asking her for permission.

I touched her picture for the last time and walked away without looking back, her eyes following me. The exit of the cemetery came into view, and I felt the ground running under my feet. The door was half closed.

A big, handwritten sign hung from one of the metal brackets. It said, "Open between 8:00 a.m. and 7:00 p.m."

It was almost 7:00 p.m. The sun was ready to settle into the horizon. I bolted to the car, opened the door, and sat at the driver's seat, exhausted. The need for a drink overwhelmed me. I needed something strong to make me relax, to help me overcome the day. As I turned on the engine, I realized that drinking had become more of a refuge recently. I never got drunk, but I had been drinking more, sometimes in the middle of the day.

With the car in gear, I stomped on the gas and felt the engine struggling to catch up. The car lunged forward, spewing dust behind, and launched onto the paved road with a bumping sound. I followed the coast road looking for a place to drink.

I could not concentrate. It was as if I had left half my mind behind, staring at my mother's picture, while the other half was craving alcohol.

"Red!" my brain said as I sped toward an intersection.

*Forget the red*, I thought for a second and then woke up.

I slammed on the brakes, forcing the car to screech to a stop, leaving smoke behind. I smelled tar as I looked around, disoriented. I heard the curses from a few men sitting at a café nearby, who looked at me with their hands raised in protest.

I drove slowly the rest of the way to a little tavern—nothing but a small kitchen that opened onto a deck next to the water. The scene was beautiful, and the tavern was known for the great drinks and octopus.

The deck was full of tables dressed in blue-and-white plaid tablecloths. The wooden chairs at each table were painted blue and made the whole place look like an extension of the sea. There was only one other group sitting at a table, drinking and laughing.

I sat far away from them. I was not in the mood to laugh or talk; I just wanted to drink. I turned my chair and my back to them, and looked toward the small fishing boats no more than ten feet from me. They rested one next to the other, trembling from the summer's evening breeze and the slow churning of the water.

*Maria*, *Niki*, and *Nicholas* were printed with bright colors on their wooden bows.

None of them was named Georgia, my mother's name.

The waitress, a young girl with brown hair and deep brown eyes and a friendly smile, who couldn't have been more than sixteen, came to ask whether I wanted to order.

"Grilled octopus and ouzo," I said, returning the smile.

She was wearing thick glasses and a top with a big "I Love NY" across her full bust.

"Of course," she replied. "Do you expect anyone else?"

"No."

"Are you visiting someone?"

"Yes, at the cemetery."

She looked uncomfortable. "I am so sorry. Are you from around here?"

"Yes, I was born and raised here, but now I live in the United States, in California."

There was a short pause of uncertainty.

"Are you Mrs. Katehi?" she said shyly, her local accent becoming stronger as her voice dropped considerably.

I freaked out.

"The newspaper was writing about you lately," she said and blushed.

My mind woke up from its hallucination, and I was on the alert. *Why here?* I thought. *What were they talking about?* My frontal lobe was synthesizing different scenarios, remembering anonymous comments I had received from UC Davis recently.

"We are so proud of you!" I heard her voice as if coming from the deep bottom of the sea.

"You are the only one who has been able to go this far," she continued. "I wish I could be like you. I love New York. That's where I would go if I could study in the US." She looked at me with admiration.

I was confused.

She paused, as if she wanted to ask more questions, but turned around and ran back to the kitchen to give the order.

*I know what she is doing,* I thought. *She's probably telling everyone in the kitchen that I am here. Probably talking about the most recent events she read on the internet. Should I leave? What if I just run away, get to the car, stop at a gas station, get a bottle of ouzo, and then drive back to Athens?*

I fantasized for a moment, but I knew that I would not dare to drink and drive. I ordered my legs to get up, but they were numb as well. They seemed to have a mind of their own lately, and they made a point of defying me again. A few minutes went by in anguish.

The young waitress came out, followed by an older man who was carrying a tray with the grilled octopus, cut in small pieces, and a small bottle of ouzo with a bucket of ice.

"This is my dad," she said, and took the tray from him to place it on my table while I looked at the ouzo.

"Mrs. Katehi, we are so honored to have you at our restaurant," the man said and took my hand, which I shyly extended to greet him.

He lowered his head as if to receive communion, placed my hand on his lips, and kissed it.

I was startled and heaved out of my chair, looking at him with surprise.

His eyes were as dark as my mom's.

"I am so happy to be here, even if my visit to the cemetery was not a happy one," I said, noticing that my voice now had the distinct local accent.

"I knew your mother well," he said while cradling my hands. "We were kinfolk. Our grandfathers were brothers. We ate food from the same table," he went on in a trembling voice. "Your order is on us."

He looked at me, and after a brief hesitation, he gave me a bear hug.

"Thank you," I whispered, my voice still trying to find its way out of my mouth. I took his hands in mine. I could feel the warmth of his heart pushing new blood into my veins. He told me I was one of them, something that I had not heard in a long time.

It felt good to be among my own people—a simple people who believe in God's will, who respect their families and their values, who work hard and with pride to support their kin.

I ate a piece of octopus and closed my eyes, trying to focus all my senses on its taste and to forget about everything else. I drank a little ouzo with plenty of ice, and the alcohol went through my veins like water in dry soil.

As the alcohol filled my veins, I sensed my hands fondling my memory book, aching to turn the pages and let my mind be absorbed by its images, sounds, and the salty smell from the sea on the cool wind. I felt the book's power enchanting me deep into the magic world of my childhood.

My cousin Eleni (right) and I (left) during summer camp as
preschoolers in Saint Nikolas in Salamis, circa 1958.

# My Childhood

MY EARLY MEMORIES ARE LIKE the pages of an old book written and illustrated by me. Pictures are drawn in countless colors and letters written in numerous styles. When I was young, I liked to draw what I hoped would become real, and these drawings have become part of my memory book. They show beautiful flowers, trees that move in the wind, animals that talk, and happy kids running and playing.

On one page, a princess wearing a long, airy dress with colors that change with the wind into blue, pink, and purple brings memories of long hours drawing and redrawing this dress. Its long train flows softly over the steps of a long stairway that stretches up to a beautiful blue sky, where the princess's castle, crowned by a majestic ivory tower, sits on a white puffy cloud.

On another page, children play under a bright sun across from my grandmother's house. It is Easter Sunday. Their voices call me as they approach, "Linda, where are you?" I sit quietly, covered by long, golden stems of wheat, ready to grab their feet and scare them. The page's scent of the sweet, warm Easter bread resting on my grandma's kitchen table fills every corner of my mind.

These are the pages my book begins with to trick me to turning over to those other ones, dark and threatening, some stuck together to hide their secrets, some ripped apart, and others smeared by my mother's tears. No matter how many times I have tried to burn it, bury it, throw it into the waves of the summer sea, hoping never to see it again, it always comes back. The book hangs over me, urging me to touch it, awakening my curiosity to go through its pages once again. Its aged, thick-leather cover is soft to the touch, and its deep engravings fire the desire in my heart to open it again. I forget that it controls what it shares, that it promises more than it gives, that it possesses me every time I touch it.

## JUST ANOTHER GIRL

I was born on January 30, 1954, at a hospital in Athens. Our small island's clinic at the naval base was for personnel only, and the military doctor on duty the night my mother went into labor told my father to take her to Athens because the delivery would not be easy. Almost all the babies on the island were delivered by midwives, sometimes unsuccessfully for both mother and baby. Most young women and their mothers feared childbirth for the ultimate price they paid in their fight to preserve the species. Those who died were hardly remembered for their sacrifice. The widower husbands would quickly remarry to give their children a new mother and to start a new family.

My grandmother had lost all the men in her life, and every time her daughters went through childbirth, she felt both the threat of losing a daughter and hopeful that the child might be a boy.

I was the fourth of her granddaughters, all born in a row without a grandson in between, and she was angry that she could have lost her daughter just for another girl. According to Mom, my grandmother's anger melted the instant she held me in her arms and felt the young life trembling as a butterfly that tries to fly for the first time. That moment, her heart was flooded with a primitive sense of love and strength.

"It was Saturday afternoon and the church bells were ringing when you were born," my mother used to tell me on my birthday every year.

She always made me a chocolate-vanilla birthday cake, her own recipe, under my watchful eyes. I could see the intensity on her face as her mind filled with the sound of the church bells swinging from the weight of the laughing altar boys who pulled the weathered ropes.

"It was the day of the three Hierarchs, the three saints who gave life to you and spared life for me," she continued. "I knew then that this was a message from God, and you would become educated, you would become a teacher!" Her voice disappeared again behind the flapping sound of the soft cake batter she kept turning over with a long wooden spatula, whose color had darkened from years of use.

The heavy ceramic bowl that rested on the top of the small kitchen table made a ringing sound every time the spatula hit its yellow rim. I loved watching the circular movement of the spatula while listening to my mom's story, and I giggled every time I got away with a quick sampling of the batter by darting my finger into the bowl. That place next to the table where I would play quietly while Mom did her daily chores was mine and mine alone.

Our kitchen was small but quite comfortable, built behind two rooms that served as our bedroom and living room. It had thick, stone walls that kept us warm in the winter and cool in the summer. The stone floor was kept warm by a large wool rug made by a family friend as my parents' wedding gift. The stove under a large hood built across from the table was part of a small fireplace that kept the room warm during the cold winter days.

"There was another sign that told me you will become important," Mom continued as she poured the cake mixture into the dark cooking pan made of heavy iron. "The last day we were to leave the clinic, I found 400 drachmas, almost double your father's monthly salary, in the drawer of my nightstand," she whispered with a voice soft as a prayer. "There was nothing in the drawer the night before. It was empty." She crossed herself three times and added, "It was God's act and a way to tell me that you would become educated and rich. Remember his will."

"Yes," I nodded, trying to visualize God placing the money in the nightstand. She never asked how the money got there and rarely mentioned the wealthy woman who had been in the bed next to hers during their stay at the clinic.

Mother was always calm, never angry, but often sad. A smart woman who, despite the scars the war had left her with, knew how to raise me. Her deep faith in the grace of God, and the power of truth and justice over evil helped her survive an impossibly harsh life. She used story-telling to express her hopes, dreams, disappointments, and fears. She was convinced that I was not going to follow her steps in life but break away from poverty and become educated, independent, successful, and important. She made sure she told me this as often as she could.

I was born into a matriarchal family, not because of culture but because of war and disease. It was a family of strong women who married young, bore many children, buried their husbands and sons, and lived on to take care of the rest of the family. These women were determined to survive and raise their daughters with discipline and honor. They were sensitive but tough, empathetic but uncompromising, poor but respected, judg-mental but fair, and (most importantly) proud of what their families had contributed to their community for hundreds of years. Before the outbreak of the Second World War, their fathers had been community leaders, their brothers had served as mayors on the island, their husbands had served the military with pride, and their sons had been educated and readied to become the next generation of community leaders. Despite the wrath of the war that brought death, poverty, and humiliation, these women remained faithful to their values and personified every ideal they hoped to inspire in their children and grandchildren.

## MY MOTHERS

"Eve had two sons, Abel and Cain, and many daughters," my great-grandmother used to say. "It was the sons who fought and died, and the daughters who were left behind to lead the kin and tell their story."

The family I got to know when I was young included my great-grandmother, Grandma Penny, along with her five sisters and four daughters. My grandma, the oldest of the four daughters, was Grandma Eleni. She had four daughters, of whom my mom was the third—five years older than her youngest sister and five years younger than her eldest. All these women were mothers to me.

My mothers came from a long lineage of people from the north. They say it was around 1200 AD, during the Crusades, when a group of families moved from the mountains of northern Greece to the island. They brought with them their culture, their dialect, their food, their clothes, and their songs—monotonous recitation of stories of love and hate, hope and despair, pride and humiliation. Their songs embodied all the feelings that make us human and imperfect.

My mothers were strong. They had little to no education, yet they were proud, wise, and determined. They honored their culture with conviction and spoke their language with pride. This language, an old dialect deeply rooted in thousands of years of history, spoke of war and peace, mourned the dead, blessed the newlyweds, cursed the traitors, and celebrated the heroes. This proud past followed the mothers' paths through time and space to find me the day I was born.

All my mothers looked after me with an eagle's eye. I feared them as I loved them, respected them as I teased them, and unwillingly grew up to become like them. As a child, I mixed up their names, great-grand-auntie for great-grandma or grand-auntie for grandma; they would laugh but always correct me. Growing up I resisted their will, disliked their advice, and hated their discipline, but they loved me nonetheless, with tough love.

My grannies did not know how to read or write formal Greek. The little they learned in the first few grades at school they soon forgot. When I was born, they were disappointed I was a girl, but they were ready to raise me to be as tough as they were. "One more of those," Grandma Eleni said. "How could I lose my daughter for a girl? Who needs more women when the soil is thirsty for men's blood?"

Even if they believed that a woman's place is in the shadows of her men, they all knew how to quickly move into their new roles when their men were taken away by death. With the coming of my generation of girls, their efforts focused on making sure we were educated and independent, without forgetting that we were supposed to get married and have families of our own. So, my mothers taught me how to sew, stitch and knit, wash dishes, make my bed, clean my room, and iron my clothes by the time I was seven. However, deep in their minds, they had a different plan for me.

"Let's go to visit Grandma Penny," my mom said one Saturday afternoon. "Go get your dress and shoes and get ready."

Before she had finished her sentence, I was going through my clothes in the small wooden closet that stood tall next to my parents' bed. I found my dress, hung nicely among my mom's clothes, and my shoes immediately below, resting next to hers on the floor. I tried to change, but my dress stuck on my head, and with it hanging off, I ran to her with a silly laugh. Rarely did I need her help to dress, but this time I was too excited to accomplish the task alone.

"Hey . . . you silly little girl!" she said as she unbuttoned the dress to take it off my head. "You have to know how to dress yourself by now," she went on in a warm voice touched by the distinct local accent, "and you have to fold the old dress and place it carefully on the chair so it is ready to wear when we come back. Now you are old enough to learn how to make your hair look nice as well." With that, she spent a few minutes tenderly brushing my short light brown hair. "You should also push your hair away from your eyes," she added, as she gently brushed my bangs away from my face and placed a hair pin on one side to keep everything in place.

Holding hands, we walked down the steep path to the bus stop. The bus was there waiting, with the engine idling and a few passengers already seated and chatting with each other, trying to catch up on the most recent news. We would always bring something to my great-granny, usually whatever goodies my mom had baked that morning and packed into a small basket covered with a white napkin. Today we had cookies with us, and I proudly held the basket as we got on the bus and found two seats.

I loved helping Mom make cookies. I was thrilled with the idea of rolling them into shapes: a circle, a heart, a little bow. Sometimes I tried to be creative and make a cat, but I always got disappointed when the cat-cookie lost its shape when it was baked. Mom would lay the dough on the table, covered with a plastic tablecloth, and then she helped me cut a small piece from the dough and roll it out. We would then place the shaped cookies on a baking sheet in rows, and she would brush them with a mix of egg and sugar. After that, we would take the cookies to the neighborhood baker to bake them in his oven. The baker's wife was always happy to do it for us.

The bus ride was short, even though it took us to the other side of the island to a town by the water facing the west. Grandma Penny's two-story house was small and beautiful, like a toy. "Appropriate for a great-grandma," as Mom used to say. A tall wall with a heavy wooden door in the courtyard protected the home from the cold and unkind eyes of passing "strangers," which was what Grandma Penny called everyone outside of the family.

A big, metal doorknocker in the shape of a hand, rusted by old age and the salt of the sea breeze, was attached to the frame of the door. It served as a reminder that you had to show respect for the family and knock before entering. This rule was always followed. Mom stood on the stone doorstep, raised the heavy metal hand, and let it fall back to its metal base, making a thunderous noise.

"Grandma Penny!" she called after a while. "It is us, Georgia and Linda!"

She raised the hand again and was about to let it fall when we heard slippers dragging on the floor. "Here she comes," my mom said and looked at me in a way that meant, "Be a nice girl."

The door opened, and a woman dressed in a long black dress with a black headscarf filled the doorway. She was tall and thin, with two piercing eyes, black as olives, and lips that had once been full and colorful but were now just wrinkled skin. She had the eyes of a hawk, and two long gray braids hung below her headscarf. For a moment I wondered whether birds of prey had braids.

"My ladies! What a surprise. Welcome, please come in," she said in a steady voice with a smile that bore the marks of time and suffering. She made space for us to come in and closed the door after us.

The beautiful courtyard had a freshly painted white tile floor and tall stone walls, also painted white, which shielded the space from the eyes of passersby. Standing on the walls were all kinds of potted shrubs, and jasmine climbed regally in its white dress, spreading a deep scent that could numb your other senses and make you dizzy—a scent deeply embedded in my memory book.

It was always my job to give Grandma Penny the basket, but her great, dark presence stunned me.

"Linda do you have something to give to Grandma?" Mom gently urged.

I raised the basket, holding it up until she grabbed the handle. I kissed her hand and then looked at her with fear. She kissed me on my forehead and watched me with piercing eyes. "*Chi bun, moi?*" ("How are you, my dear?").

"*Me-re,*" ("Good") I replied.

"She understands our ways and tongue," she said, looking at my mom with approval. "You raised her well."

The room on the ground floor had a fireplace, and next to it was a comfortable-looking narrow bed covered in pillows. A shaky wooden staircase led to the bedrooms on the second floor, and it made the whole house squeak every time it was used. Grandma Penny always had the same place for me to sit when we visited: on her bed by the fireplace.

"How is my daughter doing?" she asked my mother, referencing my grandmother. "I have not seen her for a long time."

"She is doing well," Mom responded nervously, "and she is very busy, working all day long at the naval base and bringing work home over the weekend. The wife of the admiral is very demanding, and cooking and cleaning their house is a full-time job with all the parties they have almost every day," she continued. "Every Sunday Mom brings home his uniform to clean and iron. It takes her the whole day to do that."

Mother took a deep breath, trying to avoid Grandma Penny's intense glance, and went on as if she did not want to give her grandma time to respond.

"She worries too much about having a dowry for the youngest one, Ismini. She saves all the money she makes from her work at the base to build a house for her; otherwise, Ismini will not be able to find a husband," my mom continued in a long and rushed monologue.

"Your mother is responsible for her destiny," I heard Grandma Penny say behind gritted teeth, many of them in good condition for her age. "I told her not to marry your father, but she was not in the mood to listen to me."

I sat silently as they spoke of family matters, both old and new. I looked at my hands and listened attentively to my mom's heavy breathing whenever she was not speaking. There was tense silence for some time, until I suddenly heard Grandma Penny's voice directed at me, calm and inviting.

"So, my young lady, how about you? What do you want to do next?"

Without thinking, I said, "Eat a cookie."

I was always the first one to taste the goodies we brought her. Grandma Penny pulled the napkin from the basket, placed it on my lap, and asked me to choose one of the cookies. I took a deformed cat cookie and held it until she nodded permission to eat it. Playing with the cookie in my hands kept me busy while she put a pot on the wooden stove to brew Greek coffee for us. I was dying for a cookie dipped in coffee. When I close my eyes, I can still smell the ground coffee in my great grandmother's old grinder and the warm sweetness of the dipped cookie in my mouth.

"Can I go out?" I asked after finishing the cookie, which I had dipped multiple times into my mom's coffee. I looked first at my mom and then at Grandma Penny, who was busy cleaning my hands with a white napkin.

"Of course," Grandma said with a soft voice, "but do not disturb the cats; they are not very nice today."

I ran out, leaving the two behind me talking quietly. The two cats, resting lazily near the wall, looked at me and hissed, curving their backs and raising their tails. I understood the signs: no play today. I looked around, mesmerized by the colors of the jasmine flowers planted in numerous pots. I loved jasmine, so I cut a small bouquet and took it to my mom.

"Put it in your hair," I insisted, but instead she looked at her grandma asking for a nod.

"Yes, put it in your hair. Your daughter is asking you," Grandma Penny said, smiling broadly for the first time.

Mom took it, pinned it in her brown hair just above her ear, and looked at me with a charming but serious look, one I still remember. These moments have been some of the happiest in my life. I felt safe and loved then, protected, and had a sense of belonging. In my early years, these small moments filled my whole existence, as if yesterday did not exist and tomorrow was not important.

## Mama Georgia

Mother was born in September 1925 on the island, the fourth of five children (a son and four daughters). Grandma Eleni became a widow when she was thirty-two years old, with children from the ages of twelve to two. My grandfather died when he was thirty-six years old from a disease that could have easily been treated today with simple antibiotics. In 1932, however, the people on the island knew little and tried to treat him with medicinal plants and prayers. He died within six months of falling ill, leaving behind a family with a small pension and a young widow distraught and desperate. My grandmother's father, according to the local custom, was given custody of his daughter and her five children.

For a few years, life was difficult but bearable. With the help of her father, the children all lived with dignity. However, six years later, in 1938, my great-grandfather, Grandma Penny's husband, died from tetanus, and my grandmother's brother took custody of the family.

He, an unmarried man who could not keep a job, stopped working after he had access to my grandmother's pension. He ended up spending it all in bars and strip clubs, often coming home drunk and broke. Over a short time, his health deteriorated, and he was eventually diagnosed with schizophrenia, a condition he acquired from syphilis. He made life for his family unbearable until he was sent to a mental institution, where he died a few years later, leaving my grandmother with a huge debt. For a short time after that, the custody of the family went to my uncle Isidor, a twenty-one-year-old law student who succumbed to tuberculosis in the winter of 1941 during the German occupation. He was my grandmother's only son, and his death devastated her and her young daughters.

Mom was sixteen in the spring of 1941 when her family went through its most difficult test of survival. At four-feet, five-inches tall, with long golden hair worn in tight braids around her thin, sickly face, she looked much younger. Every day she wore a black mourning dress, which was hard to keep clean while carrying rocks from dawn until dusk in the labor camp under the watchful eyes of the German guards, whose yells could not be distinguished from the barking of their well-trained dogs. At the end of every long day, she would walk six kilometers back home with a slice of bread and a piece of foul cheese or meat—her pay for the day's work. It was all the food she could share with her family; four mouths open, hungry as hatchlings. There were times, however, when hunger was more tolerable than the intense headaches caused by the sounds of Wagner's operas, which the German guards played over megaphones while people were laboring.

The German occupation ended in 1944 after bombings by the Allies that killed more civilians on the island than the Germans did during their invasion. The piercing sound of sirens in the dead of night warning of Allied planes meant danger for those who could not find safe cover. Only after the sirens stopped at dawn did people come out of their hiding places, like horrible shadows in the early morning mist, searching for those who would not see the sun that day.

The day the Germans left the island, the Greek liberation army (EAM/ELAS) came in and took over the abandoned naval base, signaling the beginning of a four-year civil war between the guerrilla forces and the military, which was controlled by the palace. The people on the island went through a new round of killings and arrests, this time of those accused of collaborating with the royal military forces or with the Germans or running the black markets. There were no courts, no defense: only a verdict of death by fire. The cemetery opened again for more funerals, which now were done secretly, in the middle of the night, to protect the families from further humiliation.

When the navy came to reclaim the base in 1945, a third round of arrests and military courts sent many who opposed the king to political prisons that filled quickly. By the time the civil war ended in 1949, the people could not recall the last time they felt safe or happy. Nine years of war had become a lifetime, during which boys turned into savage men and girls turned to widows and single mothers, all now trying to find a new order and, if possible, a new start.

My parents met in 1947 after the navy came back to their base on the island. My father came with them from Alexandria as a young petty officer. They met through my father's close friend Yiannis, a friend of Mom's brother Isidor who had stayed beside his deathbed in 1941. Yiannis had promised Isidor that he would look out for his mother and sisters, and he kept his word.

My parents got engaged in 1947, under Yiannis's strong encouragement. Two souls suffering from the memories of the war but hungry for hope and redemption, they decided to get married in 1950. My mother and father seemed to make a good match in one respect: both were young and healthy and eager to leave the war behind. But the war, like a terrible ghost, hovered relentlessly over their minds and souls. It whispered horrifying thoughts in their ears and brought unbearable fear to their souls. Their marriage was not a happy one, and I was the sole witness of this. I was too young to understand the suffering the two of them had gone through during the war, especially that of my father, whom I blamed for everything.

My parents were so different in personality and lifestyle, and so obsessed by their own war demons that it eventually became obvious to them, and everyone else around them, that they were not happy together. Mom, shy and measured, was a saint at home and in the community, yet always felt unappreciated and rejected by my father. Dad, a cosmopolitan who tried to hide his gruesome past behind a thirst for adventure, selfishly lived in the present and ignored the future. No one could recognize the signs of a horrible post-traumatic stress disorder, so no one was able to understand or help him.

I grew up close to my mom. I was the only child, and Father was mostly gone, so the two of us developed an unbreakable bond by spending all our time together. We knew my father's navy friends and their families who lived near the base, like us, and when Father was at sea, we would occasionally visit them to learn about his whereabouts. He never wrote to us, even if he was away for many months at a time.

## GOING TO SCHOOL

"Linda!"

I heard a harsh voice behind me.

It was not Mom's, but I did not dare look back. I started walking faster and was soon running, looking down at the ground passing under my dusty little boots.

"Linda," the voice continued, this time even stronger, "stop and come back immediately. Go back home. Where is your mom?"

I kept running until I turned the corner and could not be seen. My heart was beating hard, and my temples were throbbing. I was on a mission; no one would stop me. I had planned it all the night before when my mom tucked me into bed.

In the preceding days, I had missed my friends terribly. They all were going to school and had begun ignoring me. We'd had such a great time before then! I remember those days, when I would wake up in the morning, quickly drink a cup of hot chocolate with a piece of bread dipped in it, and then run out to meet my friends at Demos's house.

Demos, a year older than I, was my hero. He saved me once from his family's turkey, which had attacked me without warning one day. That darn bird was taller than me, and it threw me to the ground and stuck its beak in my thigh. Demos had gotten a knife from the kitchen and run out, threatening the beast, ready to cut its throat. He would have done it had his mom not run out, crazily cursing him for trying to kill their precious turkey. I could not understand why she would defend that ugly bird! In any case, Demos had become my guardian and mentor.

One morning, a few days before I had hatched my plan, I saw my friends passing our house early in the morning.

"They are going to school," Mom said.

"School? Why? How about me?" I cried. "I want to go to school too and have fun with them!"

"You cannot go to school yet," she responded with a softness in her voice that made me upset. "You are too young. You will stay at home with me, help me do chores around the house, and keep me company until you are ready to go to school with them next year." She tried to kiss me, and I ran away screaming.

"No! I want to go to school now! I do not want to do chores with you. It is boring!"

She ignored me and continued sweeping the floor with a broom, calm and assertive.

"I hate you," I said. I ran out into the backyard and began throwing rocks triumphantly at the kitchen's wooden door.

"Linda!" my mom screamed from inside. "I will tell your dad!"

"So? He isn't here anyway. You will forget," I wailed at the top of my lungs.

And so it went. I missed my friends. Every morning I watched them walk to school with their bags under one arm and their snack, well wrapped in newspaper, under the other. I cried when I saw them laughing and teasing each other. Every day I waited for them to come back and play. But we never had enough time, as their moms would angrily call them back to do homework.

On a Sunday morning, Grandma Eleni visited us after church, her hands full of large pieces of altar bread the priest had distributed to the parishioners. I loved this bread; it was soft and sweet with powdered sugar sprinkled on it. Grandma knew how much I liked it and would always get two extra pieces for me.

"Tomorrow I am going to school," I announced, interrupting their conversation.

They both looked at me silently and with a smile that showed doubt and amusement.

"What are you doing here then?" my mom challenged me. "If you are this smart, go!"

Her comment was meant to provoke, but for the first time in as long as I could remember, I did not overreact. Instead, I came up with a plan. That night, while I was hiding under a warm blanket on my cot trying to fall asleep, I decided. *Tomorrow morning, I will go to school and tell the teacher I want to learn how to read and write*, I thought, half asleep and half dreaming. It felt like a real conversation I was having with myself. I knew where the school was, and my friends had told me that the name of their teacher was Mrs. Mary.

I woke up early the next morning and had my hot chocolate and a piece of bread, as usual. Then I ran to the window, where I waited to see my friends walking by on their way to school. I waved at them cheerfully. Mom was surprised by the change in my attitude.

"What would you like to do today?" she asked. "Do you want me to show you how to stitch, or visit Grandma, or read a story?"

*None of them*, I thought. Without responding, I ran out the kitchen door to the backyard, where the cats were waiting for our morning games.

The neighborhood was small, with perhaps fifteen houses packed tightly next to each other and a few dirt roads wide enough for a horse carriage to drive on. Except for my parents, who had rented our house when they got married, the people in the community all knew each other very well, having lived there for generations. The neighborhood was free of cars, which were a rare commodity on the island in those days. Only a few bikes would run on our dirt roads, which were used primarily by the donkeys and mules that pulled the carts of street vendors who sold fresh fruits, vegetables, eggs, milk, and yogurt.

Almost every man in our small town who worked at the naval base walked to and from work, leaving before sunrise and coming back late at night. Most of them walked together, in old trousers and jackets that bore signs of wear and military service even from a distance. They carried lunches in fabric bags, which also brought back any leftovers from the base cafeteria, as well as the day's small wage. All of them spoke of the admiral's generosity and good nature. He had ordered the distribution of the cafeteria leftovers, recognizing the community's poverty and unmet food needs. I remember almost everyone speaking of him with respect and affection.

In this safe neighborhood, my mom trusted me to run around on my own. No one was a stranger, and visitors were few and infrequent. Everyone in our small town knew who I was, and I knew all of them. *All of them are spies*, I thought bitterly. *They tell Mom everything I do.* Yet, that morning, despite the many risks involved in the plan, I decided to join my friends at school.

"Linda!" I heard the voice behind me again. "Where are you going? Where is your mom?"

I ignored the voice and kept walking, my heart racing all the while. I knew who it was. It was one of the neighborhood mothers, one who always butted into other people's business. Once I told her that her children were going to be hungry if she did not go inside immediately to cook for them. "Oh, you little devil," she had said, and smiled at me.

"Linda, I am gonna tell your mom," I heard her, yelling with more urgency.

*Yes, like I don't already know that*, I thought and ran faster.

I turned a second corner to my left when I saw the white walls, red tiled roof, and round dome of the church, its bell tower standing tall in the middle of the courtyard. I knew I was close to the school because it was connected to the church. It was a big and tall structure, with two courtyards for the kids to play in. Strangely, it sounded quiet, which was not something I had anticipated. The courtyards were empty, the doors closed, and the whole building cloaked in silence.

*How weird! How come they do not play?* I thought. *This is not how school is supposed to be.* I pulled the knob of the metal door that provided entry to the courtyard and let myself in. A few more steps and I would be there. I would see my friends. Finally, I would get my chance to tell the teacher in person that I wanted to go to school too.

For a minute, I felt complete pride. I had made it! I could hardly believe I had come this far without problems, besides that of this gossiping, loudmouthed woman who continued to pursue me and yell at me.

I stood in front of the door of the main building, which looked big and heavy, a massive blue metal frame holding thick, opaque glass. I pulled the knob, but the door stayed firmly closed. I pulled again, and then I pushed forward, but nothing happened. I was ready to try again with greater force when a hand grabbed me by the shoulder and pulled me back. It was as if a wind had blown over me with tremendous force. Mom's voice hit me like a powerful tornado.

"What in heavens are you doing here? You bad girl! Why did you leave home and come this far without telling me? I will tell your dad, and you will be punished as never before!" I looked at her, startled and angry.

"I want to go to school," I heard myself say, my own voice rough and sobbing. "I want to be with my friends, not you. You are boring!"

She looked at me intensely, her dark eyes like two black holes spitting fire, short brown hair flapping in the wind. Her hands were still wet from washing clothes, and one of them held my hand firmly. I focused on her dust-covered sandals, my hand beginning to hurt from her grip. I raised my head to look at her, and it seemed as though she was trying to decide whether starting a fight in front of the school was worth it. As if suddenly changing her mind, she relaxed her hold and we started on our way back home without another word.

We remained silent as we passed the gossiper's house, the one who no doubt had told my mom about my adventure. She was standing by her front door, smiling broadly, triumphant for having defeated me. I stuck my tongue out at her. I felt humiliated and sad.

## MEETING GABRIEL

I was introduced to Gabriel by Mom when I was very young. I am not even sure when. Probably before my young brain could record time or place, when only feelings and voices mattered. Over time, her descriptions became so specific and references to Gabriel so frequent that I became convinced I had seen her and heard her voice before.

According to Mom, Gabriel was tall and slim, but strong. She had long, curly, hay-golden hair and wore a white robe. Her right hand always held a long sword. She was always serious and sometimes even scornful and angry. You could tell her anger from the flapping of her wings, but you could feel her approval in the calmness of her familiar voice.

Gabriel was not just any angel; she was an archangel, one who chose to be my guardian, something that made me feel unique and valued. She was a general in the army of angels. Generous but tough, understanding but not forgetful—if you were to push her buttons, she could be unforgiving. Mom tried for many years to have a child and was convinced that I would not have existed without Gabriel's help. She told me that it was holy water from the church of the Virgin Mary in Tinos and a sacred herb from Archangel Gabriel's crypt, brought by her youngest aunt, that helped her get pregnant with me. I do not remember how young I was when I rejected this story, but it was one that Mom loved to repeat. She told me that I was vowed to the Virgin Mary, and Gabriel would always protect me.

Mom had a way of expressing her wishes, anxieties, and fears through supernatural stories. This was not unique to her; she expressed the ancient superstitions and beliefs of her people. Yet for me, in my early years of life, it all made sense. Mom was very effective in making me fear the wrath of Gabriel every time I wanted to break the rules. Numerous times I tried to engage Gabriel in a rational discussion about the things I wanted to do, but she refused to participate. It was always when I did not want her around that she would show up with contempt or anger, and a few times, approval.

I was enchanted by Gabriel. She sounded like Mom, calm and understanding, but she could get furious enough to fight like a man. One gray, cold winter morning, I kept Mom company while she cleaned the greens she had collected from between the rocks in the hilly backyard. I loved the salad she made from these boiled greens, sprinkled with olive oil and vinegar. I tried to bring the discussion to Gabriel.

"Is she a man or a woman?"

"Who?" Mom asked, glancing at me.

"Gabriel! Is she a man or a woman?"

"Both," she whispered after some time, "she is both."

"Are all angels both?"

"Yes! All of them!"

"Does she have a family?" I continued. "How about these baby angels I see in church? Are they her children?"

"No," Mom said quickly, as if she wanted to stop the discussion, "she does not have children, and these baby angels just run errands when Gabriel is busy."

"Busy doing what? Keeping little kids company?"

"No, fighting!"

"Fighting?" I asked, excited about where this was going.

"Fighting the Bad Angel . . . the angel who fell from the sky. When she fell, her white wings turned gray like the bat's, her hair turned white, her skin wrinkled, and her nails curved like an eagle's talons."

"Will this Bad Angel come to me?" My nearly frozen voice barely escaped from my lips.

"Maybe, if you become a really bad girl and do not listen to your mom. You know what she does?"

I shook my head, terrified.

"She comes and speaks to you in a nice voice, and she puts bad thoughts in your head . . . If you follow her advice, she owns your soul, and later, she owns your body."

The rest of the day and that night, I could not get the Bad Angel out of my mind, especially her nails. I was afraid that sometimes I would not be able to tell her voice apart from that of Gabriel.


# A WINTER NIGHT

It had been a cold and wet winter. Most of the day, Mom and I had tried to warm ourselves by sitting next to a brazier and stirring the glowing coal around with a fire iron. Lighting the brazier was Mom's job. She would place pieces of coal in the burner, light a fire with some kind of liquid—later she told me it was benzene—and then she would wait until the initial flare turned into low flame and the coal turned into red hot balls that broke easily into ash. This fire could last for hours to keep us warm.

I still spent my days at home, while my friends went to school and grew close as a pack of young wolves. They saw me as a silly little girl, too young to play with them. They made me angry. I respected and hated them at the same time, and on top of this, I was jealous. They were going to school; they became smart while I remained a little girl. They could count and spell, but they refused to teach me, as if that made them better and more powerful. When I pleaded with Mom to teach me how to count, add, subtract, and multiply so I could be as smart as my friends, she refused, insisting I be patient and remember that I would learn it all when the time came.

It was much later I realized how self-conscious she must have been about her sixth-grade education. Her schooling had been buried under the wreckage of the war. The fact that I often corrected her when she tried did not help.

That day it was particularly cold. Mom was not feeling well; she slouched and complained of a fever. She also worried that Dad would come home any minute and that she would not have any food ready for him. The past few days we had eaten very little. My stomach hurt from anxiety about not having enough money, even if I managed to stay well fed because of the generosity of neighbors. Mom refused their invitations to meals, but she would send me to play, hoping that they might feed me, and they did.

A couple of days before, our neighbor—a nice plump lady who wore the same apron every day, as if it were part of her body—called me around lunch time to go and keep her daughter company. She had been bedridden with high fever.

She told my mom, "Georgina is so happy when Linda is around. Can Linda come today to play with her while I try to feed her? The last few days she has refused to eat."

It was noon when I went to Georgina's house. She looked thin and pale under the thick bedcovers. She smiled when she saw me.

"Come next to me," she whispered, gesturing to a spot next to her with a pale, bony hand.

I climbed onto her bed and sat next to her. She took my hands in hers and told me that she wanted to play again.

It had been a long time since I'd last seen her play outside. Even if we were a few years apart, we often spent time together on the hot summer days, playing all kinds of games. Those days seemed far away as I held her burning hands in mine. Her mom brought two plates full of food, which she placed in front of us on the bed. I had never seen so much food on one plate before. We both glanced at the meal and giggled, covering our mouths with our hands, to show that we intended not to eat. I was very hungry, but I did not want to make Georgina feel sad, so I played along. Her mom looked at us with eyes full of tears before finally taking the plates away.

We spent a lot of time together on her bed, and I told her stories intended to make her laugh. I liked telling her stories, and I spent hours that day telling every little story I knew, and others I made up on the spot. Her eyes remained shut the entire time. Her hands would squeeze mine every time she wanted me to talk more.

"Do you think I am going to . . . die?" she asked me suddenly, in a voice I could barely hear.

"No," I rushed to respond. "I was sick like you a few days ago, and I became better." It was a lie, but I was trying to cheer her up.

"Really?" she whispered, trying to smile. "Maybe we can start playing together when the sun comes out. It is so dark these days."

"Yes, I can teach you some new games I learned," I lied again.

"What happens when you die?" she asked, as if she had already forgotten about our plans to play again.

"I do not know," I responded in a low voice, wondering why my mom had never told me clearly what happens to people when they die. I went on, "Gabriel will not let you die. She protects *all* kids. This is what my mom told me."

Georgina smiled and fell asleep so quietly that I could hardly hear her breathing.

When it was time to leave, her mom gave me a plate full of food to take with me.

"It is a bad omen to leave food behind," she said in a shaky voice. "Go home and tell your mom that Georgina may be with us only for a few more days," and she turned her face away to hide her tears. I did not understand.

"Where is she going?" I asked. She looked at me with sadness that I had never seen before.

"She will go to God . . ." After a pause she added, "Now, just go home . . . and give the food to your mom."

I felt sad that I would lose the only friend I had left to play with, now that the others were going to school.

"Maybe I could plead with Gabriel to tell God not to take her," I told Mom. And at night, before I went to sleep, I prayed to Gabriel and asked her to help my friend. She did not respond.

A few days later, I heard a lot of commotion coming from Georgina's house and saw people going in and out all wearing black. Something was wrong, but I was afraid to ask what.

"Let's go and see Georgina before she leaves," Mom said with a breaking voice. I noticed she was wearing black too. I took her burning hand in mine and walked to Georgina's house.

So many people were there. Most were quiet, some softly crying, others whispering, others chanting songs in my great-grandmother's tongue. I looked at Georgina's bed and saw her sleeping, all dressed up in a white dress with flowers on her long hair, her hands crossed on her chest.

"Linda," her mom said, "would you like to come and say goodbye?"

I nodded and went to Georgina's side. She looked older, dressed as a bride. I reached to touch her hands as we had done so many times when playing together. Her hands were cold, her face frozen, her eyes shut.

"Why is she sleeping? Is she going to wake up?" I asked Mom, my eyes locked on Georgina's white cheeks and long black eyelashes.

"No, she will not wake up again, she will be with Gabriel," she whispered.

"Gabriel is a traitor," I said in a voice that made Mom jump with surprise.

"Do not say that, and keep your voice down . . . do not let the Bad Angel put words in your mouth."

"Why? Gabriel never liked Georgina," I responded, irritated. "She did nothing to protect her, even if I prayed hard. What kind of angel is she?" My voice made a few heads turn around.

Sad and furiously mad at Gabriel, I kept my eyes on my friend as her mom covered her pale peaceful face with a white lace veil. I kept holding Georgina's hands until someone pulled me away, whispering that it was time to take her.

We went back home. It was early afternoon, but the dark clouds made the day look almost like night. I felt that Gabriel had betrayed me or was dead herself.

"Maybe Gabriel was never strong, and the Bad Angel won the fight," I told Mom, who responded with a stern look.

Over the course of the next few days, Mom complained of feeling sick. I saw her shivering. She became as thin and white as Georgina had, and her hands continued burning. Gabriel had either deserted us or was dead for good.

The evening came too fast. The shadows crept up the streets, leaving many corners in total darkness. Gray clouds hung threateningly over the horizon, and the sea grew dark and angry. Dad was supposed to have come home days ago. I kept looking through the window at the steep, wet path, waiting to see his hat emerge from behind the fence that partially obscured the view from our house. Those days when he was expected back home, I could always see his hat first, then his slim uniformed body turning onto our street as he walked up to the house.

Hours went by, and our home became engulfed in a dark fog. Mom lay in bed, sick, and could not light any of the acetylene lamps we used at night. I looked at the rusty streetlight, which made a creaking noise every time the wind blew it away from its wooden pole.

I was afraid of the dark and its secrets. I was afraid of the Bad Angel. Gabriel had not shown herself to me and neither had she responded to my pleas to save Georgina. The vision of her fighting the Bad Angel over Georgina's body, their wings flapping and their swords hissing fire every time the steel crashed together, grew stronger, and the room filled with the foul smell of their sweat. I heard their swords clashing and sparking and saw their eyes piercing through the night. I was equally afraid of both the good and bad angel.

I turned away from the window. I could see my mom's face in the flickering light of the candle that burned all day long in front of the Virgin Mary's icon. She was talking and crying in her sleep. Her face and her hands continued to be hot, and I remembered Georgina before she went to God. I placed my hands upon Mom's face and shook her.

"Mom!" I cried.

She woke up and looked at me with eyes I could not quite see in the dark.

"Are you going to die?" I asked in a voice lost in tears.

"No," she whispered, "just go to the neighbor and ask for help."

I ran to the front door, but the latch was too high and too hard for me to slide out of its holder. Furious and scared, I went back to the window to see whether anyone was coming by, fighting to look through the fog of my breath on the cold glass. With eyes barely over the window frame, I started pounding on the window with both hands, crying and yelling.

"Someone help, my mom is dying . . . please!"

Suddenly there was a loud knock at the front door. I jumped in fear but the voice that followed sounded familiar.

"Linda, open the door. It is me, Yiannis, your dad's friend."

I recognized his voice and suddenly felt relieved.

"Mom is dying," I said loudly from the other side of the door and started sobbing, "and I can't open the door."

"Go to the back of the house and open the kitchen door. I will meet you there."

I ran through the dark house, feeling my way to the kitchen. The door there was unlocked. I called for Yiannis, and we hurried to the front room. My mother was unconscious.

Yiannis was shorter than Dad, but he looked similarly thin and wore the same uniform. He always smiled, but now he was frowning, his face as dark as the rest of the room.

"I am going to call for help and will be back soon. Do not be afraid. Just stay put until I come back."

Before he left, he stood at the door, turned to me and asked, "Where is your dad?"

I did not respond, but he seemed to guess the answer because he turned away and left in a hurry, leaving the front door unlatched.

Time dilated, turning minutes into hours and hours into years. I avoided looking at the shadows in the corners of the room and instead stayed at the fogged window, eagerly scanning the street for signs that Yiannis was returning with help.

My grandmother came first. I heard her steps, then saw her running down the wet road. Her house was not far from ours—a mere ten-minute walk. She emerged from the shadows clad in a black dress, short and stocky, physically and mentally strong. I always remember her wearing black, her white hair pulled back in a French bow behind her young and tired face. Behind her were Yiannis and the doctor.

They swept into the room, and the doctor spent some time with my mother. I remembered him, but not very fondly. His presence always tasted of medicine, and his face reminded me of the pain of his needles. He stood tall in front of me, and as if he could read the question in my eyes, said, "Your mom will be fine."

Grandma stayed behind after Yiannis and the doctor left. She slept with us that night, as she always did when either one of us was sick. All three of us slept on the same bed. I crawled between her and Mom, who still burned with fever but was finally sleeping peacefully.

Sleep refused to come easily to me, though, as the fight between Gabriel and the Bad Angel took a new turn. In the darkness of my dreams, it was difficult to know who was winning amid the smoke from their fiery breath and the blood that spilled from their wounds. I did not trust Gabriel to win anymore. After I saw her lose Georgina, I felt that she was weaker than the Bad Angel.

"Is Dad owned by the Bad Angel?" I asked my grandma as we lay in bed. "Does the Bad Angel tell him not to love us? Not to be with us tonight? Is he with the Bad Angel tonight?"

Grandma looked at me in surprise and then smiled, though there was unhappiness in her face. She took me in her arms, gave me a hug, and told me softly, "Don't think about him now. Just try to go to sleep. We all love you."

I did not see my dad for another week. He came home, broke and angry as always.

# THE FIRST DAY AT SCHOOL

The first day of school came as a promise for a new life, a life I had dreamed about, planned for, and waited for impatiently for a long time. First, I wanted to reunite with my friends and join their gang from which I had been excluded for a full year. Second, I wanted to learn how to read and write. I was anxious to read the picture books with fairy tales the neighbor had given us as a gift from Georgina; all the books she had accumulated during her short life were now ours. I placed them in a box, and I had my mom read them to me repeatedly. Several times I caught her jumping pages, something that made me furious. Her penalty was to start from the beginning.

It was now the summer of 1960, just a few weeks before the beginning of school. I remember the day when Dad brought me a small leather bag with a pencil holder, a notebook, a drawing pad with colored pencils, a sharpener, and a small rectangular blackboard. There was chalk attached to it with a string and a little sponge big enough to fit in a holder carved into the wooden frame. The blackboard had three thin lines in white paint on it that, according to Dad, would help me write cursive letters in a straight line. I was so happy when I got his gift that, for the first time in as long as I could remember, I told him I loved him. He smiled at me and then laughed in a way that sounded, somehow, like crying. I loved the smell of the leather bag. I opened it regularly just so that the scent of new leather would waft over me and to make sure that everything was still inside.

The day finally came. I woke up early that morning after a restless sleep, dreaming that I had missed school and that I had lost my bag and could not find my clothes. It did not matter that every time I opened my eyes, I could see that it was still dark out and that my bag and school uniform were on the chair next to my bed. The uniform had been another gift, this one from my grandma. It was a dark-blue, cotton dress with a removable white collar that she had made specifically for me. Now it lay cleaned and ironed on the chair, as ready as I for the big day.

"Linda," my mom said as I wolfed down my breakfast, "make sure you always respond when Mrs. Mary asks you a question and that you always tell her the truth, no matter what."

She continued, looking at me intensely. "Do not allow the Bad Angel to whisper in your ear. Be a good girl at school and do not argue with anyone."

I looked at her and was anxious to promise her everything she wanted. "I will not get into trouble," I said quickly. I thought for some time that this promise was something I could try to keep.

She combed my hair, straightened my dress, gave me my school bag and a sandwich for lunch, then opened the door slowly, as you open the cage to let a young bird fly free.

The school was a long building, in which three medium-sized rooms connected to a long corridor. It had been built by the community next to the church, with the same orientation from east to west, as if it were an extension of the House of God. The project had cost a lot of money, which the community had painfully collected during the ten years after the German occupation.

As I had noticed in my earlier adventure, the building was flanked on either side by two courtyards: a small one to the north and a larger one to the south. There were three teachers: Mrs. Maria for first and second grade; Mrs. Katerina for third and fourth grade; and Mr. Zafiris, the headmaster, for fifth and sixth grade. The building was big enough for about eighty students—all the youth this small town could educate during that time.

On the first day of school, the priest came to bless the building, the teachers, and especially the students, to make sure, he said, that God would turn "these wild piglets into civilized Christians." We gathered in the long corridor that stretched from the east side of the building where the teachers' room was and ended at the west side at a strange staircase that went from floor to ceiling and then stopped.

"Where do these stairs go?" I whispered to an older boy who stood next to me while we waited for the priest's blessing.

"Nowhere, stupid," he responded, seriously annoyed. "They are there in case they want to build another floor."

After the blessing, Mr. Zafiris went halfway up the stairs, looked at us carefully, and waited until all became quiet. Then he explained the rules of the school. All the girls were to play in the north courtyard and the boys in the south. If any of the boys were found among the girls, they would be punished with caning. The older kids were supposed to protect the younger ones and were not to bully them for fun. No one was supposed to stay in a classroom during recess, and everyone had to come back in as soon as the bell rang that marked the end of break. We had to make sure that we did not run, did not yell, and always kept our hands and ears clean. I could never figure out why having clean ears was important. *There is probably a good reason*, I thought.

We started moving to our classrooms in a line. As we approached the door, our teacher checked the hands, ears, and haircuts of the boys and then the school uniforms of the girls to make sure everything was clean and proper. Those kids who did not have an appropriate presentation were not disciplined; instead, the headmaster would visit the family to personally complain. These visits gave the mothers of these kids an additional reason to pull their ears in front of the teacher, even if it was not the kids' fault that their nails were long and dirty or their ears plugged up with wax. Mom had already explained to me that if for any reason Mr. Zafiris or Mrs. Mary were to visit our house, I would pay dearly. So, I became very picky about my dress, hands, and ears.

We all started misbehaving from day one. Even I, after all the promises I had made Mom, had a hard time trying to quiet the Bad Angel, who whispered to me constantly. It seems she was able to displace Gabriel, who must have been off somewhere licking her wounds.

Some kids teased the teachers, and I wanted to smile. Others made fun of those kids who came to school dirty or without shoes, and I wanted to make fun of them too. Mrs. Mary was always kind to those children, however, and gave them pencil and paper every time they showed up without their own. They all looked sad and thin, and they hated school.

Many of them would leave in the middle of the morning and would not show up until next day. Mr. Zafiris, I was told, went to their homes and threatened their parents, promising that unless they sent their kids back to school, fed them properly, and kept them clean, he would send the police to arrest them.

Some of the moms would come every day to prepare breakfast and serve us. Usually, it was a cup of cold milk and a piece of hard chocolate. It took me a while to realize how many of the kids in our community survived on very little and that they skipped school not because they were lazy but because they found school to be a distraction from what really mattered—finding food to fill their stomachs.

One day, Mom and I walked by the home of one of those kids, dirty and cluttered with junk. I grabbed her hand and said, "I do not want to be poor!"

"Then go to school and be a good student. This is the only thing that can save you," she responded.

## THE MAGIC OF NUMBERS

I loved numbers. Not only did I love writing them, I loved reciting them and playing with them. Numbers meant something to me that I cannot explain. I could *feel* them. I could remember them, and I could talk to them.

I was always the first to finish math assignments in class. I would finish quickly enough to pay attention to the assignment of the second graders. Not only could I understand the second-grade math, but I could solve the problems faster than any of the second-grade students.

Every time Mrs. Mary gave us a problem, I would know the answer, as if Gabriel had decided that this is what she could do to repay me for her negligence and being absent for such a long time. It was as though she whispered the answers to me. Many times, I would give the right answer but could not quite explain why it was correct. It became apparent to me that Gabriel was good at math and felt guilty for not being able to save my friend. She also tried to rebuild her reputation, but I told her that she had lost my respect, and it would take a lot of work to rebuild my trust in her motives and powers.

"Did Gabriel go to school?" I asked Mom one day as we sat having lunch at our kitchen table.

"Probably, yes," Mom said.

"How about the Bad Angel? Did she?" I asked, remembering her long dirty nails and her ugly face.

"Definitely not! She hates school and cannot read or write," Mom answered quickly. "She also whispers bad things to little kids to make them become like her, and she tries to keep everybody poor, without any money, any pride, any hope for a better life. She does this so that she can own them and make them her slaves."

This is the second time she had mentioned enslavement to the Bad Angel, and it made my hair stand on end. It was then that I promised myself that I would never allow the Bad Angel to own me, and that I would do everything I could to be an excellent student.

Being at school made time go fast. The bright fall days were quickly replaced by gray skies. The blue sea became angry with white caps, and most of the trees lost their leaves. Only the proud pine trees kept their greenness and continued to shine brightly and smell intensely, especially after every rain. The happy children playing outside during the afternoon hours soon migrated indoors, and the days grew shorter.

Our school had no heating, and we had to keep our coats on to keep warm. We wore gloves that were open at the fingertips. Mom had knitted mine from an old, bright-green wool sweater that I had outgrown. Each of the gloves had a little crocheted pink rose that appeared on the back of the hand, a pattern I had selected myself.

Many of the kids became sick that winter, and there were a few days when I woke up in the morning to find a thin layer of snowflakes on the wild grass that grew all around our home. This serene, white coat made our neighborhood look clean and our homes noble.

One day, I woke up cold. My feet felt frozen. The little brazier was burning, but the heat could not reach my bed five feet away. I got dressed in a warm sweater my mom had knitted for me and a warm skirt I had gotten from my cousin, Eleni, when she grew out of it. I pulled on my socks and shoes and went to the kitchen to have my breakfast. Mom no longer took me to school, and all the kids from the neighborhood went together in a pack.

I was so proud to be one of the young wolves, which is what we called ourselves. I waited for the group to come by, and when I saw them approaching, I ran out to join them. My feet were still cold. That day, we all went to school carefully, as the white streets were icy. We left behind us footprints, like a flock of black birds on a white sky, sometimes grouped together and other times spaced apart as though dancing to their own tune.

At school, we all gathered as usual in the long corridor to say our prayers before dispersing to our classrooms. There was more noise today than usual. Our teachers were not there, only the headmaster, who walked up and down the corridor with his ruler raised in a threatening manner. It was this ruler he used to show the letters or numbers on the board, and to point out Greece on the map. "Big and impressive with its 2,500 islands," he would always say. With the same ruler, he spanked us for discipline: the girls on our hands and the boys on their thighs.

He walked slowly up the stairs and then turned so he could see all of us. With a ceremonial seriousness in his voice, he announced that our two teachers, Mrs. Mary and Mrs. Katerina, were sick with the flu and would not come to school for a few days.

Proudly, he added that he had decided to keep the school open. After he allowed the voices of the disappointed students to die down, he reminded us that, for as long as he was alive, the school would never close, not even for one day. That was bad news for many. The whispering grew louder and louder until he had to yell, "Stop!" at the top of his lungs to quiet us.

"Go to your classrooms immediately, as you do every day," he ordered, and came down the stairs to guide the first graders in.

We walked to our classrooms, curious to see what would happen next. Our desks were in the same place, but the wooden doors that separated the three rooms were wide open, so all the six grades were together. The pandemonium that followed was indescribable. The older kids started throwing paper balls to the first graders—not that they had enough paper to waste, but they found it entertaining. Mr. Zafiris threw the ruler and hit a few of the boys, who screamed like bitten dogs, then sat in the middle of the room and looked around viciously.

"Do not even *dare* doing that again. Today, I own you. Not your mom, not your dad. I do. Today you are mine."

I thought it was a mistake to take away what the Bad Angel had already claimed, "Unless he is the Bad Angel," I told a friend, who looked puzzled, as though I were speaking another language.

"What Bad Angel?" she tried to ask, but our voices were swallowed by the headmaster's thunderous scream.

"We will all read and write together, and then we will do math separately."

We looked at him in amused confusion. One of the older boys laughed, and the rest of us giggled. That was the last straw for this Bad Angel incarnate. He went to the boy, grabbed him by the ear, and pulled him all the way to his desk. By then, the boy's ear was dark red. The headmaster pushed him into the corner and told him to stay there for the rest of the class. Seventy boys and girls became deadly quiet.

The headmaster walked up to our teacher's desk and looked left and right like a hawk.

"Let us start with the first grade," he announced. "Who wants to read today's lesson?"

Silence. Everybody looked down.

"Linda, my child," he said with a poisonous politeness, "can you read today's lesson from your book?"

I was stunned that he had picked me. My voice left me. I looked at my book and opened it to the day's lesson, but the letters flew left and right in a frenzied dance. I could not read them. The words came out of my mouth in a stutter. I had never stuttered before.

"What is the problem with you?" he said.

"N-n-nothing," I replied.

Trying to deflect his attention from my reading, I dangerously suggested something else. "M-m-may I recite numbers instead of reading?" I asked with trepidation.

He looked at me with ambivalence, clearly debating whether he should yell me back to my seat or continue ordering me to read. Either way, I would be totally humiliated.

After some silent seconds had gone by, he made a gesture with his ruler and said, "Whatever—go ahead."

I started counting. I went from one to twenty, and then backward.

"Stop!" He waved his ruler in the air, uncertain about what to do next. "Do you know the multiplication tables?" he asked, trying to catch me unprepared.

I nodded and started reciting the tables forward and backward.

"Stooooopppppp! Enough; sit down," he screeched like a hawk. "In fact, no, come here, up front," he added, as if the Bad Angel had whispered into his ear a new idea.

I went up front and stood by the chalkboard. Nausea gripped me, and I felt ready to run home and never come back. He kept looking at me, his left index finger on his lips, thinking. While he was thinking, I debated my next move. Was it worth pretending to be sick? It seemed like a bad idea. Finally, the headmaster turned and asked a boy from one of the older grades, almost double my height, to come up front with his math book. The boy did so hesitantly and opened his book to that day's lesson, looking at the headmaster for further guidance.

"Copy the first problem from your homework on the board and then solve it. You may ask Linda for help," he said, smiling at me and making me blush up to my ears.

The other children did not make a sound as the chalk made its screechy run across the board. The whole school was waiting for the second act. I do not remember the problem. I do not remember the boy's answer, other than that it was wrong, nor do I remember the answer I gave when he asked for help. All I remember was that the headmaster's face turned white as he looked at me, stunned.

"How do you know?" he asked.

I was sweating and shivering at the same time. I was ready to reveal Gabriel's mischief, but I remembered Mom telling me that the story of Gabriel was just for the two of us. So, I said nothing.

For the rest of the time that the grades were all together, the headmaster had me do math with the older kids. Even after the teachers came back to school, recovered from the flu, I continued doing math with them. By the end of the school year, I had mastered everything in our school's math curriculum for all six grades. No one thought of me as weird, and no one mentioned it to my mom, until Mrs. Mary told her before the summer break that I was gifted in math.

It was the first time that someone had told me I was gifted in anything, and I felt proud for having something no one else had. Never had I believed I had any gift worth talking about. My gift in math was the first one. Math made me love school more than before, even when my problems with writing and reading persisted.

Math made me happy. It made me forget my dad's temper, his absence, and our poverty. Solving math problems was not just playing a game, it became an escape from reality. Every day after finishing my homework, I made up my own math problems and spent the late hours of the night trying to solve them by lamplight. Mrs. Mary supported me by giving me extra paper almost every day for my math games, since Mom could not afford it herself.

As spring arrived and we prepared to finish school for the year, Mom told me that we would be moving to Crete, another island far away from our own, because dad had been transferred to a ship at a different naval base.

I was very sad. This was the first time I had to leave my friends, my grandma, and my cousins. I protested fiercely, but we left nonetheless.

# GROWING UP

In the fall of 1961, my family underwent the first of many relocations between three separate bases. Moving around every year just before school started created more hardship for our family than anyone could have imagined.

Being away from our neighbors and the support of my mom's family, to say nothing of my father's continued absence and our meager amount of money, made our situation almost unbearable. School became my only escape. I let it become my life, my entertainment, my whole world. Even Mom came second to it.

I rejected Gabriel's good intentions, and I ignored the Bad Angel whose tricks I could easily recognize and carefully avoid. I came to realize that the two of them were more similar than I had been led to believe; they were both powerful, arrogant, and uncompromising. They were both deceitful and liked to play with my mind and threaten my soul. Good and bad, bound in an eternal relationship, are painfully similar and inseparable. Their twisted coexistence confuses, corrupts, and destroys, all the while offering a sense of power, self-worth, and self-righteousness.

The two angels continue to fight a battle I sometimes still see in my dreams. The two of them—forceful and fearless—clash in an endless fight over my soul with their wings burned, their hair entangled in a golden and white mess, their swords broken, and their bodies covered with my blood.

I woke up, my body shivering, and shook my mind free of the pages of my memory book. I found myself sitting on the deck of the small fish tavern, my eyes lost in the blue of the sea and the small boats that kept quivering in the soft wind of the summer evening. I felt engulfed in their serenity and, for a moment, I became one of them. The sun was ready to set, and my order had remained on the table untouched, still carrying the warmth of the old man's heart.

I tried to reduce my existence to one sense only and dispel any other thoughts, but my brain found a way to sneak a signal into my memory:

*This is exactly what your father would have ordered had he been here next to you.* I heard the angel's voice that sounded like Mom's.

*This is what he would do if he were in the mood to love me,* I added as I raised my glass.

"This is for you, Dad," I said aloud. "Cheers."

Our house in Panoussa, Tinos.

## CHAPTER FIVE

# TINOS

**August 28, 2016**

I SAW MYSELF LOOKING AT THE CLOCK, but I could not read the time. The clock hands were spinning, as if time were accelerating. Every molecule of my body began to age instantly. My hands trembled, their blue veins so prominent that I thought they wanted to break my skin and set themselves free. My face reflected off the glass surface of the clock, and I saw an old woman with long white hair looking at me, uninterested and tired, appearing to wait anxiously for the clock to run through time until she could disintegrate into dust.

My head filled with the buzz again, this time louder, longer, and more painful. The view of the older version of me sat frozen, her reflection on the glass oblivious to time. I opened my eyes to the glowing hands of the clock in the darkness of our apartment in Athens. The buzz went off again, and quickly I slapped the clock, knocking it to the carpeted floor; the minute hand pointed up, the hour hand rested at six, and the second hand steadily ticked between them, unperturbed by the fall.

"Goddamn it," I heard Spyros hissing between his teeth in a sleepy voice. "Could you not find another alarm? This one's sound can raise the dead from their graves." He pushed his head under the pillow and turned to the other side.

"That's exactly the point," I whispered as I picked the clock from the floor.

The old woman was gone; only my sleepy face remained, still tired. *Wake up! We have a boat to catch, remember? We're going to Tinos,* I yelled in my head. The words rang in my ears, and I felt the old woman inside me yearning for this trip to the island, as if it were to be her last one. I tried to cheer myself up.

"In less than three hours, we'll be in Tinos, if we make it to the boat." I raised my voice so Spyros could hear me. My intense, high-pitched voice did the trick. He stood up and frantically started packing his bag, cursing the boats for running so early in the morning. My bag had been packed since the night before and sat ready by the door.

We threw our bags into the car and drove to the port of Rafina on the east side of Athens. The ferry was ready to leave, its engines running almost at full power. The sea water churned deep down beneath the boat, and white foam overflowed onto the landing dock. Our car was the last to drive on. "Thank God we made it." I heard my voice full of anger. "Why couldn't we make it earlier?" I muttered, "I cannot take the stress."

"It's the clock," Spyros said. "It refuses to buzz earlier than six o'clock. It complains that it is deprived of sleep."

Going back to Tinos felt like a pilgrimage to a place of peace and redemption. I had been to Tinos every summer since July of 1997 when our thirteen-year-old son Erik, ten-year-old daughter Helena, and I visited my cousin Eleni in her new house. It was an old ruin of a wine cellar built in the seventeenth century, which she had transformed into her summer home. The house was in an old village comprising no more than fifteen homes on the top of a hill almost 1,300 feet in elevation.

"Welcome to my tiny house," Eleni said with a broad smile. Her velvet-black, almond-shaped eyes set within her richly tanned face looked bigger and brighter. Those eyes captured all the love that she had for me since she first saw me when I was a few days old, and she was a curious two-year-old brunette. It was then that she declared that I was her little baby and gave me her heart as a gift to keep forever.

Helena was the first one to enter the tile-floored living room. Two divans covered by colorful pillows made a warm and inviting sitting place from where we had a view of surrounding hilltops through two small windows. The whole room was decorated with Eleni's art that was placed carefully and tastefully near the fireplace. It was a small but beautiful abode, like those in the fairy tales. It had thick stone walls painted white and a wide, ancient arch, which had been the only thing standing when she purchased the property.

We followed Helena, who disappeared up to the second floor via the narrow staircase that led to Eleni's bedroom—another small but airy room that ended with a small veranda, the house's bridge to the vastness of the steep hillside. From there we could see the many small canyons around the foothills, like avalanches of green and brown coming to rest below the old Castle of Exomvourgo. We stared silently at the breathtaking sight until Helena, making sure that nobody would miss it, raised her hand and pointed at the castle. "Look," she said, her voice blending with the whistle of the wind.

I remained still, with my hand shielding my eyes, lost in my thoughts as I saw the procession of the old garrison, banners flowing in the air, horses breathing hard in the dusty air as they marched up the steep hill eager for food and refuge inside the gates of the fort. The horn blowers upon the castle walls announced the arrival of the Order of Solomon. The knights sat tall on the horses, their swords reflecting light under the hot sun, their white robes red from blood and wine, their loot clanging loudly on the backs of their horses, and their faces marked wild with the signs of war.

"Do you know the story?" Eleni's voice brought me back.

"Not yet," I said, implying that I wanted to hear it.

"This is a very old castle," she started. "Nobody knows when it was first built. Some say that a few of the rocks in its foundation go back to the pre-Hellenic times." She looked at Helena who was listening anxiously. "I will tell you the rest of the story when we visit it."

The Castle of Exomvourgo has been built, destroyed, and rebuilt numerous times over the centuries. Though its beginnings are lost in the fog of time, its thick walls give a deep sense of its history; a mosaic of old and new cobbled together in a temporal patchwork. In some places, the restorations were done with care, while in other places the work was done hastily. Between the fifth century BC and the eighteenth century AD, the fort had accepted many masters who ruled the small population living inside its walls with little empathy. From the fourth crusade in 1207 AD until the castle's final destruction in 1715 AD, it was under Venetian rule. The Venetian masters cared only about three things: producing silk from the island's famous silkworms, the fertilizer from the pigeon droppings, and imposing harsh taxes on the natives. The production of silk and fertilizer is still visible in the architecture of the island's homes and its unique pigeon houses—structures incredibly elaborate, even more so than the island's churches.

Famous for its beautiful green and white marble, during the Athenian rule in the fifth century BC, the island provided everything that was needed to build the houses and temples on the island of Delos and in the city of Athens. However, almost a thousand years later, by the time the Venetians claimed the island, these resources had already been expended. Despite the war-torn history of the island brought by the marauding Persian and Athenian ships, the Roman and Byzantine armadas, the crusaders, the pirates, and the Ottomans, it was disease that kept the population under control. During all that time, the castle stood strong, slowly growing in size with the families who sought refuge within its walls.

After numerous failed attempts, twice the Ottomans took over the island, first under Hayreddin Barbarossa (1537 AD) and then led by Canum Pasha (1570 AD), but both times the invaders failed to capture the castle with its 680 houses. In their last attempt, in 1715 AD, the colonizers finally took it over by heavily bribing the Venetian garrison, who left secretly in the dead of night, leaving the two thousand locals in the hands of the frustrated new owners.

Today you can see the ruins of the small homes, like holes in the rocks, untouched since the day they were blown up. No one survived the barbaric killing that followed. All the dead were piled and burned atop the destroyed castle, a confirmation that no one could avoid the wrath of the Ottoman sword. According to documents of that time, the Venetian Republic, exposed for their weakness and greed, accused the commander and officers of the garrison of treason and sentenced them to public death by swallowing liquid silver.

Today, mounted proudly on the highest point of the hilltop is a large white marble cross surrounded by the old ruins and the destroyed church, a reminder of those who were betrayed by greed and died from the sword of the arrogant and bloodthirsty new owners. Standing by the cross you can hear the voices of the dead in strange whistles and murmurs of the wind as it blows through the hollow openings.

The island, like a Homeric siren, made me feel connected to her rocks and hard soil, as if I were an olive tree planted right there, thousands of years old with my roots deep inside her stone heart and my branches opening wide to touch her blue skies. Standing on the castle's highest point underneath that white cross, I fell blindly in love with Tinos.

"I wish I could build a house here," I whispered, absorbed by the beauty of the view. I saw Eleni turn to me with a smile.

Two years later, on a freezing Michigan morning, while I was looking through a pile of papers in my faculty office at the University of Michigan in Ann Arbor, I heard the phone ring. It was Eleni's voice, as if coming from the depths of the Aegean: "I found four acres of land in Tinos very close to the sea, with an unbelievable view of the sunset." She paused. "Twenty-five thousand dollars. Do you want to buy it together?"

I was not sure I had heard her correctly, but I said yes nonetheless.

Over the following five years, Eleni helped us build a summer home on the island. Her architectural talent made it easy for us to design this house. She knew what we wanted before we even had the opportunity to draw it on paper. We wanted something small, simple, and appropriate to the locale. We wanted it to blend with the island's rocks and aged terraces. But she made it better than that: a simple but beautiful house that stands tall on three levels against the southern Aegean Sea looking steadfastly westward, waiting to witness the sun blow out its fire as it dives every evening into the deep dark blue water in a wondrous display of magenta and violet.

Our house sits on a steep slope full of sharp rocks that for thousands of years have borne silent witness to the progress of human life on the island. The slope faces southwest, with a view of Tinos's sister islands— leftovers from a promised land that some call Atlantis, the Cyclades, which are the most beautiful islands in the Aegean.

Our home was made of stone that was cut out of the hill. Master Builder Antonis decided where to place the foundation, despite the many back-and-forth arguments between him and Eleni. Antonis was in his mid-forties, masculine, and tall with curly gray hair and blue eyes. He was heavily tanned and wrinkled from the sun and salt, and he commanded respect.

No matter what Eleni was instructing him, he always did his own thing. This is how he had built many houses on the island, and he was not ready to receive directions from an educated architect who had never built a house with her own hands. Antonis learned the trade from his father whose apprentice he became when he was twelve years old. As the first son of his generation in a long lineage of builders, he took the responsibility to teach his younger brother and their sons a profession that has more secrets than an architect could tolerate. He built homes his own way, at his own leisure, and "without these funny sketches that make no sense," as he used to say with contempt about Eleni's blueprints. He knew what worked and what didn't, and the moment you left him alone, he would decide where to put in a window and how to build the stone arch. There are very few people in Greece nowadays who know how to build a stone arch, and Antonis brought them from the northern part of the country specifically to build our house.

I met all the workers during construction. They were quiet and shy but worked nonstop and treated my cousin and me with great respect. I am sure that they talked about us after we left, making note of how little we women knew. The next day, the door was where they wanted it and the fireplace was in the opposite corner from where it was supposed to be. Eleni had to ask Antonis to change it, who knows how many times, until she gave up. I am afraid that my house was the reason Antonis and Eleni did not speak very much after they finished it.

In the summer of 2004, the house was ready, almost two years after we started digging the foundation and five years after we bought the land. This is how long it takes to build a house in a place where the builders have a mind of their own, many times in conflict with the modern building code, and where "city planning" sounds like an elite term only found in books. In fact, Tinos does not have a city planning office. You have to take a two-day trip to the capital Ermoupolis, on another island, Syros, to be able to speak with an official. A phone call does not help. Despite the internet revolution, business on the islands is done the good old-fashioned way: face-to-face, with emotion and gusto. You cannot be in a hurry when you build here. Life on the island has its own clock, the same one she's had for thousands of years.

The Cyclades, with a total population of 120,000, is one of the most historic, beautiful, and diverse groups of islands in Mediterranean. Mykonos, the closest island to Tinos (a thirty-minute boat ride) and Santorini (about two hours away by the fast ferry) are internationally known and visited by millions of tourists every summer. They are only two of the thirty-three islands in this group. Tinos, on the other hand, with a total population of 8,000, is the sixth largest of the group by population but the largest in area, with fifty small villages spreading like splashes of white color on the steep hillsides.

From our house, on days when the air is not filled with the dense summer mist, we can see Ermoupolis on the island just south of us, with its churches, squares, and snake-like roads that take you to Ano Syros, a medieval town built by the Venetians after the forth crusade. At night you can never miss the city, its lights flickering like a small Christmas scene.

Despite the short distance that separates Tinos from most other islands of Cyclades, moody Poseidon makes it difficult to travel by boat. When he is in a bad temper, something that happens often throughout the year but mostly in August, he stirs the waters with his trident, churning the sea into big waves with thick white caps and forcing the boats to stay docked for many days at a time, making everyone, tourists and locals alike, curse him for his misery-making.

When we moved into the house in the summer of 2005, Eleni made sure it was finished and decorated. Like any Tinian house, the kitchen and family room make one space on the middle level, with the divan next to the fireplace and a large wooden table in the middle of the family room that can easily fit eight people for a meal. It has four bedrooms and two bathrooms split between the upper and lower levels; and each level opens to a breathtaking view of the Aegean.

We invited Antonis for our first lunch, according to the local custom. He came with his son, his new apprentice, a shy twelve-year-old boy with his father's hair and eyes, anxious to follow in his father's footsteps. In less than two hours, Antonis told us everything that had happened during construction.

"Did you build a strong house?" Spyros asked him just to trigger his passion.

"In the name of my father and the health of my son!" Antonis crossed himself three times, his blue eyes wide open, wrinkles on his forehead deep as his dimples.

"Master Spyros," he said with a seriousness in his voice, as if he were confessing, "the head of the rooster is buried under the column at the right east corner of the house. We thanked the gods properly." He lowered his voice and added, "But, to make sure, you may also want to ask a priest to come and bless the house."

Spyros and I looked at each other with a smile. *Half of the evil is cast out following the ancient ways and the other half following the Christian ones*, I thought. The old and the new were tied in a formidable bond that cannot be broken; a bond that is called "culture" and can only be respected.

The house was built the way the locals build their homes: without air conditioning or central heating. It has one fireplace in the family room. The heat in the summer is the biggest problem, so Eleni and Antonis decided to build windows you can open during the night for the cool breeze to come through as the waves lap against the small sandy beach about a hundred feet below. All the windows and doors have wooden shutters painted in cobalt blue, the color of the Aegean sky in the summer dusk.

The house is a dramatic mix of white and blue, pinned to the rocky cliff that drops down into the blue waves. It is distinctly visible from the ferry every time we visit the island—a safe signal that we are approaching the port.

## ALL OF US TOGETHER

Our first day in Tinos always starts with the opening of the house. First come the windows and doors that have been shuttered for a full year, then the chimney and the outside wood oven that provide shelter to all kinds of birds and animals during the cold winter nights. The dusting and cleaning of the whole house comes last.

On this visit, Eleni, who had left Davis a couple of weeks before us, had already come to the house and had already brought someone to open it and clean it. I felt so thankful to her. Once more she was taking care of me. *How can I ever pay her back?* I thought.

I was not in the mood for intense work. Even the idea of it was appalling to me, for the first time. Usually I find cleaning relaxing, and I do most of it, but not this time. Even opening the suitcases and hanging our clothes felt difficult.

I climbed the narrow stone stairs to our bedroom upstairs and opened the blue shutters to the veranda that looked out over the south Aegean Sea. The breeze fondled my body and made me tremble with yearning. I heard the waves call and felt the sea's cold embrace that holds you tight until you surrender body and mind. She seduces you to enter her world, calm and powerful, vicious and dangerous, sometimes unpredictable but never deceiving. I longed for her.

I heard the disrupting ring of my cell phone and realized for the hundredth time that I needed to change the tone. This one made me anxious. It reminded me of all these times in the past few months that it meant trouble. I looked around the bedroom I was trying to tidy up before opening the window, but I could not locate it. The ring sounded remote. I ran downstairs bumping on the narrow walls, wondering why in old homes the stairs were so narrow, and for a moment I regretted our decision to build an old-style house. I grabbed the phone from its cradle, "Hello?"

"Hi," a soft voice said in Greek. "How are you, when did you arrive?" I heard a warm smile hiding behind the voice on the other side of the airway.

"Ritsa! How are you? I am so glad you called," I said as the picture of a woman with a diva style, always beautiful and extravagant for her age, appeared in front of me: full lips, large almond eyes, two distinct dimples on her cheeks that make her face uniquely attractive. I always admired Ritsa when I was young. Eleven years older than me, she was my idol. Her mother, my mother's oldest sister, made the most beautiful dresses for her, which I secretly tried on in her room every time I could find myself there alone.

"I want to see you," I said in a voice full of determination. "We're in Tinos, and I don't want to travel. If you want to see me, come here."

"I would love to. I will be there tomorrow." She paused. "But there is a small problem," she continued.

"What's that?" I asked, suspecting that it had to do something with her sister. The face of Eleni the Older, with its witty look, dark eyes like my mom's, and determined stiff lips appeared for a moment.

"My sister wants to see you too," she said reluctantly.

"I know! I spoke with her in the morning and I invited her. We have enough space here for everyone."

"Can you manage being with both of us for a few days?" she asked. Memories of long arguments crowded my mind and forced a smile on my face.

"Of course, I can. See you tomorrow, I will pick you up from the boat."

I could not believe I had made all these invitations without telling Spyros. I needed to find a way to break the news to him. "Who was on the phone?" Spyros asked as he came in from the yard. He had been pulling the weeds that had grown to an impressive height, and he was clearly tired. "These weeds are growing faster than anything that I have seen," he complained.

"Ritsa called," I said.

"And?" he looked at me with fear.

"She is coming, tomorrow, and her sister too," I said quickly and ran upstairs before he had time to respond.

When I was born, I was the fourth granddaughter in a family of all women. We cousins grew up together and spent most of our summers together, eating at the same table, sleeping on the same beds, playing hide and seek, teasing each other, scaring each other, and fighting with each other when we were in the mood. For the first time since I had left Greece in 1979, all four of us would be spending time together. I felt nervous. I did not know whether this would have a happy ending. Eleni and I made exit plans. In case things between the two sisters went south, we would split them between our two homes. For the time being, we planned to have them stay with me and Spyros.

This was a special event for us. Seeing each other without rushing, supporting each other without reservations, and healing the wounds our separation had created in our hearts could bridge the distance time had built up over almost four decades. We would have the opportunity for the first time in almost forty years to learn about the moments we missed, the people we lost without being able to grieve together, the babies we had birthed and raised separately.

Our bond—a thin, fragile lace of connections we were trying to keep alive over the years with letters and phone calls—demanded time together to get stronger.

The next morning, I saw her coming off the boat. I waved, holding with my other hand the fence that separated the docks from the people who were there to receive their visitors. You cannot miss Ritsa; always fit and well dressed. Her years as an actress and dancer had left a mark on her personality. "I am on a special diet," she said when we got in the car to drive to the house. "Is my sister here?" she asked nervously.

"She's coming this evening. We'll pick her up from the boat."

"By the way," I continued, "You and she will have the two rooms downstairs, is that okay?"

"Of course," she said, "I want to see her. It has been such a long time!"

Her sister—Eleni the Older, as we used to call her to differentiate her from our younger cousin—had remained fit and fast like a cross-country athlete. She was the opposite of Ritsa: a tomboy when she was young, wild in her manners, but direct and disciplined when needed. She grabbed me when she came off the boat and kissed me on both cheeks. She reminded me of those days when, as a child, she was double my size. She always grabbed me to kiss me with such a force that it would stop my lungs from breathing air. She was the most fun when we played, and always the leader of the pack of all the cousins who lived nearby. We had a clan of almost twenty wild kids.

Though she was older now, Eleni had not changed much. She had always been strong, outspoken, and fun. She came down from the boat with a big smile. "Is it okay if you ladies share the two rooms and bathroom downstairs?" I asked again politely, just to make sure that both parties were in agreement. "No problem," both sisters said. "We came to see you." For as long as I can remember, the two sisters always had some form of competition. They love and hate each other in a way I have seen nowhere else.

Over the following few days, the four of us spent a lot of time together. We cried and laughed, we argued and cooked, we set the table, ate, and got drunk, washed dishes together and placed them back in their place. Spyros and Elias tried to stay in the background and mostly out of sight.

We spoke in code, the one we had developed almost half of century ago when I was five, Eleni the Young was seven, Eleni the Older was twelve, and Ritsa was sixteen.

It was interesting to observe how quickly we reverted to our old roles. I was the youngest and most taken care of. After so many years, they came together because they sensed that I needed them. After so many years, drinking unearthed the same old feelings, and I was like an animal waking from hibernation hungry for the old food.

"Do you remember that you always cried when my sister and I were fighting?" Ritsa asked me over the calming sound of the waves breaking on the beach below. The glasses in front of us were filled with wine from the third bottle we had opened that night.

"I cried because you were scary," I said, laughing and recalling their violent arguments that played out like an ancient Greek drama. "I thought you were going to kill each other—"

"You are exaggerating!" her sister Eleni interrupted, her voice filled with the smoke from her cigarette.

"No, I'm not!" I protested. "When I was in first grade, I stayed over at your house for the weekend and saw you chasing Ritsa with a wire cord, the one you pulled from your iron." I heard Eleni chuckle. "I remember your sister screaming like a wounded animal."

"I did not hit her," she noted, avoiding Ritsa's intense glance. "She was always screaming and *pretending* she was hurt."

"You were always hurting me, mentally and physically," Ritsa replied, irritated.

"Yes, but you have to say why," her sister said. "You always wore my clothes without asking! You owned everything I had. Sometimes even my boyfriends."

I felt the storm coming, so I raised my hands in surrender. "Enough of this. I have another story." Everyone remained quiet.

"One evening we were playing hide and seek in your house," I told the sisters, who were trying to restrain themselves with a discipline I had not seen before. My tone attracted their attention. "I was very young, but I still remember it. Our mothers were sitting in the backyard under the trellis," I continued. I remembered the thick vine, heavy with fruit, overhanging the trellis providing the most enjoyable shade during the day. Our mothers used to enjoy sitting under the vine during the cool summer evenings talking quietly while we, the cousins, were making mischief.

"I was afraid of the dark, and I didn't want to play. Eleni raised me in her arms and held me for some time until she got tired and let me stand on the kitchen table almost at her height. Then someone turned off all the lights."

"Who?" they both asked with true curiosity. I ignored them.

"I kept asking, louder and louder, 'Why did we turn off the lights?' Eleni whispered to me in a creepy voice. 'Dogs came from the moon to eat people, we do not want them to find us.' *Hoooowl*! I heard a dog howling and got terrified! I started yelling hysterically, 'Mom, help . . . Mommy . . . I am scared!'"

"How do you remember all of this?" Eleni the Older asked defensively. "You were too young."

"Our mothers rushed in angrily," I continued without acknowledging her question. "'Who scared the baby?' your mom asked, looking at both of you with piercing eyes. 'Not me,' Ritsa cried. 'Why does it have to be me all the time? It is her!' she said, pointing to you." I looked at Eleni the Older. "Ritsa said, 'She hates everyone because she is so ugly. She scared the baby.'"

"That's Ritsa," Eleni the Older said with contempt.

"Your response was immediate and violent," I continued, my voice getting stronger. "You threw a plate at Ritsa that could have cracked her head. You were lucky that it missed the target. Ritsa started screaming, and soon enough we were all crying. I know Eleni the Younger was there but too young to participate. She was crying too. Your mom punished both of you with an extended grounding, and my mom and I went back home both very unhappy. Eleni went to sleep at Grandma's place."

This story has remained vivid in my memory after all these years, and

I have always wondered whether the dog's howling was a coincidence or part of the game. That night I found the opportunity to ask the sisters for the first time. They laughed and confirmed that it was a coincidence. We all remembered that we never played this game again.

"You were taking play too seriously for us to have this kind of fun with you," Ritsa noted with a smile hanging off her lips. "You always found a way to ruin the party!"

That night, we stayed awake talking about fun times from the past. Each one of us bringing a story from the depths of our past that made us laugh until tears blurred our eyes. When it was over, silence fell like a black veil. We were left with a deep sense of loss for the people we loved but were not with us anymore, the dreams that never came true, the moments we missed, and the happy times that went by like a flicker.

I have engraved in my mind and my heart the moment when Mom asked me to stay with her on Christmas Day, about eight years ago, as I was about to leave for California. I told her I couldn't. I remember her standing by the door, looking at me as I left with a smile full of tears. I would give everything I have to go back and change that moment. I wish I could go back and tell her, "I'll stay."

The following morning, I found the sisters talking quietly in the kitchen over a cup of coffee Ritsa had prepared for them. "Did you sleep well?" I asked, thinking that with so much wine the night before they must have fallen asleep immediately. "We stayed up talking after you left," Ritsa said cheerfully. She was wearing a flowery caftan, her brown hair tied up in a loose bow.

"We tried to catch up," her sister said as she took a deep inhalation of the cigarette she had just lit up. She wore jean shorts and sported short brown hair; she was still impressively tall and fit.

I got a cup of coffee and sat next to her.

"Eleni is going to join us," she continued. "She called us to say that she will bring fresh bread for toast, so we will have breakfast when she comes. A cup of coffee is good enough for a start."

I nodded while keeping my eyes fixed on the thin blue line on the horizon that barely split the sky from the sea. The morning promised yet another gorgeous day, but nothing could light up my heavy heart.

"So, how are things with you?" I heard the younger sister's voice for the first time that morning. She sounded uncertain about the question, which she knew I feared. I was at a loss for words. I looked at the blue sea, but the only thing I could see was my soul, lost in fear, anger, and resentment.

"If I say 'well,' be sure I'm lying," I responded in a voice almost inaudible, even to me, and feeling a sudden cramping in my stomach. "I don't really know how I am doing."

How could I describe my feelings when I had no idea how I felt? The only thing I was sure about is that I wanted to wake up from this bad dream. I wanted to jump into the future as a new person with a new name. I would even settle for a brain injury that would erase all my near-term memory, take away the past seven months, and let me feel happy with a big hole in my memory book.

My eyes sought the thin white line between the sea and the sky that had almost disappeared, leaving in its place a blue continuum. The uninterrupted merging of two different worlds melted the boundary into a strong bond at the place where the sun sets.

My thoughts disappeared into random memories from the past that were fighting to capture my attention. I did not quite know where to start from, how to tame my feelings and how to find the words that stubbornly hid.

"It's a long story," I managed to say before I fell into silence.

As a graduate student at UCLA, with my son in the
shade of a tree across from Kerckoff Hall, June 1984.

## CHAPTER SIX

# THE SIRENS' SONG

IT WAS SEPTEMBER 10, 1979 when I left Greece for the United States, "the land of the free." I heard the voice of my second-grade English teacher creeping up from the past like a siren's song. I was afraid and anxious and had little money, but I was excited. Isn't this the story of every immigrant? My F-1 visa attached to my passport, stating "UCLA-international student" in bold letters, was supposed to be with me the whole time.

Despite my excitement about the adventure, leaving Greece was like ripping my heart out of my body. My visa became the only real reminder that there was a way back, Gretel's breadcrumbs out of the fearful forest.

The start was difficult. The place felt foreign and the people behaved differently. Before a week had passed living in Los Angeles, I was already regretting my decision. *This is not for me*, I kept thinking, *I do not fit here*.

"I want to come back," I told Mom when I called her a week later, paying one dollar and twenty-five cents a minute for a call that was mostly interrupted by noise. I do not remember how long her silence lasted on the other end of the line.

"Just give it a few more weeks. You spent so much money to get there. Do you really want to come back empty handed? But I miss you so much. Let's talk next week." She hung up with the sound of a sob that, like an echo, bounced from one side of my head to the other, building slowly into a migraine.

I do not remember our call the following week or the week after. Weeks and months went by living in two different worlds of the UCLA campus and my small, dark apartment. The first one vibrant, interesting, challenging, and intense; the other a mattress and a small black-and-white TV in a one-bedroom apartment with a view of the back of the next building. This was the only apartment I found where the building manager, a woman originally from Israel, was willing to rent it to a woman who had just arrived from Greece with limited income and only offering a promise to pay the rent on time. She told me that I reminded her of herself a few years back.

Within a few weeks, my desire to go back home was conditional on getting my doctorate. I could not go back without it. Spyros anxiously waited to finish his military service and join the Chemical Engineering department at UCLA, where he was admitted as a graduate student. Connecting my return to Greece to my graduation from the PhD program gave me a timeline and a goal.

In the following months, coming to California felt as if I joined the world and not just the United States. I made friends who had come to graduate school from China, India, Poland, Scotland, England, France, and Turkey. My American friend Cynthia took me under her wing. She fostered me as a sister. We were the only two women in the master's program in electronics until I met a third woman who came to the program from what was then known as Yugoslavia. Cynthia invited me to her family's ranch in Arizona for Christmas in 1979, and when I told her that I could not afford the ticket, she used her air miles to help me buy one. We became very close friends. By the end of January 1980, I was already happy waiting for Spyros to join me after his military service in Greece. It was March 1, 1980, when Spyros came off the plane at LAX.

The days were replaced by months and the months by years. We were poor graduate students but happy, filled with excitement, and free to be together. Like all other graduate students, we lived on a paycheck while trying to save enough to pay our international tuition, a total of $10,000 a year for both of us combined. None of our friends had more money, but that did not seem to bother us. We were excited building our future. At twenty-five years old, we were the only married couple among all graduate students in electrical and chemical engineering. I felt loved, safe, and intellectually stimulated. Everything else was secondary. My desire to go back to Greece faded away, and the emptiness of the early days was filled with the excitement of experiencing everything new.

My five years in graduate school were some of the best years of my adult life. Years full of dreams and filled with hope that I was moving up the staircase, getting closer and closer to the top of my dream tower. I did not wear a long floating dress, as in my memory book, but it did not matter. I felt light, like a small white cloud in the bright summer sky, seeing no boundaries and feeling no constraints. I did not realize then that I was living in a bubble.

In all these years, going back home was a reassurance my visa was holding true. The fact that Spyros and I could not stay after the completion of our studies made me believe that I could go home any time I desired to. What I did not realize was that this desire was slowly leaving me. Like in *The Odyssey*, the sirens' song had brought me thousands of miles away from home, and now Circe's power was clouding my thoughts. Yet my heart was telling me that the journey I had started at the airport in Athens was not supposed to end in America. It had a destination, and this destination was back home. I tried to repeat this to myself every time I felt the desire to stay.

In the fall of 1983, we found that we were expecting a baby. The news hit us like a bomb that spread a mix of terror and happiness. We were twenty-nine years old, a year away from our PhD degrees and quite naive. Despite the complexities a baby would bring to our lives, we convinced ourselves that we would find a way to manage the new addition to the family and let our hearts feel joy at the thought of having someone else in our lives whom we could love as much as we loved each other. For me, the baby gave me hope that now we had one more reason to go home.

"The university has a daycare where they accept babies three months and older," I told Spyros one evening, glowing with the amazing luck that we had such a facility on campus. "There is a waiting list, and I'll put down our name. I was told that their office is behind the tennis courts, and I can go any time to sign up."

Our happiness evaporated a few days later when I was told at the daycare office that the list was almost twenty-four months long. "What do you mean?" I asked with a half-smile hanging from my lips, an expression that angered the middle-aged, red-haired woman who was sitting behind a desk going through a box of baby toys.

"We are not elephants!" I joked. "Human babies take nine months to be born full term!"

"Most educated people, smarty," she said, voice thick from cigarettes, the stubs of which were lying in a big ashtray, "plan for a baby and for the baby's daycare ahead of time."

"What happens if they don't have the baby on time?" I asked with real curiosity.

"They lose their place on the list until they come back to place their name on it again." She pulled a new cigarette pack from her bag and started pulling off the plastic film with a pleasure that made her puffed-up face glow. "People are desperate for high quality and reasonable cost daycare," she continued. "Any private facility will charge you a minimum of five hundred dollars a month," she added, holding the cigarette she pulled from the fresh pack with her front teeth, in an accent I could hardly understand.

"Five hundred dollars a month!" I repeated in disbelief. "That is all we make every month." I heard my voice ringing like an echo.

"Exactly. That's why we are so popular!" she said triumphantly. "What's your name, sweetie?" She pulled out a yellow pad with names and phone numbers written in two clear rows. "We'll call you when we have an opening for you. In the meantime, you have to find someone else to take care of the baby."

I decided not to tell Spyros until I had an alternative solution, which I feared would be hard to come by. I was almost a year away from getting my degree, and there was nothing I could do to accelerate my progress.

The only person I could confide in was my thesis advisor, who was calm, cool, and very supportive. I knew he was not going to explode.

"Don't worry," he told me when I described the situation at the daycare. "You can take off for a few months when the baby is born and then you can continue to finish with your degree after you find a daycare solution."

It was nice on his part to provide this solution, but deep in my heart I knew I wanted to finish on time. I did not want to become a "lifer" in the PhD program. I knew many examples of students spending ten years trying to finish. I was not going to be one of them.

The thought of a baby coming without delay forced Spyros to progress faster than we had expected. He miraculously turned his anxiety into energy. He spent sleepless nights in his lab taking measurements. His only break was a piece of pizza from the student union with a large coke, which I took to him every night around 11:00 p.m., before I caught the last bus home to our one-bedroom apartment in the married student housing complex at the corner of National and Sepulveda boulevards in West LA. By Christmas 1983, he had collected all his data, and he had started writing his PhD dissertation.

My progress was a lot slower. My computer programs were complex and extensive, and finding program errors required a detailed and time-consuming effort. Furthermore, I couldn't cut down on my sleep. On the contrary, I added a few hours to my normal six-hour routine.

In January 1984, I was visibly pregnant. It was big news for engineering. Spyros and I were the only married graduate student couple in engineering who were expecting a baby. The graduate students got really excited and started betting whether the baby was a boy or a girl to raise money for a stroller. My advisor's wife donated her maternity clothes to me, since after having their third baby two years before then, they had decided to have no more children. My department's administrative assistant gave us the crib she had used for her two young children, with all the bedding accessories. With the warm generosity of our friends, we were able to get everything we needed for the baby. As the idea of having a third member in our family took hold, we started looking forward with hope and a feeling of being truly loved. It was a great time of our lives.

Just before Christmas 1983, Spyros came home one evening glowing, as if an internal light had turned on just above his eyes.

"I spoke with a recruiter from the General Motors Research Labs who wants to hire me."

"Where is General Motors?" I asked, holding my breath, fearful of leaving LA, which I had ended up loving so much.

"In Warren, Michigan!" he responded as he grabbed me in a bear hug.

"Where is Warren, Michigan?" I asked with my voice trembling.

"Somewhere north," he said emphatically. "Near Canada! Don't you want to see some snow? Didn't you get tired of the twenty-four-hour sunny weather?" He giggled.

"No," I heard myself saying but knowing it was the only option we had.

After that evening, things moved really fast. With my advisor's suggestion, I applied to the University of Michigan for an assistant professor position in the Department of Electrical and Computer Engineering. In January 1984, Spyros and I were invited for interviews. I borrowed a coat that could wrap me and the baby well, and we flew to Detroit for our interviews, hoping to get firm job offers. I had not realized then how prestigious these jobs were. My feelings were clouded by my desire to go back home, yet the baby was demanding a better income and more stability in our professional and personal lives. Home had nothing to offer us yet professionally, so our timeline for the return to Greece was moved out by a few years.

On January 30, 1984, when our parents called to wish me a happy birthday, we told them that our family was growing. There was pause on the line as they tried to understand the meaning of what we were saying before they erupted into happy laughs.

"Do you want me to come and help you?" Mom asked with some hesitation.

"Of course, I do. Please come," I responded, ready to plead on my knees as a pilgrim in front of an icon.

"We solved the daycare problem," I whispered to Spyros who was trying to overhear our conversation.

On April 26, 1984, Erik was born at the hospital at UCLA; a healthy boy who cried all the time. My mom had come to stay with us for a month, but realizing that I still needed to finish my dissertation and that we had an upcoming move from LA to Michigan, she offered to stay with us longer until we would settle into our new place.

In August 1984, Spyros, Erik, Mom, and I took the night flight from LA to Detroit. I boarded the plane, fearing that I would never see LA again. The move from Greece to the United States had already shaken my trust in my ability to adapt; this new move made me fearful that I would hate Michigan and its weather. The only comfort was that my family was with me this time. *Maybe,* I thought, *if we spend a few years working in America, we can find good jobs back in Greece and move back there once and for all.*

The first day in my department, I was told that I would share an office with another assistant professor who had joined the same lab with me—the Radiation Laboratory at the University of Michigan. The lab director, in his British accent and with short sentences interrupted by pleasurable draws on his shining wooden pipe, made sure to explain to me every part of the lab's history. In a formal voice, he said that having faculty sharing offices was not common, but he figured that, since I had a newborn, I would be gone most of the time, so sharing would not be that bad for my colleague and would help the department, which had limited space. I tried to express disappointment, explaining that I planned to be in the office every weekday and possibly weekends too, and that I was hoping to have my own office. "We'll see," he said and turned his attention to the paper he was reading before I had entered his office. I left quietly, under the watchful eyes of his assistant who was typing away with a constant rhythm.

A few days later, I went to the director's office to ask him for advice and to understand his expectations of me relative to teaching and research. He seemed surprised at the question. "My expectations are not important," he said with some annoyance in his voice. "The question is what your plans are."

I had no immediate plans. My future US plans had involved only my appointment as an assistant professor. My real plan to go back to Greece was not one I would share with him. "Do you have any advice for me?" I asked with hesitation.

"No," he responded. He started cleaning his pipe with all his focus on his lightly trembling hands, going through a process with a precision that showed years of experience.

I left his office puzzled and walked back to my desk in our shared office, where my colleague was speaking on the phone with a loud voice and even louder laughs. "Have you spoken with the director?" I asked him, after he hung up.

"You mean Tom!" he said with a hidden sarcasm in his voice. "Tom is a wonderful guy," he added in his thunderous voice.

"Is he okay with you calling him by his first name?" I asked, remembering the director's casual comment to me that he prefers formality.

"Yes, of course," my colleague responded. "Tom insisted that I be informal with him. By the way," he went on, his face showing concern, "he doesn't expect both of us to get tenure." After a pause, he added, "And I don't plan to fail."

The tone of the conversation reminded me of my first-year experience as an undergraduate back in Greece and filled me with a deep sense that I did not belong and people did not like me. I feared that all these years at UCLA gave me a false sense of reality.

As the weeks went by, the situation grew gloomier. The director was communicating with me through the lab administrator, who also served as his secretary. Wanita, a tall and sturdy woman with a proud and beautiful face scarred by a hard life in a northern Michigan Indian reservation, served as my mentor and tried to soften the blows from the boss's behavior. She kept excusing his demeanor in an effort to protect me.

"He's moody, but that has nothing to do with you," she kept telling me, "this is who he is with everyone." Yet, his actions showed something totally different.

In October 1984, I wrote my first research proposal to the Army Research Office on the request of the program manager who had funded my research during my five years as a graduate student. With two national Best Paper Awards in 1983 and 1984 by IEEE (the Institute of Electrical and Electronic Engineers) and almost a dozen publications over a period of five years, I was his best researcher, he insisted. He was a wonderful man, as gracious and honorable as my advisor.

When the twenty-five pages of my proposal were finished, typed, and proofread by Wanita, who insisted that she would love to help, I was very proud to have completed my first major research proposal as an assistant professor in just a couple of months after I joined the department. After all, this was my first ever proposal: ideas conceived by me, text written by hand, figures drawn carefully with stencil and sketches, and all references assembled after multiple runs to the engineering library. It was my first intellectual product in my new institution with ideas I owned exclusively. Wanita was also very proud of her typing, and she assured me that this proposal was a winner.

A couple of days before we mailed the proposal, Wanita called me in a low voice; she needed to speak with me about something important. I hung up and run to her office. The director's door across from her desk was shut, and only the heavy tobacco smell indicated that he was in. Wanita looked at me concerned and stretched out her hand with a written note.

"He wants to be the PI [principal investigator] in your proposal," the note read in her fast handwriting. "He asked me to tell you that the proposal will not go out without this change," she completed her note in a low voice while looking at his door.

"That's not possible!" I responded with fury in tone matching hers in volume. "He knows nothing about the subject." I tried to find the words that matched my anger. "Adding his name as a PI in my proposal is like him stealing my work."

She shook her head. "He refused to sign the proposal on behalf of the department, and he is the lab director to whom we both report," she added, concerned. "You won't be able to send your proposal out."

"Who else can sign in his place?" I asked, looking at her for suggestions.

"The department head, when the director is out of the office," she responded with a slight smile on her face. He will be out in a couple days, if you can wait that long."

I thanked her and rushed out of her office hoping to catch my research program manager before he left for the day to inform him about the delay. I would explain that I needed to make some additional changes to the text. Thankfully, the proposal left a couple of days later, with me as the principal investigator.

This proposal was funded by a large amount for that time, making me proud. But my relationship with the director went to an all-time low. I could have transformed into a ghost and attracted more of his attention. He totally ignored me, as if I had left the university. For a period of three years, he gave me six different courses to teach, one of them never taught before. He swayed all the new graduate students away from me, and it was only during my second year when the first graduate student asked to work with me at the suggestion of the department head, against the lab director's objections. For two years in a row, my salary raises were zero, at the director's recommendation. I had no idea that others had received increases. I thought we were on a salary freeze, as I never wished to check the salaries of others. In the summer of 1986, a member of the college's executive committee told me that the new dean overruled the director's recommendation and gave me a hearty increase because I had the highest productivity among all the assistant professors.

In the late fall of 1986, we found that we were expecting a second baby. The news came as a sunny break in the middle of a heavy storm. For months, working in the lab, while productive, was emotionally draining. Every day I was driving to work with tears in my eyes, and every evening I was driving back home both physically and mentally exhausted. The news that I was pregnant moved my attention away from the darkness of my working environment to the new addition in our family. The bliss of expecting a baby girl came mixed with worries about suffering from placenta previa, a medical condition that requires rest during pregnancy. I did not want to lose this baby, and I was determined to do anything I could to keep her healthy. The doctor suggested that I stay at home, preferably on bedrest for the duration of the pregnancy, an idea which I dismissed immediately. With a two-year-old who needed daycare five days a week, a two-bedroom rented apartment, and two cars for our long commutes to work, our $75,000 combined salary could not be halved by me staying at home. At that time, there was no maternity leave for faculty, and the only option I had, according to the lab director, was unpaid leave.

In early December 1987, the doctor offered to provide a letter saying that for the baby's and my health, he had recommended home rest or, at a minimum, avoiding standing, raising weights, or doing any other physical exercise, including going up and down stairs. By about the same time, the lab director had assigned to me yet another new course to teach during the spring semester of 1987, scheduled to start that coming January. Knowing that it takes an effort to assign faculty to various courses, I decided to contact the director immediately after I received the doctor's directives. I contacted him through his new secretary. Wanita had left on an early retirement, wanting to spend more time with her family and grandchildren, and her departure left me without a real friend. Before she left, however, she introduced me to the department chair's administrative assistant, Pam, who quickly took me under her wings.

In my department of eighty-six faculty at the time, there were only two other female faculty distributed among the various labs, one of them in computer science and the other one in optics. I was the only female faculty ever in my lab. My only friends were the women on staff who, experiencing how differently I was treated all the time by faculty and students, were protective of me. I was not treated as a faculty member but as another member of the staff. Even the students preferred to call me by my first name, regardless of how many times I had corrected them. They were coming to my office asking me for appointments with the other faculty members whenever the other administrative assistants were busy. A few times, when I suggested that they go back to the lab staff, these students complained to their faculty that I was not helpful. One of my colleagues reprimanded me for not being student-friendly when I refused to make an appointment for him. My officemate, during the time we shared an office and afterward, always asked me after faculty meetings to clean up the donut crumbs and empty coffee cups from the table because he needed to use the space for meetings with his students. It did not matter how many times I told him that this was a job he could manage himself; he kept doing this in front of everybody else, and no one corrected him. With every incident like this, the idea of leaving that department was taking hold in my head.

The day of my appointment with the lab director to discuss my medical condition, I recited the conversation I was planning to have with him. Knowing that our relationship was rather combative, I wanted to make sure that my interaction with him was to the point and professional.

I walked into the visitor's area in front of his office, and I saw his door three-quarters open. I looked at his assistant, who nodded me to go in. I knocked at his door, and I saw him rushing toward me. I thought he was going to show courtesy to a pregnant woman and open the door for me. To my surprise, however, he intended to shut the door.

"I believe we have an appointment," I said trembling, a wave of red heat coloring my face.

"I'm busy right now," he said, placing his hand firmly on the doorknob.

"I have a private matter to discuss with you," I continued. "May I come in?"

He looked uncertain, but he rushed to respond, "I'm too busy for an extended discussion right now. What is it all about?" His voice carried a tone of dismissal.

"I have a medical condition I need to discuss with you," I garbled, visibly shaken, "and the doctor suggested a lot of rest. Is it possible not to teach this semester but then teach an extra course in the fall?"

By then, I had already forgotten what I was planning to say and my face felt hot. I looked at the assistant whose eyes showed fear and dismay.

"No," he said without thinking. "The teaching schedule is set, and we have no one but you to teach this course." He tried to close the door, but I put my hand on it trying to stop him.

"So, what should I do?" I asked, feeling shamed and desperate.

"That's a question for you, not for me!" he said, and he pushed the door shut, forcing me to step back.

I do not remember whether I said anything or rushed back to my office. What I remember is that I shut my door and let hot tears run down my face in anger, shame, and desperation.

I taught the class that semester while sitting on a chair and trying to use the board as little as possible. By then, I had solidified my decision to leave. I had multiple papers published, three major proposals funded, two Best Paper Awards and the NSF Presidential Young Investigator Award that was given to me by President Reagan. My advisor from UCLA, who was aware of all the issues I had at the University of Michigan, insisted that I apply for a transfer to UCLA. By late spring of 1987, and while I was eight months pregnant with our daughter, UCLA made me an offer as an associate professor with tenure. The offer was amazing, and I really wanted to go. There was, however, a catch. There was nothing for Spyros in Los Angeles except a possible postdoctoral position, a serious professional downgrade for him both in status and salary, which was an issue with moving back to a very expensive area. We both were anxious and confused, but we decided that it was important to go for my own mental health and emotional stability. My parents who were visiting to help us with the second baby were equally anxious and upset about the situation, but they stayed silent, respecting the space Spyros and I needed during this difficult time.

In May 1987, I informed my department chair that I was leaving and offered to meet with him to discuss the reasons, if he wished to do so. Late afternoon a couple of days later, I was in my office trying to finish my work before driving back home, a thirty-five-mile drive that in late spring would take me about forty-five minutes. Getting close to my delivery date of June 25 put an extraordinary amount of pressure on me because I knew I had to clear my desk before June 10 so I could stay at home during the last two weeks before delivery, as my doctor had suggested. I was absorbed in my writing when I thought I heard a faint knock on my door that was kept half-open all the time. I saw a slender man come into the office, a man whose face looked familiar but, for a second, I did not recognize.

"Chuck Vest," he said with a smile. "The new dean, but don't worry if you don't recognize me. Administrators are supposed to stay invisible, otherwise they become a barrier." I believe I looked dumbfounded because he asked me not to stand and whether he could sit. "Yes," I said, when I found my voice.

"Linda," he said in a serious tone, "I heard you're leaving us. Do you want to talk about it?"

I looked at him in disbelief. *Maybe he's checking his boxes*, I thought. His boss, the provost, who was the previous dean who hired me, may not be that happy and this new dean wanted to cover his back. "Yes," I said with a steady voice. "I will be pleased to do so."

"Do you want to talk here? I'm available," he said. He let me think for some time while he glanced at my bookshelves full of engineering books I had read and reread over the years.

"We can talk tomorrow in my office, if you want," he offered as an alternative, sensing my discomfort. His face showed concern.

I did not want anyone to see the dean in my office because the rumors would fly around with the speed of light.

"Yes, I prefer to come to your office," I responded.

"How about tomorrow morning at ten?" he asked.

Next day, I was at his office at 10:00 a.m. He told me he had all the time I needed to share with him whatever information I felt comfortable relative to my leaving the university after three very successful years as an assistant professor. "We do not want to lose star faculty," he said. "What happened?"

I decided to share it all with him. Everything I had experienced since the day I came to campus and over the period of the previous three years. He remained silent while his face became progressively more serious. He said nothing until I finished.

"Will you give me a chance to correct this?" he said. "Could you wait for a couple of weeks?" I looked at him in disbelief. "I am not asking you to commit to stay," he continued. "I just want the chance to undo the wrong done to you."

*Either this man is a great politician and a total liar,* I thought, *or he is naive and thinks he can fix things.* "I can wait for two weeks," I said with a smile. "I have already waited for three years. In any case, leaving solves my professional problem but creates a family one. I will be glad to stay under different conditions," I added and thanked him for trying. I left his office convinced that two weeks would bring no resolution.

A week after my meeting with the dean, the department head's secretary, Pam, called me excited.

"Linda," she said, "did you hear the news? Your lab director is out of his position, and the new lab director is a great friend of yours, Fawwaz Ulaby."

"Fawwaz became the lab director?" I managed to utter. "What happened?"

"The dean cleaned house," she said with a laugh that filled the phone. "Are you staying?" she asked anxiously.

"Yes," I said and started crying.

I will never forget Chuck Vest's intervention. His strong leadership changed my life. It was a lesson that has remained with me until today. Following that change in the lab leadership, I stayed at the Radiation Lab for fifteen more years before I started on my own administrative path. In parallel, Chuck moved to become the provost at Michigan, then the president at MIT, and then the president at the National Academy of Engineering before he passed away, too early for those of us who depended upon his support and encouragement.

I told him many times how much I appreciated his leadership during a time when I needed someone to believe me and support me. His actions changed my family's life and mine for the better. I do not know whether he ever appreciated the impact of his support because he never mentioned it to me again. Great leaders do good and then move on to help others. They do not act expecting a return, or a favor, or recognition. They act because it is consistent with their values and their commitment to serving people.

I followed Chuck in his career, and he became my mentor and advocate along with a few other great men who saw value in me, who trusted me, and brought out the best in me: my advisor Nick Alexopoulos, Dean Chuck Vest, President Jim Duderstadt, and Lab Director Fawwaz Ulaby. They supported me, they guided me, they taught me to be fair and stay true to my values. The encouraged me to be a fighter for my students and for all those who depended on me. Their teachings have made me who I am.

We stayed in Michigan eighteen years, building a professional reputation that brought many career opportunities. There were very few women in the engineering faculty in the 1990s who had survived the hardships of being the first woman in their professional spaces. Many found explicit discrimination unbearable and chose another professional path. By the time I left Michigan, I was the most senior female faculty member in engineering. My visible presence, forceful character, and professional success split my colleagues into two camps: those who loved me and those who hated me. My friends did everything they could to support me, but my enemies found every way to take me down. Not able to touch me, they went after my graduate students, especially the female students I had in my group. By the spring of 2001, I was exhausted by having to defend my female students' research work, despite the multiple national awards for their papers presented at conferences and published in scientific journals.

Feeling exhausted and discouraged, I started looking for a change. In June 2001, I had an offer from Purdue for the post of Dean of the Schools of Engineering in West Lafayette, Indiana, while Spyros had an offer from Rolls Royce in Indianapolis. By June 2002, the whole family had moved to Zionsville, a suburb of Indianapolis, except Erik, who moved to Ann Arbor as a freshman at the University of Michigan.

During all the years in Michigan, the professional stress and anxiety was moderated by my life at home. For our family, the times in Michigan were the best I had, and I always remember them fondly. My parents visited almost every year, for many months at a time, to help us with the children. Either Spyros or I drove Mom to evening classes at a nearby college to learn English, which she did successfully. When she was six-ty-five years old, she took her first ever driver's test and started driving the kids everywhere—to school, soccer practice, and sleepovers. Mom became the children's official driver for almost the whole time we stayed in Michigan. Dad was always there to help too. He loved our children the way he could not love me. He gave them everything he had. He was able to find atonement in loving Erik and Helena, and I appreciated him for that.

Together, in our seven-seat van, we drove everywhere on short and long vacations, including Chicago, Washington DC, northern Michigan, South Carolina, Canada, and New York, among so many other places. During one of these trips, Mom told me that I had given her every-thing she had dreamed of and beyond. In Michigan, we lived some of the happiest moments while my parents were alive. It was a time when going back to Greece became a faded dream, and I felt that they brought Greece to me whenever we were together.

By the time I was approached for the dean's position at Purdue, the children had grown and my parents had aged to the point that traveling to see us became a struggle. The last time they visited, accompanied by Spyros's mom, was in 2005 for Helena's graduation from high school. We were living then in Zionsville, Indiana. Mom was almost eighty and Dad eighty-seven with some early signs of dementia. That was the last time they visited the United States.

My time as the engineering dean at Purdue was one of excitement, progress, support, and productivity. I had excellent colleagues who were proud of their university and eager to make it the top engineering college in the country, an effort they have sustained over the years with great success. I was treated exceptionally well by everyone, and I felt that I had earned my way out of small academic politics and continuous anxiety and stress that I had suffered in my previous years. I made great friends at Purdue whom I remember fondly.

It was a time of progress for me, both as a female engineering dean and as a researcher. When I was announced as the Purdue Dean of Engineering in the fall of 2001, I received an email from Denise Denton that included one line: "Thank you for increasing our number by 25 percent," and underneath she had listed the four other female deans of engineering at the top 350 engineering schools in the country: Denise Denton at University of Washington; Christina Johnson at Duke University; Jenny Fouke at Michigan State University; and Ilene Bush-Visniac at John Hopkins University. In fact, there were five deans, counting Eleanor Baum at Cooper Union who became the first female engineering dean in the country in 1987. I was the sixth, making the percentage of women engineering deans 1.5 percent of all engineering deans in the United States. We all sat at one table during the dean meetings of the American Association of Engineering Education, a group of more than 350 participants.

Getting together was a rare occasion but one we were looking for, even if we rarely complained and almost never spoke of the hardships, believing that it was a privilege being a dean and that talking about problems could be perceived as weakness, a characteristic none of us wanted to show. Yet, I kept hearing the low-level rumors about each of the other women, making me often wonder what was said about me. The comments were very similar, implying less experience and lack of emotional stability or foresight.

In 2005, Jenny Fouke emailed our small group an announcement that Denise was selected to be the chancellor at UC Santa Cruz. The news raised a round of warm congratulations for Denise that wished her great success and asked her to stay in touch. However, the support from Denise's circle of friends and supporters was not enough to counterbalance the force of the politically conservative mob who decided that an openly gay woman chancellor was the wrong choice for a university community too settled in its ways.

In June 2006, Jenny sent another email to our small group that included a story in the *LA Times,* stating: "The chancellor of UC Santa Cruz, a prominent advocate for women in technical fields, criticized for seeking expensive perks and helping her partner obtain a UC job, apparently leaped to her death from the roof of a 43-story building in San Francisco on Saturday morning . . ."

I froze in my chair. I kept rereading the email as if the words had tricked me into receiving the wrong message. I had seen Denise almost three weeks before then at an awards luncheon in San Francisco, and she seemed okay, even if I found her uncharacteristically quiet.

"Who would know?" my friend next to me whispered as we patiently waited for Denise's memorial service to start in an amphitheater at UC Santa Cruz. It felt like an out-of-body experience.

"How did this happen?" I responded, trying to find an explanation.

A woman to my left said, "First they come after you, then after your students, and at the end they come after your family." Her voice caused a few heads to turn.

"Who is she?" I asked my friend sitting to the other side of me.

"That's Mary Ann Fox, the chancellor at UC San Diego," she whispered in my ear as the UC President walked to the stage.

I wished I had remembered Mary Ann's words when I was approached to consider the position as chancellor of UC Davis in 2009. Unfortunately, I did not believe something like that would ever happen to me. I believed that Denise's treatment and the end of her life and career was an anomaly in the UC system. The years that followed proved quite the opposite.

The day I was announced as a chancellor at
UC Davis, May 2009.

# CHAPTER SEVEN
## ON THE WAY TO UC

**June 13, 2009**

I LOOKED OUT THE CORNER window of my second-floor office without being able to focus on anything. Spring had come late, and the trees were trying to catch up with their growth. You could almost hear the leaves bursting from their branches as the trees awakened from winter's quiescence. On any other day, such a view of the beautiful white and pink flowers outside would make me feel happy and thankful, and I would be quick to open the windows to let the sweet scent fill the space. *Not today*, I thought.

That morning, I felt anger and anxiety making my stomach hurt with a strong, piercing pain that came in waves with growing intensity.

I put two Tylenol in my mouth and chewed them hard, tasting my hand's salty sweat mixed with the pills' bitterness all the way down my throat. I remained still for some time and held my breath long enough to feel the pain subside. "Almost thirty years of hard work seem to have vanished as salt in water," I uttered to Debbie, my executive assistant in the provost's office at the University of Illinois Urbana-Champaign. I turned to face her.

She raised her eyes from the document she was reading with concern and looked over her glasses at me. She and the rest of the communications staff had summarized the newspaper clippings for me as part of their morning routine. She performed this task with pride and care, the best work I have seen in my many years in academia.

Debbie was not just my executive assistant. She performed the duties of a chief of staff without any expectations for a new title or higher salary. Her work reflected the Midwestern ethic, as well as pride and loyalty to the university, to my office, and to me. She was always upbeat but firm, demanding but cheerful.

Today, the list was long, and her smile had been replaced by a frown I had not seen before: a mix of annoyance and contempt. I glanced again at the identical copy I held in my right hand. I gripped it so tightly that my sweat had made the paper soggy and the ink smudgy in many places. The paper was full of comments and yellow highlights to help me scan the most interesting statements. The comments from the *Davis Enterprise*, the *Sacramento Bee*, and other California papers, some I had never heard of, were cited carefully wherever my name was mentioned.

Debbie raised her head. She had nice features framed by thick, red hair that was cut short with style. She solemnly reminded me that this explosion of comments had started the day of my announcement as the UC Davis chancellor. She also noted that despite the few weeks that had passed since then, the critical comments had not subsided. On the contrary, over the course of the past four weeks, almost every newspaper article had been negative. "First," Debbie recalled, "the Davis newspaper put your picture next to a cow's picture when they announced your appointment. Our office staff thought it was weird. In fact, the cow won the prize for capturing readers' attention. Her picture was way bigger than yours, and she looked so sad. It matched the title of the article that announced you. It was funny to look at you under the article's title next to the cow . . ."

Rolling her pen in her fingers nervously, she went on, "A few days later, they called you greedy for your salary and asked you to give back part of it." She snickered in disbelief.

She started looking through a folder filled with paper clippings and summaries from the communications staff and stopped at one clipping. "Have you read that they have complained about Spyros's position as a lecturer? If I am not wrong, he is faculty here and an assistant dean. The lecturer's position is a downgrade. They did not mention *that*, only that your husband 'stole' someone else's position."

She hesitated under my angry glance, but then quickly went back to her commentary. "Now they call you unethical, implying that you were involved in the Blagojevich scandal with university admissions in 2003 and 2005. Where were you then?" she asked animatedly.

"At Purdue," I replied, as if she did not know.

"Exactly the point," she remarked and then paused as she became absorbed reading down the list.

"Did we tell them that?" I walked nervously back toward the window. There was a lot of commotion in the tree, its branches moving left and right as a couple squirrels chasing each other playfully flew from one branch to another. "I never thought squirrels could fly," I said.

"They do in Illinois," Debbie added, with her head still bent over the list. She removed her glasses, looked at me seriously, and turned to the next page of the list to look at the comments.

"You asked whether I told them? Of course, I did," she raised her voice. "I mean . . . I did tell them that you were not here when Blagojevich enrolled his nephews in our law school.

"As a matter of fact," she continued, "I mentioned this several times to the reporter from the *Bee*." She paused, trying to remember the details of her conversation. "She did not seem to care. The only thing she asked me was whether they will investigate you. When I told her that you cannot be investigated for something that happened before your time here, she responded aggressively that this wasn't her question."

"What did you know about that issue? I mean the Blagojevich nephews' admission to our law school," I asked her, my steps taking me slowly back to my desk to look at the day's meetings.

"I knew nothing. No one from our office knew," she responded categorically. "Do you think that they would tell us? I learned about it at the same time you did, a week ago, from the paper."

"What did you know about the I-list?" I asked, referring to the university's admissions waiting list.

"Nothing!" she retorted aggressively. "Don't you believe I would have brought it to your attention?"

We both remained silent for a few minutes.

"Do you really want to go there? UC Davis, I mean," she said. "Where in the world is it, after all? This is the first time I've heard of it. Why don't you stay here? There is still time to say no."

I did not respond. I was confused by the same question swirling in my head like a fly around stale food.

"Debbie, please ask the reporter to speak with me the next time she calls. For now, let's talk about the meetings today. I am still the provost here and I have work to do."


## June 15, 2009

I heard the doorbell ring. I woke up and found myself in our bed in our house in Indianapolis. I heard the bell ring again and again, and I could feel my heartbeat accelerating. It was the weekend, still dark. *I wonder where Spyros is*, I thought. Feeling alone and scared, I walked into the foyer to see our daughter's tall, slim figure waiting behind the glass front door, still ringing the bell frantically. I wanted to let her in, but my legs would not move. "Mom, open the door!" she screamed.

I woke up sweating. It was hot and humid. The darkness of the room did not remind me of our house. It was small and had a weird smell. I had the sense that the ceiling was touching my head. It took me a moment to realize that I was in a hotel. I heard the cell phone ringing, the same sound as our doorbell, its screen glowing. I looked at the time—2:00 a.m. The number started with a 916 area code. I realized it was a call from California, and I responded reluctantly.

"Hello?"

"Linda?" the female voice asked cautiously.

"Yes, who is this?" I responded in a hoarse voice that I tried to clear up with a cough, wondering how she knew me by my first name.

"This is Diana Lambert from the *Sacramento Bee*."

"It is two in the morning. Where did you get my number?" I asked, agitated.

"Your assistant gave it to me. It's important that I contact you." She didn't seem interested in the time. "I have a deadline in about one hour, and I'm writing an article about your involvement in the Illinois scandal."

"I am not involved in the Illinois scandal," I responded in a harsh tone.

"Yes, but admissions are under you," she said.

"True, general admissions on my campus are under the provost's office, but admissions in the law school are processed by the staff of the law school directly."

"What do you know about Blagojevich?"

"The governor of Illinois? Not much. I never met him in person."

"What do you know about the I-list?"

"Every university has a list like this so that we can manage admissions carefully."

"Do you select the students from that list?" she continued.

"No, I do not. The selection is done by formula and the staff performs this task without interference from my end."

"This is your staff," she continued. "How come you do not know who they're selecting from the list?"

"There are hundreds of students on that list. By policy, the provost does not interfere with admissions," I responded, growing irritated.

"Did you know that Senator Leland Yee has accused you of being responsible for the scandal? He has asked you to resign. What is your response to that?"

"I do not know Senator Yee, and he is wrong. I do not even understand his motives. Do you?" I guess she took it as a rhetorical question because she did not answer. I could hear her typing in the background.

"I'm sorry, but it is almost two thirty in the morning, and I have an early meeting tomorrow," I said while listening to the continuous clicking of the keyboard.

I was ready to tell her that I was in DC for a meeting at the National Science Foundation, but I chose not to mention it. "Less is better," our communications staff at the University of Illinois had advised me.

I felt tired and emotionally exhausted. She mumbled something—I do not remember what—and hung up.

I threw my head back on the pillow. The small hotel room felt like a prison, hot and humid in the middle of June. I had turned the air-conditioning off because of the noise the old fan was making. I could not sleep anymore. I felt nauseated.

It had been almost a month of unwelcome news. There had been more unbelievably unkind comments from California. Dozens of emails had arrived in my personal university account—I have no idea how they found the address—calling me all kinds of horrible names and asking me to resign. Even a Greek-American priest, I inferred from his name and title, emailed me to tell me that I was a disgrace to all Greek Americans.

Many of the comments were anonymous. Few were welcoming, and most wanted me not to go to UC Davis. Still others demanded that I give up all my salary and distribute it back to the students and the public who had paid for it. Among those were faculty from the English, history, and philosophy departments at UC Davis and UC Berkeley. A couple of these messages were identical, as if they had copied each other's email, and told me to go back to my country and never show my face in California again.

After fighting so hard to get to the United States and succeed there, I was being asked to go back to Greece. *What does it take for someone to be so hateful?* I thought. *What is it about me that makes them so angry?*

Obviously, they believed Leland Yee. In the middle of a serious recession, they had found the villain they had been looking for. I remembered *The Crucible*, a film I had seen in the nineties, and a shiver ran down my spine.

I tried to relax and push any questions out of my mind. "What is the point of asking questions you cannot answer?" I said loudly, trying to go to sleep. The heat began to grow unbearable, so I turned the air-conditioning on. The fan started like the engine of an old Chevy, spilling a wave of hot air that smelled of tar. "What in the world!" I said, jumping off the bed to turn it off again just as the phone rang. It was the same number.

"Linda," the voice said without introduction and before I was able to speak, "I am just finishing my piece and I wanted to make sure that I represent you accurately."

"What is your question?" I asked, almost ready to cry from frustration.

"Is it true that you deny any involvement with the admissions scandal?" she asked, as if we hadn't just discussed it.

"Yes," I replied, "I just said that a few minutes ago."

"Okay. That's all she said." Her voice sounded unconvinced and she hung up.

I went back and sat on the bed still feeling sick. *What am I going to do?* I thought in horror. I picked up the hotel phone next to the bed and dialed Spyros's number with trembling fingers.

"Hi," said Spyros's sleepy voice. "What's up? It's 3:00 a.m."

"Can you check the *Sac Bee* for me?" I answered in a hollow voice.

"Why? Is there anything wrong?"

"I'm not sure . . . Just go to the website and type 'Sac Bee Katehi' and see what you get."

"Just a second! I'm going to the computer."

"Where are you?" I asked him, feeling uncomfortable waiting. "In Indy or Urbana?"

"I'm where you left me, in Indy," he responded while typing on his computer's keyboard. "What's the problem?"

"I don't know yet, just do as I told you."

I waited for what seemed like an eon.

"Here it is. I found something about you from this morning. In fact, there are two articles. One from the *Sacramento Bee* and the other from the *San Francisco Chronicle*."

"Look at the *Bee* one. What does it say?"

"It says, 'The woman who has been selected to be the chancellor at UC Davis claims she is not involved in the Illinois scandal.'" He paused. "I guess that's you."

"I guess that's me," I murmured. "I tried to explain. She only needed to check the dates to see that I told the truth."

"They do not care about the facts; they just want to sell papers." Spyros sounded calm. "The truth does not sell. Just try to relax. You are going to make yourself sick if you worry like this."

I was nearly weeping. "Yes, but what am I going to do?"

"Just @#!& them and go to sleep." His voiced trembled. I hung up. I could not speak with him any longer.

My mom and I in July 2009, when I was debating whether to join UC Davis.

## Chapter Eight

# Looking for Answers

**July 10, 2009**

IN MID-JULY, ATHENS CAN BE very hot but never humid. It is a dry heat that comes in waves. By the early afternoon it feels like the earth has melted beneath your feet and your shoes have become one with the tar that covers the streets. *How did we live without air-conditioning?* I wondered. *It seems that either the weather was milder, or we have become spoiled and intolerant. Maybe both. Comfort makes people feel frail and entitled.*

I have started hearing her voice back in my head. The same one I used to hear when I was young, sometimes asking me, other times scolding me, most of the time giving guidance, or even engaging in long debates. As a young girl, I was convinced it was Gabriel's voice trying to keep me away from trouble, but we had parted ways some time ago, and I was convinced that I was finally free from her and her unreasonable expectations. Recently, though, her voice had come back, and she was getting on my nerves. She hadn't changed—only her voice had become identical to mine and her attitude had worsened. As aggressive as ever, she was trying to get me engaged in long discussions and quarrels about UC Davis and my choices.

Spyros and I had just resigned from the University of Illinois in Urbana-Champaign and were on our way to UC Davis. In the beginning, we were very excited and nervous. No change comes with excitement only; it brings along anxiety and uncertainty as well. Yet this time, when I was told that I was selected to be the chancellor at UC Davis, we were truly happy.

Going back to the University of California was a dream come true. It was a dream we'd had since we graduated from UCLA and moved to Michigan to start our first jobs in the United States. We always wanted to come back to California, to the Golden State.

This time, however, the blue California sky of our dreams was full of thunderous clouds. The threat of a violent storm was everywhere. From the newspapers' constant accusations to the unwelcoming emails to the blogs that were calling for my resignation to save the institution from a "corrupt bureaucrat," the signs were clear that what we once thought was opportunity was quickly turning into a nightmare.

If it were not for my "Greek Pride," an outdated principle that should have died with my mother's generation, I would have saved myself from the seven painful years that followed. I asked Gabriel what she thought about pride one day, and I got angry with her mumbling. *First,* she said, *pride is what we make it,* forcing me to sigh with dismay. *But after a second thought,* she continued, *pride can be good until it hurts you.*

"How about that for consolation?" I yelled, and she disappeared.

Yet, thinking back, maybe she was correct after all. It was pride and my fear of humiliation that made me decide not to resign as soon they started accusing me of the Illinois scandal. But I hoped the truth would triumph and things would change for the better. It was my first experience that taught me that truth does not matter when it comes to politics. "Talk to your family," her voice told me when she came back. "You will find the answer in their words."

Going to Greece was not the plan that summer; it was not even a vacation. It was an attempt to escape the attacks and to distance myself from everything that was happening. We needed a quiet space to finalize our decision, not recognizing that every day that was passing by was further limiting our choices.

The public outcry about my salary, then the accusation about my involvement in the Illinois scandal led by Senator Leland Yee, and the *Sac Bee* assertions made me feel the need to get away from a campus I had not even joined yet. It was not just the *Bee* that kept chewing the same old bone. A new wave of Davisites came out in public to write opinions and letters to the editor of the *Davis Enterprise*, blaming UC President Mark Yudof for his bad choice and asking me to have the decency to resign and never come to their city. They wanted the previous chancellor back.

It was one of those sleepless August nights in Athens, hot and noisy. Spyros and I were lying in our adjacent beds, the ones his mom had bought when we were engaged and then placed in the same room after we got married. I was so stressed that I could hardly hold myself in one place. In shorts and a t-shirt, I rolled in bed, breathing like a wounded animal, tired and ready to give in to the huntsman.

"The faculty want you," Spyros tried to cheer me up. "Twenty or so senior faculty, many of them members of the National Academy of Engineering, signed a letter in the *Davis Enterprise* showing their support for you. What else do you want?" he asked emphatically.

"And this is happening before I've even started," I responded.

I rolled to face him. "They're trying to help me hold my position before I've even shown my darn face. Do you know what this means?"

"What?" Spyros asked in a provoking voice.

"This is the beginning of the end. The end of a story that has not even started. What is the word for it? Hopeless?"

"No!" he responded pugnaciously. "It is called tenacity. You cannot do these jobs if you do not have the stomach for it." His voice sounded like that of a lecturer on the podium. "Do you not understand that they do this to attack the UC? It is all political."

"I do have the stomach for hard work, but not for dirty political games. No one told me that I would have to defend myself against something

I have not done. No one prepared me for this. It is like trying to fight a ghost," I said, thinking of all the years I had played by the rules.

I wish I had Gabriel in front of me to throw her theories back in her face: "Work hard, think bold, sacrifice for the greater good, make a difference, respect people."

What for? So that these people come back to accuse you of whatever they find convenient? I wondered what her answer would have been now. But of course, a coward, she never showed up to be confronted with her mistakes. My head was spinning.

"The years of discipline, hard work, commitment, and going above and beyond mean nothing now," I complained. "Tell the truth, follow the rules, and work hard—I was told this was the recipe for success. Not really! Not anymore. I was prepared to live for a world that does not exist. I learned the rules of a game that no one plays anymore, and I believed in principles that no one respects. There we go!"

The phone rang. I heard it clearly, and I was almost prepared for it as if I knew it was coming. "What time is it?" Spyros asked.

"One in the morning," I said, "afternoon in California."

"If Marc Yudof is on the phone, I will tell him I am reconsidering," I said sarcastically. "No, don't!" Spyros hollered. He was now next to me with his hand holding mine away from the phone. "Where is your pride? Stay calm and just listen to him."

"Hello?" I answered, trying to keep my voice low.

Being in a flat with the doors and windows open in a summer night is the way to make sure that everyone in the apartment building can hear you speaking on the phone. I had heard a few complaints already from the sleepy neighbors.

I heard a familiar voice on the end of the line. "Linda, this is Nick Barboulis. I'm sorry I called this late."

"It's the chair of the faculty senate from Illinois," I whispered to Spyros with my hand over the phone.

"Hi Nick. It's okay, I was not sleeping anyways. What's up?"

"Linda, I'm calling to tell you that you should not go to UC Davis.

AFSCME placed on their website a statement from Senator Yee that says you were heavily involved in the Illinois scandal and asks President Yudof to fire you. They have fifteen thousand members. Do you know what this means?"

"But it isn't true!" I said, shivering.

"Well, it does not matter whether it is true or not. Now this is the truth for them and that's what matters," he said.

We both remained quiet for some time. Finally, he broke the silence.

"Come back to Illinois. Your future is here, not in California."

"But I have not done anything wrong."

"I know, but they do not care. They do not want you!" he said, slowly making sure that I could hear every vowel clearly. "They will not give you a chance."

"By the way," he continued, "the ASUCD student president or a member of the student senate, I don't remember who exactly, is also collecting signatures asking you to resign. They have already collected 1,500 student signatures in less than a day."

"What does this mean?" I asked as a wave of nausea gripped my stomach.

"It means it's over," he said in a calm tone.

"Thank you, Nick. I will think about it. Thank you so much for caring about me."

I stared at my phone's screen long after he had hung up. Finally, I stood up in the dark, my thoughts running away from me.

"What did he say?" Spyros asked, irritated.

"It's over. He said it is over."

"No, it's not over until you make it that way," Spyros replied.

"There is no way back. If you do not go now, everyone will think that you are a liar and a coward, and they will believe that you were involved in the scandal. You have no other choice but to go on. Where is your courage? Where is your pride? Are you going to fight for the truth or just give up?"

## July 16, 2009

I woke up around noon. I was a total mess. My head hurt, and my stomach was cramped and howling from the numerous cups of coffee that had soothed my anxiety. I slowly stood up from the bed and felt my way to the door. The room was dark and stuffy. The air-conditioning was off again. *That's my mother-in-law*, I thought. *Every time she finds the opportunity, she opens the door, pokes her head into our room, mutters something about "Siberia" and runs to turn the air-conditioning off until one of us wakes up sweating and vehemently complaining.*

She was in the kitchen cooking. She was short but always in high heels, even when she was cleaning the house, which made her at least two inches taller. A voluptuous beauty in her youth, she still looked much younger than her seventy-plus years, curvy and busty with a beautifully aged face surrounded by thick, deep-red hair, always well-colored and combed.

"What is the problem?" she asked as soon as I entered the room.

"I could hear you talking all night long," she said while stirring the green bean casserole on the electric stove.

"Are you hungry? The food will be ready in thirty minutes." She started looking through the shelves next to the stove for herbs, complaining that she did not have enough of them. It seemed she had already forgotten her questions or was no longer interested in my answers.

I was not in the mood to start a discussion. The heat in the kitchen reminded me that I was thirsty. I opened the refrigerator and grabbed a can of diet soda. I sat at the kitchen table looking through the open door to the veranda and the green backyard of our flat. It was beautifully shaped, with a couple of terraces, almost at our level, full of lemon and orange trees and surrounded by flowerbeds. The roses were in full blossom, and the air coming through the door was lightly scented. That smell made me feel happy momentarily.

"It's amazing," I muttered, "how small distractions from misery become so noticeable when at other times they go by so unnoticed."

"What happened last night?" she asked.

I knew she would not give up.

"They called me from Illinois about this situation with the newspapers in California," I said, too tired to repeat the same story, provide the same explanations, and express the same doubts about going to Davis.

"Why do you bother your beautiful head with this nonsense?" she asked while she set a glass in front of me. "By the way, do not drink from the can. They are all dirty." She turned to watch the food simmering on the stove.

"Are you going someplace?" I asked, glancing at her shoes. She was also wearing a heavy necklace and earrings.

"No," she said. "I just came back from the bakery. Why are they calling you all the time? Do they not know you are on vacation?" She pulled up a chair and sat at the table across from me, expecting an answer this time.

"It is not working like this," I said, "not with my kind of job."

"Well, I told you. These jobs are not for women. Can you run a university in high heels?" she asked. "We women are not successful in these positions. People hate you for daring, but they will not admit it. They will call you all kinds of names and look for reasons to take you down. They will wait until the opportunity comes. People are unforgiving and resentful of the mistakes women in your position make, and when the moment comes, they will try to hurt you as much as possible just for their satisfaction." Her eyes focused steadily on her chipped nails. "I have an appointment for my nails. Do you want to come?" she asked as if her previous thoughts had suddenly disappeared.

"How do you know what people will do?" I replied, visibly irritated.

"Oh, I know, trust me," she said as she vigorously rubbed her nails. "I saw what they did to my oldest sister, Theone. She was the first woman in our town to become a lawyer, back in 1937. I was a young girl then, but I still remember what happened. They drove her crazy, called her crazy, even made fun of her in cartoons they published in the local paper. She never married. The whole family had to leave town to survive the ridicule. Why? Because she dared to do something no other woman had done before."

She took a deep breath. "That was a lesson for me and my sisters."

"Well, that was Theone in your small town sixty years ago. I live and work in the United States. Things are different there."

"They are different until you realize that they are not. People do not change easily. They may wear different clothes, speak different languages, live in different homes, and have different jobs, but both men and women hate those who challenge them. They fear those who are different. They want them out."

I lashed out at her. "Well, I don't want to have this discussion with you this morning!" I stood up and left the room. She was still looking at her nails.

The rest of the morning went by quietly. I did not expect a call until later in the evening when the sun would go up in California. I had a few hours to think, but my thoughts were foggy and chaotic. I picked up the phone and dialed my mom's number.

"Hello?" I heard her familiar, warm voice.

"Mom," I said quickly, "I'm coming to stay with you for a few days."

"Is Spyros coming?" she asked curiously.

I paused. "It will be just me. I will be there in a couple of hours."

My mother-in-law stood by the doorway, listening. "Are you leaving? Without eating lunch? This food is good for you, there is no meat or chicken and it is not fattening!"

I walked by her without answering. *She can manage without a response,* I thought. I grabbed a bag from the storage room and threw in a few pieces of underwear, a pair of jeans, a couple of t-shirts, and my make-up. I took my electronics with me, the car keys, a couple hundred Euros, and ran to the door.

"Where are you going?" Spyros asked as he put aside the book he was reading.

"I am going to Mom's for a few days. Can I use the car?"

"I guess," he replied reluctantly. "Be careful, don't go fast, and call me when you get there."

I bolted from the apartment like it was running out of oxygen. I drove on the Attiki highway from our apartment in Holargos through the city of Elefsina to Perama, the port to the island of Salamis, without paying attention to signs. I knew this way well enough to drive it with my eyes closed. Always the same way, from Spyros's house in Athens to my mom's place on the island.

I got off the highway at a place called Megara, a famous Greek city. In ancient times it had been a friend of Sparta, owing to their common Dorian heritage, but an enemy of Athens and Salamis, who were Ionian. Though Megara and Athens believed in the same gods, they had very different language and culture, which made for a good reason the two cities did not see eye to eye. This difference was enough to create a rivalry that led to many wars in the pre-Roman years. This rivalry lives on to the present day, in the form of a modern feud in the minor soccer league. The names of the soccer teams being "Vizas," the famous Homeric king of the city of Megara, and "Ajax," the famous Homeric king of the island of Salamis. The two cities are known now for their products and not for their wars: Magara for the production of eggs and poultry, and Salamis for fish and octopus.

The road from Megara to the island is less than five kilometers, but it is divided by a narrow channel of the sea of Saronikos, less than half a mile wide, that takes an hour to cross if you miss the ferry and must wait for the next one. I could swear it would take me less than half an hour to swim from one side of the channel to the other. This time I was lucky; the ferry was there with a couple of cars already loaded waiting for other cars or trucks to come. I drove over the ramp without stopping and turned onto the open garage of the ferry, where I parked.

The young man collecting the fare helped me maneuver into position. He was in his late teens, had tanned skin like cinnamon, green eyes, and long brown hair in a ponytail. He had a tattoo that stretched from his neck down his arms. Without the tattoos and the long hair, he reminded me of my friends in grade school who had dropped out of school before sixth grade and ended up working on the ferries for the rest of their lives. I could barely recognize them now, with their white hair and wrinkles, their skin worn from the salty water, drinking, and smoking. A couple of them whom I knew well had already passed away, according to my mom. Both took their own life. Suicide on the island had been a serious issue, but no one would talk about it. Religion forbids it, and culture condemns it. The priest would refuse to bury the bodies in the cemetery, so the families would keep it under wraps. For a small, hardscrabble community like this, there is no worse penalty for giving up a hopeless life than refusing to bury you in the cemetery.

The road from the port to Mom's home started narrow, meandering through a thick forest of conifers, a variety of Mediterranean pine trees that grow under warm and dry conditions and spread their needles in a think carpet that smells of resin. This cover of pine needles runs down the hills to meet the salty waves of Saronikos at the white-sand beaches. The road takes you by the gate of the famous Monastery of Faneromeni (meaning "the discovered") dedicated to the Virgin Mary. Legend has it that it was founded by a monk in the middle of the sixteenth century who built the monastery right where he found her icon.

When Mom was a young girl, before the war, her family had a cabin by the monastery where they used to spend their summer months. It was a small, wooden structure raised on a concrete foundation, surrounded by the forest. There was magnificent shade during the warm hours of the afternoon, those times when your limbs feel numb and your mind gives in to the dreams of a short siesta.

Driving through this forest is uplifting, but that day, my mind was confused with questions I could not answer, questions that fogged my heart with a veil of darkness and uncertainty. The forest ended at the outskirts of the city of Salamis, also known as "Koulouris"—an unofficial name from ancient times signifying the round shape of the bay that made the town along its shore look like a ring.

Koulouri, the capital, had fewer than five thousand people—almost 50 percent of the island's population—when I lived on the island as a young girl, but slowly it had grown to almost forty thousand now, not counting those who have summer homes and visit the island during weekends and vacations.

My whole family on my mother's side was born and raised in Koulouri. The family had lived there for over 700 years. Nobody knows where our ultimate roots are. The genealogy is obscured by the fog of the thousands of years of unwritten history on the island, and the stories of the people who have populated it—a history that is carried from one generation to another by tales and songs.

Very few people of our generation have the experience of a history dictated by oral tradition. You hear the words before you are born, you feel the distress, happiness, or fear before you can speak the words; you know your history before you can read the books. Oral tradition defines you as an individual and as a member of your community. Anything that contradicts it you reject, and everything that supports it you embrace during your lifelong fight with evil and death.

The narrow road to Mom's house took me by my great-grandmother's house, the one my mom and I used to visit regularly when I was young. Now only the large wooden door that separates the road from the yard of the house remains standing. The whole house, rubble covered by grass and weeds, stands there idle but proud, the result of a fight between the city that wanted to demolish it to widen the road and the family that now owns it and wants restitution for loss of property. "It will not be settled until we all die off," my mom used to say.

I parked the car in front of the fenced yard of the house my parents were now renting on the island, halfway between Koulouris and Palou-kia. They selected this location between the places where they had lived in the past as a compromise for the memories my mom wanted to cherish. A few years before then, Mom and Dad gave up their apartment in Athens and moved permanently back to the island, away from our old house and closer to where my aunts lived. They seemed happy there.

A thick line of lemon trees separated the fenced yard of the house from the road, soaking the air with the refreshing smell of citrus. The veranda, two small steps over the ground, was heavy with pots of geraniums, gardenias, and carnations, all in full bloom. Two of the four house cats were waiting by the open door, whose beaded curtain stopped the bees and mosquitoes from getting into the house.

"Mom!" I called as I pushed the curtain aside to enter the small living room, the cats a step behind me. Mom came out of the kitchen wearing her colorful apron, a big smile on her face, black velvet eyes, and her soft cheeks. Her hands extended to hug me. "Mom," I said again, relieved, and kissed her on her neck, the place where I used to find rest and consolation as a young child.

Her familiar smell found its way to my brain, where it turned into a soothing feeling that ran along my spine.

"I love you, Mom," I said while holding her.

"Come," she said quietly. "I have prepared something for you." I followed her into the kitchen, where she pulled a round pan out of the oven.

"Spinach pie!" I cheered with joy. "Can I have a piece?"

Before she had any time to answer, I grabbed a piece and shoved half of it into my mouth. "I am so hungry," I uttered with a sigh.

"What brings you here?" she asked. "I thought you would stay in Athens for a few days."

I took her hands in mine and looked at her, feeling safe again. "Two things. First, I missed you." Her smile hid doubt. "And second, I need your advice." I saw her eyes grow serious while her smile remained in place.

"I do not want to go to UC Davis!" I said.

She did not react immediately. She looked at me as if she had known what I was going to say and opened the refrigerator to put a carafe of cold water in the middle of the table. "I knew you were coming to tell me something important. Have a seat. Why?"

"They don't want me," I said while I chewed the last piece of the spinach pie and sat comfortably on a chair. I faked as mile of indifference. "They are calling me all kinds of names, they insist that I was involved in a scandal I had nothing to do with, and they are asking me to resign before I've even got there. Can you imagine? This is just the beginning."

I grabbed the carafe and filled the glass in front of me with cold water, spilling a bit on the lace tablecloth. "Sorry, Mom," I said in a low voice. "I do not even feel that the office staff—the people who will eventually become my colleagues—care about me either."

She looked at me, as if she wanted to know more.

I continued. "The other day, I called the person who is supposed to interact with the media and nicely asked him if he could call back the journalists who were calling his office for comment. I suggested that he have a statement ready, so they do not call the University of Illinois complaining that UC Davis does not respond to them."

I noticed I had been raising my voice, something I do when I get upset. I drank some more water to pace myself. "You know what he did? He yelled at me, blaming me for being such a big problem. He said he was busy and would call the journalists back when he had the time. He is supposed to work for *me*. He is three levels below the chancellor, yet he spoke to me as if I were his servant. How do you like that?" I took a deep breath, feeling tired again.

"Do you want to give up?" she asked me in a calm voice.

"I do not want to give up. I just do not want to go *there*." I felt my anger growing.

"Is this not the same?" She paused. "If you decide not to go, it means you are giving up a chance you may never have again." She sat next to me and took my hands in hers. "Do you know how many times in your life you have been unwelcome? Many! Countless many! Those you remember and those that I do. You never gave up. You had the strength to keep going. You had no choice but to fight all the way until the end. I taught you never to give up. Giving up is only for losers." Her voice trembled. "Have you done anything wrong?"

"No," I said raising my voice again, "unless I have lost it and do not remember the bad things I have done. I have done none of the things they accuse me of."

"Then go to UC Davis and do your best," she said. "That's what you have been trained for, to do your best every time, all the time." She smiled. "I ask you to do this," she said in her calming voice. "You have worked for this position your whole life. You gave up your country, your family, your friends. You left everything behind for a chance to make a difference, to achieve your dream."

She stood up and removed something from the corner stand, where a small vigil lamp burned day and night in front of the icon of Virgin Mary.

"This is for you," she said. She casually placed a small square of folded paper in my palm and gently curled my fingers to hold it tight.

"It is sacred, from the Virgin Mary's crypt where they found her icon in the monastery. It will protect you."

I took the folded paper in my hands and looked at the old dribble of wax that kept it sealed. I kissed it lightly and felt the strong smell of Livani, an incense burned in Greek Orthodox churches. I opened my purse and put the packet in a side compartment.

She continued to look at me, her eyes shining like two black beads.

"What?" I said with a goofy, childish smile.

"You finally made it!" Her broad smile showed two perfect rows of white teeth. The skin on her face, lightly covered with freckles, had a fine surface, like porcelain. I was ready to tell her that I wished I would look like her in my eighties, but her intense glance reminded me she was waiting for a confrontation. "If you refer to my career," I responded with a sarcastic tone, "unfortunately, I am ready to disappoint you."

She kept looking as if she wanted to hear more.

"I worked my whole life just to find myself defined by some senator, someone who doesn't know me, has never seen me in person, and has never bothered to understand how universities work." Once again, my voice trembled in anger. "It seems that you work for years, and then a moment comes when *others* define you."

"No one can define you but yourself," she disagreed calmly. "You will define yourself by what you do, and you have your whole life to do it." She seemed animated, something rare for her.

"Time only shows the truth, and time is powerful and ruthless. Your grandma used to say, the good wine comes from a good vine. You just have to be patient, be who you are, do the things you want to do, and know that time is on your side."

"Where is Dad?" I asked, just to change the topic.

In a voice revealing concern, she said, "He is sleeping. He is not doing well these days. His mind is leaving him. At times he forgets where we are. He thinks we are in Athens. But he still remembers you, especially when he hears your voice on the phone. He asks about you."

"Are you sure it is me he is asking for?" I chuckled. "The other day he thought you were his sister!" We both laughed, but our eyes became wet with tears.

"The war has claimed his mind," Mom ceded. "His memories stopped when he went back to his house after his parents died and found it empty."

Tears dripped down her cheeks.

"Mom, don't. He does not quite know what is happening to him. He is very lucky to have you, despite the life we lived with him." I shushed her as I moved close and wrapped my arms around hers. She wiped her tears with the back of her hands.

"His life was destroyed before he had a chance to make it," she whispered. "His happiness was snatched away from him. He lost everything he had before he was even twenty-three years old. After that he tried to survive his agony. He could not be a better father. He was haunted by his demons," she sobbed. She stared at her wet hands, the ones I remember touching me with such love and calmness. Now they were trembling. We stayed still for some time, looking at the door leading to their bedroom where Dad was taking a nap.

My father and I, summer 1954.

## CHAPTER NINE

# MY FATHER

THE RELATIONSHIP WITH MY FATHER changed over time from distant when I was little to combative when I was a teenager and to silent when I became an adult. We never communicated our personal feelings about each other, and I refused to engage in any form of dispute, disagreement, or even a simple conversation that could lead to an argument. There were so many things I wanted to ask him but my curiosity was always defeated by my unwillingness, or maybe fear, to engage. The few things I know about his life, he offered at odd times as if he were speaking to a ghost. Those rare times, I only listened without asking, as if I feared knowing more. I still do not know which of the two kept me silent. From the moment Dad started showing signs of Alzheimer's, it was as if I never existed for him. Any information about his life froze in time. But then, even before the moment he started losing his memories, everything that he shared voluntarily took place sometime between 1940 and 1943, during a time he lost everything the he truly loved.

**September 1940**

"Vassili, wake up."

His aunt Andriana's gentle voice touched his ears. She rested a hand on his shoulder, and her other hand held a lit oil lamp. "Vassili, you have to wake up," she went on, her hand now shaking him more urgently.

His head came out from under the pillow, his eyes still shut. He sat up in bed with one hand pushed his tumbling hair backwards. His other hand groped for his watch, a gift from his mother, which he had left next to his pillow.

"Your uncle will be here soon to pick you up," his aunt said anxiously. "He sent a boy with a message. You must get ready. Quickly."

"It is early," he said. "Where does Uncle want to go? He said nothing last night."

His aunt looked distressed but maintained her calm. She held a shawl wrapped around her thin body dressed in a flowery housedress.

"Sweetheart, hurry up. You must get dressed. Your uncle is coming here. The two of you have to go somewhere, he messaged with the boy," she repeated, as if she could not believe what she was saying. With a soft, graceful hand she placed a pile of tightly folded clothes on the bed next to him: a clean pair of brown slacks, a white undershirt, a freshly ironed light blue shirt, a warm, dark blue sweater, and a pair of white cotton socks.

"Did Uncle say where we are going?"

"No, my heart," she responded, as her eyes searched his face. "His message said that you have to take extra clothes with you." She pointed to a worn-out leather bag by the bedroom door, prepared for a trip and ready to go.

"Why? I am not leaving! Am I?" he said, not quite sure what to think. He stood up anyway and started dressing while his aunt looked away.

He was tall and slim, handsome, and in his early twenties. He had a strong body with which he could move quickly and assuredly. He did not know whether he loved or feared his Uncle Dimitri. Perhaps it was both. His uncle was a tall, stocky man in his late forties with meticulously combed gray hair. He was stubborn, but fair and reasonable. He was an honorable man who never married. Instead, he devoted his life to his unmarried sisters. He was difficult to read, especially when he did not want to share his thoughts. There were times when topics were out of bounds and he would refuse to engage. Dimitri did not like surprises and was obsessed with planning everything carefully and in advance. Deciding on a last-minute trip was highly unusual and strange.

Adriana rushed out of the room, leather bag in one hand and the stair rail in the other. The stairs squeaked as she ran down them into the kitchen.

Vassili looked around his small but neat room, as if for the last time: his warm bed that had given him refuge from pain and despair so often; the wooden dresser full of the clothes Aunt Adriana had refused to throw away as he grew out of them; an old walnut table that belonged to his mom, with four artisan chairs around it. For a moment he wondered whether he was still asleep, dreaming, or really leaving.

On the second floor he met his uncle, dressed in his usual gray suit and black hat. His face was stern, lips tight, one hand holding his watch and the other clutching his nicely decorated cane. His uncle loved this cane. It had been passed to him by his father, a gift from King George for his father's services to the royal court.

"We do not have much time. We need to leave immediately," his uncle said as he glanced at his watch and turned back down the stairs.

"Vassili, sweetheart, wait . . ." Adriana wept behind him and pulled his sweater until he turned to look at her. She suddenly looked much older than she was. Her eyes were blurred with tears. She pushed the leather bag to his chest, as if he had to guard it with his life, and put a paper bag in his hand.

"Raisin bread," she said, and broke into sobbing. She grabbed his young hands, placed them on her face, and kissed them, her tears spilling down his hands.

"Follow me," his uncle said, opening the squeaky wooden door to the narrow street.

Vassili ran fast behind him. He felt a rush of crisp, cold air on his face as he tried to keep up with his uncle, who was moving fast despite his age.

"Where are we going?" Vassili asked, trying to catch his breath.

His uncle did not respond, and Vassili stopped abruptly, throwing the bag to the ground. He planted his feet in protest. He angrily waited for a response from his uncle, who had now stopped and had turned to look at him.

"I am not coming with you, not unless you tell me where we are going," he called, stubbornly watching his uncle who was now coming back toward him, eyes looking at him with determination, lips set firmly.

"You are going to be enlisted in the Greek Navy today," his uncle said.

"What?" Vassili asked, grinning as though he had heard a joke. His grin soon wavered under his uncle's deadly serious stare.

"Enlist in the navy? Have you lost your mind? Why? I do not want to go to war. Not now. We are protected by the British; I will fight the Nazis if they come to the island."

"They will come to the island, and it will be too late for you," his uncle growled, his face flushed red and lips trembling. "It will be too late for you then," he repeated. "Do you want to live or die?"

Vassili could feel his uncle's rage, his breath like the fire of a dragon, his cane held defiantly between them. "I promised your mother, my sister, that I would protect you. She begged me to keep you alive, and I told her I would. You will not be the one to force me to go against my promise. You will be safe in the navy, away from here; away from fascists."

"They are not here yet."

"They will come soon."

"Who told you that?" Vassili said indignantly. "The barber, Sior Giacomo, told me yesterday when we were closing the shop that we are protected here."

His uncle smiled sadly. "No one is protected. Not here, not anywhere else. Sior Giacomo should try to take care of his family and leave you alone."

"He is a good man, Sior Giacomo, and he said I can have his shop after he retires. He told me that I have learned the craft." Vassili wasn't sure why he said this. Perhaps the reality of the situation was setting in.

"Does Sior Giacomo read the papers? There is not going to be a shop to have," his uncle raged back at him.

"What if I enlist later? In a month, a year?"

His uncle shook his head. "You are going to enlist today. Not tomorrow, not in a month, and not in a year! Today. Do you know what is happening in Poland? In Germany? In France?" He turned around and started walking down the narrow street, ignoring the few heads that had peeked out of narrow windows to see what the argument was all about. Vassili picked up his leather bag, confused, and ran to catch up to his uncle. His thoughts were chaotic, crashing over him like waves. He began trying to reason once again with his uncle.

"What if I enlist later, after saying goodbye? I cannot leave like a thief in the night, without anyone knowing."

"The Greek navy is not coming back. The Germans are halfway to Athens. The Greeks are moving all their ships and servicemen to Alexandria. It is today or never!"

"I cannot enlist," Vassili said in a low, hoarse voice. "I am not baptized."

"Nonsense! They do not enlist priests. They enlist soldiers."

"I have no papers," Vassili stammered, desperately reaching for more excuses.

"They do not need them."

Dimitri then stopped and turned to his nephew. "When we speak with the officer, I will do the talking. You will just stay behind me, listen carefully, and say nothing while I am talking."

They kept walking until they heard loud whistling in the distance, followed by barked orders and the growing, thumping sound of mixed voices and footsteps.

"This way," his uncle said. He disappeared around a narrow turn.

Vassili followed, and soon they found themselves in the city's center, the Spianada, where Vassili had played and promenaded multiple times as a member of the St. Fathers philharmonic.

The beautiful square was ringed by old Venetian homes and covered with colorful cobblestones. Now, it was full of men lining up in three rows in front of city hall (*municipio*). The lines were long and growing longer by the minute. Young men were anxiously waiting for their turn at the narrow wooden table, where a midcareer navy officer was sitting, his back straight, his cap slightly tilted, a cigarette in his left hand.

He smelled sweat coming from the young bodies impatiently clustered around him. Most of them were there with someone, a friend or relative, who was giving them advice about what to do, how to take care of themselves, and how to come back safe. His uncle remained silent but looked increasingly stressed and uncomfortable. He made no effort to wipe away the beads of sweat that were forming on his brow. He kept looking at the navy officer and the two sailors flanking him as if he was already reciting their discussion.

"Next!"

Vassili heard a strong voice from the seated officer. The man began shaking his pen, which seemed to have stopped working. "Fucking pen," he said and threw it away. He took a drag on his cigarette, held the smoke inside his lungs, and exhaled slowly. He grabbed the new pen a young sailor put into his open, impatient hand and looked down again at his book.

"Name?" he asked, raising his eyes from the book to stare at Vassili. Vassili could hear his heart beating and the arteries throbbing in his neck.

"Vassili," he said finally.

The officer started writing. "Last name?"

"Hmm . . ."

"Katehis," his uncle responded. The officer slowly turned his head up, hearing the new voice, and his eyes focused on the new face.

"Sior Katehis," the officer said with a smile. He set the pen on the table and grabbed Dimitri's hand in an affectionate gesture. The two of them seemed to be around the same age and clearly knew one another.

"Is this your nephew we spoke about yesterday?"

"Yes. And as I told you, he wants to serve."

"I am glad! He seems strong, and if he is equally smart, he will make it," the officer said as his eyes searched Vassili's. "Your full name?"

"My name—"

"His full name is Vassilios Katehis," Dimitri interjected.

"What's your problem, son? You lost your voice?" the officer said with a laugh that deteriorated into a cough. He spat on the ground. "Hold your anxiety for later. You will have plenty of it in the war," he said, and his mouth made a grimace as if he had felt pain. "When were you born?"

"August 27, 1919," Dimitri replied on Vassili's behalf.

"Papers?"

"We lost the papers during the bombardment by the Italians that year," Dimitri said firmly, looking at the officer straight in the eye.

"Religion?"

"Greek Orthodox."

"How about his baptism papers?"

"We lost those too. We searched but we could not find them."

The officer took another puff on his cigarette, looked at them for a few moments, and then continued writing in the book. "If you live through the war, son, and find your papers, you can bring them to me," he said with a smile that showed no emotion. "You are not the only one who does not have papers today. Your parents' names?"

"Fidelina and August," Vassili replied quickly, thinking that he could tell the truth to this officer at least once.

Then, a man in doctors' attire peered at him so closely that Vassili could see every single pore on his nose. The doctor checked his eyes and ears and put his yellowish fingers around his young neck and the back of his head. The doctor curled his upper lip, displaying an array of sharp yellow teeth. With a hoarse voice that smelled of tobacco and coffee, he said, "He seems healthy, he can fight."

The officer, his eyes still on the heavy logbook, wrote "256" on a piece of paper that he extended toward Vassili. The young man's hand trembled as he took it.

"Next, you go to the old harbor. The ships are leaving in an hour."

Vassili left the table in disbelief. He never wanted to go to war. Sarah and he had made different plans, and war was not part of it.

"We've got to go to the harbor immediately if you want to find a place to sit on the boat," his uncle stated as though he were talking about a leisurely cruise.

"I need to go by the barber shop," Vassili said, as if in a dream. "I need to see Sior Giacomo. He will wonder where I am."

"There is no time. I will tell him," his uncle said.

"No, I will! Who are you to tell me what to do?" Vassili's words came forcefully out of his mouth with a spray of spit that almost hit his uncle's face. "I know what to do next. I do not need you."

He immediately felt sorry for speaking so rudely to his uncle. Nevertheless, he ran toward the Jewish quarter. He needed to see Sarah. What would he tell her? How could he explain? If he was in danger staying on the island, then she must be too. His mind was numb as he raced to the barber shop.

He found Sior Giacomo waiting by the door as if looking for something. "Vassilaki!" he said with a smile and a calm voice. "I have been waiting for you. It is already late. Is there a problem?"

"Where is Sarah?" Vassili pushed the door of the shop open, forcing the old man inside with him. Sior Giacomo was shorter, with a bent posture. He had a gentle face with brown, expressive eyes and gray hair and beard. His face showed calmness and anxiety at the same time.

"What is the problem, my son?" he asked Vassili.

"Where is Sarah?" he asked again in an agonized voice.

Before the old man was able to respond, a young woman came out from behind the yellow curtain that divided the barber shop from a small bath and kitchen. Her thick brown hair in a French bow framed a pale face, graced by hazel eyes that were shaded by thick lashes and a straight, small nose over full lips. Looking at her broke his heart. He lost his voice as he looked at her innocent, smiling face. She was wearing a dark blue dress with a laced collar, a tight belt around her narrow waist, and a pair of blue shoes—the ones they had bought together. He came close to her and grabbed her hands in distress.

"Sarah, I have to go," he said. "I got enlisted. You must leave too. You must protect yourselves. Promise me."

Her smile fell from her face, which made her somehow more beautiful. She looked at him in surprise.

"You are leaving?" she said, startled. "You make no sense!"

"I am not leaving you. I am going to fight the Nazis, and I will be back to take you with me. People in the navy can take their families with them to Alexandria, after a time. I will come back to take you with me, I promise."

She looked at him as if he were speaking a different language. She raised her hand and tried to push his hair out of his eyes.

"Please, slow down," she said in a steady voice. "We are safe here."

"No. Listen to me. You are not safe here. You have to hide." He reached for his mom's watch that he had inside the leather bag. "Sarah," he went on, forcing his eyes to stay on hers, "please keep this with you. It was my mother's. Now you know I will come back for you. I promise on the soul of my mama." He kissed her forehead.

He turned to the old man, his eyes pleading with him. "Sior Giacomo, take care of her until I come back." He looked again at Sarah, grabbed her face, and kissed her lips, praying that it would not be the last time. He turned away and ran out of the shop before his feet would refuse to move, and before the look of shock on her face dragged him back.

His uncle was waiting outside. Vassili felt a great anger bloom in his heart. He hated his uncle for taking him away from what he loved the most.

They walked toward the old harbor without saying a word. They had both lost the ability to communicate without fighting. His uncle's anger seemed to match his own. Their steps on the cobblestones were gradually joined by others that multiplied with every turn of a corner; dozens of men joined them on the path to the harbor. The noise from the boots and the murmurs of the men grew into a deep rumble. The crowd, like water from a broken dam, rushed through the narrow streets, forcing the young bodies to crash into each other. There were no complaints, no laughter, and no curses. Vassili looked behind him and saw his uncle following him, staring forward.

Clutching the handle of the leather bag in one hand and the paper bag with the now-mushy raisin bread in the other, Vassili let the crowd march him onward to the navy ships. After the narrow streets, the harbor was no better. In fact, there the crowd was stiflingly thick, pushing toward the doors of the two navy ferries waiting with the engines on, dense smoke pouring from the chimneys.

The rabble pushed left and right, trying to enter through the doors of the ferries that hung open like the jaws of a monster, a war machine feeding on human flesh. He looked for his uncle but could not find him. He looked forward again as the crowd nearly took him off his feet, as though it wanted to feed him to the beast. He felt like he was drowning in moving sand.

He let himself be carried over to the open mouth of the boat, a gray-painted war ferry with guns extruding from its turrets and sides. Blue-and-white Greek flags flapped in the wind with pride and fear.

The open mouth of the boat led to the belly of the horrifying monster. There was an overpowering stench of oil and tar. It was completely dark, and the crowds continued pushing forward. Vassili felt his feet touch the ramp of the ship and his head brush a metal cable that held the ramp in place. He bent his arm around the cable and lifted himself off the ground, trying for a last time to find his uncle. He saw him, finally, at the back of the crowd. His uncle was holding up his cane as high as he could, waving it back and forth in farewell.

"Barba!" Vassili yelled from the depths of his lungs, using the Venetian term for "uncle," his eyes blurring with tears. "Barba, Barba . . ." he cried, until his voice was consumed by the sounds of the thrusting engines.

Dimitris kept his eyes on Vassili as the thicket of the crowd surrounded his slim body and shoved him inside the boat. He wanted to cry but couldn't. The last tears he had shed were over Fidelina's grave. His eyes surveilled the ships until the crowds had filled up their metal bellies. Once they were full and heavy, the doors were shut, and they began to slowly pull away from the dock. Soon, the engines were in full thrust, and the ships were off on an unknown journey.

"Live, Vassili," he heard himself saying. "Live."

Mrak Hall houses the UC Davis administration building.
The chancellor's office is on the fifth floor.

CHAPTER TEN

# THE GREAT RECESSION

### September 20, 2016

BACK ON TINOS, THE SISTERS Ritsa and Eleni the Older had finished their breakfast of French coffee and toasted raisin bread and were looking at the calm Aegean Sea. They were deep in thought.

"So that's how it started," I said, knowing that they were struggling to understand the story I had just told them. We sat in the veranda under the pergola's shade with our chairs turned toward the sea, whose blue presence was magnetizing and overwhelming, as if you were looking into the eyes of Medusa. She could strip you of any sense of confidence and entitlement and turn you into a meaningless speck. Her vastness and her power made you feel unimportant, vulnerable.

"Well, my life at UC Davis was like sailing the Aegean in August: a few days of blue calmness followed by weeks of blustery blows and growling waves," I chuckled.

"Why did they not want you?" Ritsa asked as she leaned forward to look down the small, golden beach.

"I don't know!" I admitted. "Every time I ask this question, I arrive at a different answer. Maybe I was the wrong bride for the groom, the wrong sail for the boat. Maybe I was too forceful, too intimidating, too business-minded for Davis's culture."

"Why do you consider yourself the problem?" Ritsa asked with an innocent grin on her face. "We always blame ourselves for every unhappy incident. I am tired of feeling guilty for everything. I blamed myself for my husband's affairs, for his abusive behavior, for leaving him, for being happy when I finally felt free to start a new life." Her eyes showed the suffering of many years.

"Yes, we blame ourselves for everything," I said, feeling anger flowing through my veins, turning my face a hot red. "It is so debilitating," I continued and turned my head away, trying to control my feelings. *How many times have I told other women that we must stop ascribing guilt to ourselves, that we should embrace self-reflection and accept responsibility when appropriate?* I thought. Yet, I had failed every single time. Feelings of guilt and remorse seemed to be embedded in my amygdala as a parasite that fed on my fears and killed my confidence.

"How about that Senator Yee?" Impressed by his title, Ritsa had memorized his name. "Did you meet him?"

I was sure she did not know the difference between a state senator and a US senator. "He's in purgatory," I replied, smiling.

"Purgatory?" Her surprised face turned abruptly to me with a half-smile on her lips.

"I meant jail," I chuckled. "He's been punished for his crimes. He was found guilty of money laundering, corruption, and racketeering. He was buying guns from gangs, and he was reselling them to extremist groups."

Both sisters looked at me in amazement. "People are paid back with the same coin," they cited in one voice.

"Did this not redeem you?" the younger sister asked.

"Not really," I replied. *For those people who wanted to believe him, his faulty character had no impact on their desire to accept his accusations,* I thought. *They had not been interested in the truth. They were ready to deny it and denounce it in favor of their beliefs.*

"People need a villain," I whispered. "They need someone who will pay for their faults. Women are particularly attracted to this idea. We want someone to hate."

"This senator did something hideous and calculated," Eleni said as she blew out the smoke of her cigarette. "He thought you were easy prey. A foreign-born woman who is in a powerful position. You were a low-risk target who could place his name in the newspapers." She paused to take another drag on her cigarette. I remained silent.

She continued. "Who would care if you were taken down in favor of his political ambition? No one he would worry about," she added. "Well, forget about this nonsense. It is all a small ripple in your life. That's all!"

*This is not a small ripple. Do not be confused!* I heard a voice that sounded like the old Gabriel ringing in my brain. *This is just the beginning.* Always uninvited, she showed up when not needed.

*Go away!* I was ready to yell, but I resisted out of fear that my cousins would think that I was not only upset but crazy as well. I had a feeling that she had decided to show up in order to contradict me at every point along the way. I excused myself from the company of the sisters and went to the kitchen to wash the breakfast dishes that sat in a pile by the sink. I needed time to collect my thoughts. As the white foam swallowed every speck of dirt and grease, I tried to reconstruct my memories of those first months as chancellor.

**January 28, 2010**

It was a wet morning in Davis. One of those days when the clouds slowly lower their gray veil to cover the whole city in misty dullness. The fog on the office windows had condensed on the glass and droplets slid down it, creating straight lines of water. It was ten o'clock in the morning, but the tinted windows kept the office dark. *This office feels so cliché*, I thought with a smile as I looked around the corner office on the top floor. It was outfitted with rather heavy furniture—a combination of leather, wood, and dark fabric. Its male character from the previous occupant was prominent. The pictures and flowers I had brought from home did little to brighten or warm the room.

The desk sat almost at the center of the room, with its back to the west windows. It was only recently that I noticed the desk had a hidden emergency alert button. When I squeezed under the desk to pick up my pen's cap that had rolled onto the floor, I discovered it.

"Did anyone try to rob this office, or threaten the previous chancellor?" I asked my assistant. She seemed surprised when I pointed out the button, as though it were the first time anyone had mentioned it. "Does it work, or is it just left over from the old days?"

"It works," she replied. "If you push it, the police will show up in a few minutes."

I examined the gadget carefully, but the red flags it raised in my head made me feel uneasy about the whole thing. "I hope I will never have to push it!" I commented to her, but she did not seem to have given it a second thought. She was absorbed in a document open on her computer screen.

On the desk, I found a thick folder intended to help prepare me for the upcoming budget meeting. It was a meeting we had urgently called with members of the chancellor's cabinet, who were responsible for the campus budget.

Under normal conditions, the first few months of a chancellor's tenure on a campus require serious efforts for outreach, both internal and external. In most cases, this is a time of hope and anticipation for a better future, even if the past was already good and memorable. When I joined UC Davis in August 2009 in the middle of a serious national recession, budget cuts and tuition increases were hitting the university hard. In June, just two months before I joined the university, 40 percent of state funds had been cut, and the University of California had announced a 36 percent combined increase in tuition to compensate for the loss. During these announcements, people were losing their homes, their jobs, and their health insurance.

Starting in this role in the middle of a global recession made this outreach eminently critical and difficult. The media coverage around my salary and false allegations about my involvement in the Illinois scandal had poisoned the well. My first five months as chancellor were overwhelmed by meetings with faculty and staff who were anxious and stressed about the impending cuts and the future. The fact that I was new to the institution and arriving under the cloud of an accusation did not give anyone relief. Some were skeptical of my ethics, my salary, and Spyros's position as a lecturer in the chemical engineering department. Others remained undecided about their feelings toward me. People who knew me felt sorry for me.

Those who were vocal in their disapproval knew well that my salary was not the highest on campus. In fact, there were dozens of higher-paid faculty and staff members. On top of that, almost one-third of the faculty had spouses and children employed by the university. In short, mine was not a unique or controversial situation at the time. Yee's and AFSCME's political rhetoric, combined with the *Bee*'s articles, found fertile ground with those not familiar with the university. This was my first exposure to a political environment that thrived on rumors and twisted perceptions of truth.

When I joined the university in August 2009, I started meeting with students who were startled by the extraordinary tuition increase in the UC system. Many of them believed that I was responsible for setting tuition, or at least that I had the political power to veto it. Even the student leaders were oblivious to how the university worked, making the average student believe that I had "unlimited" power. Believing that it was my decision to increase tuition, some students and their parents asked me to give up my salary for as long as these cuts persisted; others suggested that I undo the increase and cut my salary in half. Some, under the encouragement of a few faculty in the English department and Asian Studies department, created posters with my picture on them that claimed that I was unethical, with dollar signs covering my eyes.

While I could see the argument from their point of view, giving up part of my salary would not have helped the students financially, and doing so would have placed me and the campus in a very difficult position. Such an act would have undermined the decisions of the UC regents, the president, and the other chancellors. It would have forced my other UC chancellor colleagues to do the same, and it would have been an affront to every effort of the university to help the state understand that faculty and administrative salaries in the UC were already in the bottom quartile of all American Research Universities. But beyond all this, I felt that this request of me only indicated an unspoken truth—those who objected to my salary believed I was not worthy of it.

Since August 2009, a group of about fifty student activists—organized by a few faculty members and their graduate students—had led the fight against the "Fascist Chancellor," as they called me, and the "Oppressive Administration," as they called my office. The group grew over time with the help of external instigators, some of them from the East Coast and others from Southern California. They participated in demonstrations during the day and sit-ins at night. They jazzed up their frequent marches with signs, copies of a picture of me from my days at Purdue University with dollar signs over my eyes and mouth, and a badly made effigy that I assumed was of me eating money. They marched with it in their protests, yelling as a group, "Fuck the chancellor!" and "Resign!"

At night, they took over buildings and individual classrooms and held general assemblies and lectures given by the same faculty on the economic theories of Marx, the history of protest in the USA, neoliberalism, and the international movement of anarchism. This group grew larger as the holiday season approached.

While my interactions with most of the students were positive and upbeat, my outreach to the activist students was always defeated. They were not interested in a discussion or a debate. They wanted to break into meetings and use their phones to record an exchange in which most of them were yelling slogans and then upload an appropriately modified version to YouTube that eliminated all the ugly aspects of their behavior.

The only way I was able to communicate with them was through the staff from the Office of Student Affairs. The relentless demonstrations and our efforts to manage them effectively quickly made it clear how thin our resources were in student advising services. We only had two staff working during the day and night, sleeping in cots in their offices just to make sure that the students were safe during their protests and sit-ins.

By the holidays in 2009, the stamina of the staff had been depleted.

Contrary to my meetings with students and the managed interactions with the activists, meetings with the faculty and staff had taken the form of therapy sessions in which I felt like I was both the therapist and the problem. It was the first time I realized how deep and wide the gap between faculty and leadership had become. The cuts in faculty positions and the severe reductions in departmental funds, which had begun before my appointment, had defeated their courage and crushed their hopes. In return, they were angry and unbelievably suspicious.

Many of the academic units had suffered from chronic underfunding, as a result of multiple budget cuts that were stacked one on top of the other over a decade. Several faculty members, especially from the humanities and social sciences, saw me as an uninspiring, unimaginative engineer who had come into this job because of personal ambitions and who could not understand or appreciate the importance of the humanities in higher education and the history of politics in the United States. Very few of them understood that I could hear in their words, read in their eyes, and see on their faces the contempt they thought they were hiding. I did not blame them for their cynicism and distrust. Nowhere in any of my previous institutions had I seen such substandard conditions as those under which these men and women had worked for years on the UC Davis campus. It became obvious to me that just cutting the budget to address the state reductions would only drive the campus deeper into despair, distress, and unrest.

My outreach to community leaders both in Davis and Sacramento had also intensified. I was anxious to meet with those who worried about the new Greek woman on the block and her ideas and wanted to know what my immediate actions would be, as well as my near- and long-term goals.

"What attracted you to UC Davis?" I remember being asked by a middle-aged man with a pink, round face and a broad smile of perfect, pearly white teeth. This had been during an afternoon event organized by the campus in the courtyard of the residence as an opportunity to meet members of the Davis community.

"I always wanted to be on a campus that has an appetite for excellence," I responded proudly, and I paused to gauge his reaction. He seemed unmoved. "I want to make UC Davis one of the top ten public universities in the country and also benefit the communities that surround it," I continued with enthusiasm. I was truly excited about the ideas percolating in my mind and inspired by the potential I had seen on campus.

"UC Davis is already very good," he responded with surprise on his face, which had turned even pinker. "And," he continued, "we at Davis like our community the way it is." His face had lost its smile and his eyes looked concerned. "We would hate to see it change," he added, looking at me intensely.

"I understand," I responded. "Be sure that I and the campus will respect the community culture. I can also assure you that we will only do what is good for the university without getting involved in the local politics or creating political ripples."

He smiled and then turned away to mix with the crowd.

This was a polite gathering that left me tense and uneasy. Some mentioned my salary and others the Illinois scandal, a few apologized for the bad reception I had received from the newspapers and the students, and even fewer mentioned that they were happy that I was there.

Back in my office, on the day of the budget review meeting, I reviewed the thick document in front of me. It included multiple and sometimes conflicting recommendations about budget cuts. On top of the thick volume, there were loose pages with graphs that showed income and spending projections. The state budget cuts had already been activated in July, forcing us into a deeper deficit with each day that passed. Looking over the budgets and participating in numerous meetings about spending cuts during my few months in office made me realize that there was a fundamental gap between my philosophy and the prevailing philosophy within the Office of the Chancellor that had already defined the strategy for budgetary reductions before I had even joined.

However, the executed and forthcoming cuts were not the biggest threat to the university. The unprecedented tuition increase proposed by the University of California Regents was the real menace. This increase was suggested at the peak of the Great Recession, when people were already feeling the pain of the Wall Street crash. Worse yet, this tuition increase, even if justified by the need for more income in an effort to balance the state budget reductions, at best had a small positive impact on our budget and, at worst, forced our campus into steeper cuts.

During my first UC Regents meeting in September, only one month into the job, all the chancellors were asked whether they approved the tuition increase. I felt numb and uncomfortable, and I decided to remain silent. Never had I experienced an increase of that level, and all my instincts warned me against such an action. My predecessor had advised me during our one-hour meeting in June that this increase was necessary, and that the chancellors had already supported it when the Regents made the recommendation in the July 2009 meeting. He mentioned that he personally had supported this increase and would expect me to do the same.

"The group for your meeting has already gathered outside," Lindsay's voice sounded tetchy. She peeked through the door that separated our offices and looked at me curiously.

"Yes, I am ready. Please bring them in," I responded.

Lindsay was relatively new to this position, a young, well-educated, and hardworking woman. Yet her limited experience in the Office of the Chancellor seemed to have been significantly more problematic than she and I had anticipated. Her hard work, including spending long hours in the office to meet the needs of a position that was truly demanding and complex, was weighing on her and her young family. We both felt that we were swimming against the tide, both new to the campus and to the office, and we were struggling together to rediscover how to meet the expectations of the campus culture. The executive assistant of the previous chancellor, who carried with her all the office's history and memories of the past twenty years, had left before I joined the campus. She had decided to follow the outgoing chancellor to his new office, unintentionally severing a management continuity that was so important and critical in my life as the new chancellor.

Lindsay's head disappeared behind the door, and I heard her footsteps in the hallway running to bring the team in. I looked at the thick document again. *There is so much to discuss and debate,* I thought. *This agenda looks impossibly long.*

The group was not large that day. It included the interim provost, the vice chancellor for administration and facilities, and the director of finance who reported to both of them. The discussion was only financial in nature and only those directly related were involved. We all sat in the heavy leather chairs around the wooden table in my office, furniture that was bought by my predecessor some time ago.

"Despite all the cuts we have made so far, we are far from balancing the budget," the director of finance started, anxious to get into details. She was a veteran of UC Davis, strong in character, persistent in her convictions, and stubborn, but she knew her math. "The tuition increase is costing us a lot more money than anticipated," she continued.

I looked at her with a question on my face that encouraged her to explain.

"Of the undergraduate students who enrolled this year, about 50 percent pay no tuition and another 25 percent pay less than the full amount due to their family's low income. In addition, this year and next year the regents have limited enrollment, so we have fewer students who pay any tuition at all." She paused to distribute a packet of pages that included dense tables. "All our scholarships are need-based, and they along with the teaching assistantships have to be adjusted for the tuition increase. In addition, we have to provide the tuition differential for our graduate student research assistants, whose grants will not cover this tuition increase since it was not budgeted." She took a deep breath and drank some water from the bottle she carried with her. "That's not all," she added quickly. "Not all of this tuition income will come to campus. Part of it will be held centrally by the Office of the President."

"So, what is the bottom line?" I asked impatiently.

"If you calculate the loss of revenue from the reduced number of enrolled students and the new cost related to the abrupt tuition increase, and subtract the sum of the two from the revenue generated by the increased tuition, the balance is a small positive."

Her comment forced me to sneer. "You're saying that the 36 percent increase was not worth the trouble?" There was a pause as we all tried to digest the news. Whatever it was, it was the wrong move for the University of California.

Indeed, in the months following the announcement, the tuition increase became a political spark that created the kind of unrest at the UC not seen since the Vietnam War demonstrations. Over the academic year, this spark turned into a wildfire that engulfed all the UC campuses. It created student activism and a faculty dissent that I had not seen since my days as an undergrad in Greece during the last years of the junta. All the while, the financial benefits provided no justification whatsoever for this thoughtless action.

"Anyway," the director of finance continued, "we have no other option but to cut down to the bone. I have two proposals to make." She sounded confident as she distributed a new copy of the documents I had already read.

"I read these documents. Is there anything new?" I asked, worrying about the time left for the rest of the discussion.

"Some of the numbers have been corrected."

"Why do we never get the same numbers every time we do a new data query?" I asked, trying to understand why every time I asked how many tenure track faculty we had, I got a different number.

"Our financial tracking systems in the colleges are old and not compatible. Some of the data have to be entered by hand."

"How are we going to make decisions about cuts without access to accurate data?" I looked around as everyone remained silent. I could tell that this question had an obvious answer but no obvious solution.

The director went on. "We have to cut 10 percent of the staff and 10 percent of faculty across the board in addition to cutting a number of programs."

I knew where she was going, but hearing her proposal made me flush from anger. This was not the first time we had this discussion with no agreement. Our different opinions on the topic were deeply rooted in one of the many vulnerabilities of the modern public American university. The vast post-Cold War expansion of academic degree programs and the birth of the "research university," the proliferation of student services and sports, the substantive expansion of state and federal regulations, and the growth of the academic hospital sector in the United States have driven auxiliary services to a degree where the increase of non-academic and administrative staff has significantly outpaced the growth of both faculty and students. The modern public American university has turned into a massive public employer no different than any other department of public service, but with one exception. The university has a small academic core that defines it, namely its faculty. Without faculty, there are no students; without students there is no university. Eroding the small core during times of financial stagnation and eliminating academic programs, as if they were another auxiliary student service, would send the university into a downward spiral until it reaches the point of no return.

"Cutting across the board is not strategic," I responded, my voice trembling. "If we want UC Davis to survive this financial crisis and be able to recover, then we need to protect its quality. The core of the university are the faculty and its students. Support services and administrative structures can be dismantled and recreated but academic programs cannot." I felt my heart beating faster.

The fact that we had to revisit this discussion every time we met made me hugely uncomfortable. I had not been in a university before where the longevity of high-quality academic programs was not a priority.

"How are you planning to do a 10 percent cut in faculty positions?" I asked to keep the conversation moving.

The financial director responded, sounding confident. "We will remove funding from every position that is vacated due to retirement, resignation, or separation. This is exactly what we did last time we had a similar situation, in the early 2000s." She looked at me, hiding some degree of discomfort.

"Yes, indeed," I responded briskly. "This is why we have 200 unfilled faculty positions. They are all without money. Instead of having 1,400 tenure-track faculty as we are supposed to for the 25,000 undergrads, we have 1,200, with 200 empty positions depleted of money. This means that $20 million annually has been removed from academics to fund all other non-essential activities."

I noticed my voice had gotten stronger, and I tried to breathe. "If every time we have to cut our expenditures, we remove faculty positions, then we will have a university with thousands of students without the necessary number of instructors."

"We can hire lecturers," she responded airily.

"So, we could envision a university with thousands of students who are trained primarily by lecturers," I continued in my terse style. "Should we consider this an acceptable scenario? Because if we were to follow this way of thinking, such a future may become possible." I looked at everyone's apprehensive faces. "We have to protect the faculty positions. Could you please run another budget-cut scenario, assuming we not eliminate any additional faculty positions? Let us discuss it again when you have the new projections. Now, what was the second proposal?"

The director glanced at the papers in front of her. "This is a tricky one," she started breathing out heavily, "and has to do with our athletics department. The department has a $1.5 million annual deficit, built up over the past three years. By the end of next academic year, the deficit will be almost at $4.5 million. The faculty have voted against transferring academic funds to athletics, and fundraising efforts failed to get us the funds we expected." She paused, thinking of her next sentence, and I noticed that her neck had turned red. I felt sorry for her feeling responsible for solving an unsolvable problem. *Whatever we do, we will be criticized heavily,* I found myself thinking over and over again.

*When there is no good solution, do what is right and accept the blame for that,* said the voice of my mentor loudly in my head.

"Okay. What is the proposal?" I asked, wondering what color rabbit she would pull out of her hat this time.

"We need to cut some sports." Her voice sounded serious and steady.

"Excuse me?" I responded in disbelief. "Do you know what you are asking? That's how chancellors lose their jobs. What we need to do is stop making cuts, especially in sports, and try to generate more money. Do you have any ideas for *that?*"

In that moment, one could hear a pin drop.

## THE SPORTS DRAMA

Despite my efforts to avoid touching athletics, we had to go through with the cuts proposed by the director of finance and the athletics director. The months following that decision were busy and unnerving, as we scrambled to address the fallout.

Among those who hated the cuts was a ringleader who emerged early. In the beginning, he started sending me poems via regular mail asking me to reverse my decision to cut four sports. Later, his letters changed from poetry to threats, promising to spend the rest of his life destroying my career. His letters arrived by mail first at my office and then at home. Later, his letters were pushed under our kitchen door by hand. Eventually, he changed to emails, often sent in the middle of the night and copied to dozens of others, mostly administrative staff, faculty, and student senators. In the beginning I took it lightly, but as time went on, I ended up fearing him. He sounded mentally unstable.

The ringleader organized a group who went after State Senator Dean Flores of San Francisco, and persuaded him to arrange a state hearing in August 2010 that took place in the state's capitol and lasted eight hours, from 6:00 p.m. until 2:30 a.m.

This ringleader remained a distraction for years. His obsession had blinded him so much that he would do anything to hurt the university, the sports programs, and me most specifically. Because of his lies to students that we were misusing student fees, we did a financial audit of the athletics department in 2014 to prove to him and the students that his claims were incorrect. The Office of the President provided oversight of the audit, and they concluded that the use of student fees in athletics was appropriate and according to the student referendum.

In November 2015, the ringleader approached the Office of the President to accuse me, again, of misusing student fees for personal purposes this time. In January 2016, the Office of the President informed us about it, but in view of the recent audit, they concluded that there was no need for an additional investigation.

My cousin Eleni and I in Tinos, August 2016.

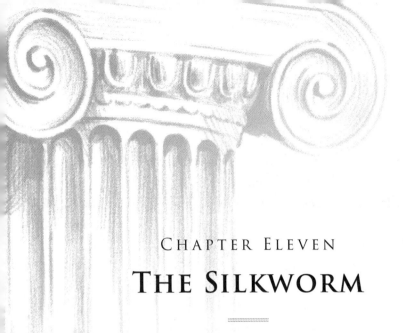

## Chapter Eleven

# The Silkworm

**September 5, 2016**

TODAY THE SISTERS LEFT. WE all felt it was time for us to part ways. The daily interactions were getting noticeably more difficult. After our first few days of sharing the memories that made us happy and connected us again, I became overwhelmed by my grief. Any effort on their part to discuss something other than what happened at UC Davis forced me into silence. They understood it was time for them to go. They packed their bags, made their beds with new sheets and placed new towels in the bathroom. Before they left, we hugged and kissed each other farewell and promised to stay in touch. They boarded the ferry and took their separate roads back to lives of their own.

My only cousin who stayed behind was Eleni. Our moms were sisters, and they had raised us as twins. We started speaking in our own language when we were little girls, playing our own games, eating together, and sleeping together. We were inseparable until Eleni went to school, a couple of years ahead of me. The separation during our school year did not stop us from spending all our summers together, which lasted until I left for the United States in 1979.

Eleni played an important part in my most beautiful memories. We never fought or disagreed. I looked up to her and wanted to be like her for much of my young life. Born in Athens, she lived in the big city with her parents when she wasn't visiting the island. She went to an Ursuline Catholic school, spoke fluent French, and learned ballet.

It was not just our mothers who sealed our sisterhood. Eleni's father was also my godfather (my *nouno*) and loved me like a daughter. I remember him so fondly, not just for his support and affection, but for his sensitivity, discretion, and humor. He knew how poor we were, and every time we visited them, he would give me surprise gifts that were quite unusual and extraordinary.

I remember one time, probably when I was in first grade, when Mom and I visited him in his restaurant. It took us half a day to go from the island to Athens. We took a small boat from the docks of my little town of Paloukia ("the boat docks") to the port of Perama ("passage") on the mainland where we caught the first of two buses, followed by a walk of a few miles to Eleni's home. I was so excited to go to Athens, even if I hated the city noise and the smell of the narrow streets—a mix of foul food and human sweat. Yet, I would give anything to spend some time with Eleni.

Eleni told me that her dad had invited us to his restaurant. It was during lunch time and the restaurant was full of people. I was so excited to be there. Rarely did we have the opportunity to eat in a restaurant. "They are too expensive," Mom used to say. Yet this time was different; we would eat for free.

My nouno had reserved a table large enough for five people, nicely covered with a white tablecloth and decorated with a beautiful little vase of fresh flowers. He saw us as we entered the door and showed us to our table. Eleni and I sat next to each other, while her dad started explaining the dishes he had prepared for us himself. I can hardly remember what we ate because food did not interest me. It was the people who attracted my eyes and whose voices overwhelmed my ears. I was mesmerized by the beautifully dressed women, most of them wearing small hats pinned to their hair, sitting at the elegantly decorated tables, all covered with white tablecloths. They and their companions were engaged in animated discussions as they chewed the food and drank the wine. I watched the waiters run around and take orders and the musicians who played in the corner.

My nouno joined us at the table. In his soft voice he asked me how I was doing and whether I was a good girl deserving of a unique gift. I responded "yes" without hesitation, while shooting brisk looks at Mom, whose face remained serious under her smiling eyes.

"Linda," he continued with a warm voice, "go to the back room where the cashier is and open the drawer. Put your hands in there and bring to me as many of the coins as you can hold in your hands." Eager to escape from my mom's attempts to push as much food as she could in my mouth, I gulped the last forkful of French fries, got off my chair, and looked curiously toward the back room.

"Mr. Tony," he added, gesturing to the waiter, who looked at my godfather as though he were crazy, "will help you open the drawer."

"Are you sure, Master, you want me to do this?" Mr. Tony asked.

"Yes, go and do as I said," my godfather replied impatiently. "I will be here waiting for Linda to come back."

I followed Mr. Tony, who kept looking back at me in disbelief. I already didn't like him. I sensed his dislike crawling like a dark shadow on my heart. Mr. Tony guided me to the back of the restaurant to a tall desk and pulled a key out from under his long white apron to unlock the drawer. The drawer was so high that even standing on my toes I could not see inside.

"You little brat," I heard Mr. Tony whispering as he pulled a stool over and nodded at me to step on it.

I stood on the stool and looked inside the open drawer in amazement. I had never seen so many shiny coins. They looked like the bubblegum we bought on Sundays at the store back on the island: large golden coins with the face of a queen on both sides. Yet, these ones looked real. I put both hands in the drawer and felt the cool shiny surface of the coins on my skin. I grabbed as many as I could with my eyes set on the frowning face of Mr. Tony. Holding the coins tight, I stepped off the stool and walked back to our table. Mr. Tony stayed behind to lock the drawer. Walking slowly so I would not lose a coin, I took the treasure back to my nouno and left them on the table in front of him. Mr. Tony managed to be in step behind me.

"Good job, Linda," Eleni's father said, smiling. "This is all yours for being a good girl!"

It did not feel right that I should get so much money. I turned to my mom looking for permission. "Roco," my mom said, calling him by his name, "this is way too much. We cannot accept it." The seriousness on her face was a mix of surprise and shame.

"This is not for you, Georgia. This is for my goddaughter."

My eyes moved from Mom's face to Mr. Tony's, who was making many strange sounds, with disbelief written on his face as though it were *his* money.

"Mr. Tony," my nouno said, "we have work to do. Why are you standing around speechless? Let's go now." He stood, grabbed Mr. Tony by his arm, and they walked away from our table.

On our way back to the island, Mom remained silent for most of the time.

"Are you sad?" I asked when we got on the boat, as the sun began to set and the wind blew a cold, salty mist into our faces. "I am happy that my nouno gave us this gift. We can spend it on food!" I whispered, holding her hand against my chest.

"I am happy too, but sad for having to accept such a generous gift. We have nothing to give in return," she whispered back as we squeezed between the other passengers who were trying to find protection from the waves inside the boat's main cabin. "The gift is more than Dad's salary," Mom said in a low voice. "Remember your nouno's generosity and, when you can, try to pay it back."

Since then, my admiration for Eleni was sealed with a sense of respect and responsibility. She was more than a cousin; she was more than a sister. She was my real angel. Even Gabriel surprisingly agreed with me when I asked her opinion; *Eleni is your earthly angel.*

With the sisters gone, I felt free to move into my world of silence, like a silkworm that is ready to build its cocoon and bury herself into the chamber of metamorphosis.

*Changing from a worm to a moth is probably a very painful transition,* I thought, wondering whether anyone had written about it. *How would anyone know? Silkworms do not speak. Who has asked the silkworm what she goes through in order to turn into a moth? Who can imagine the pain and suffering when her skin breaks and her muscles expand to grow wings bigger than her body? It probably feels like giving birth to yourself, leaving the old self behind as an empty, dry shell. I need to go through the same metamorphosis.*

I had to let my wings break through my skin and grow strong enough to fly away, free from neglect and hatred, jealously and contempt, disloyalty and betrayal; free from everything that hurt me in life and almost destroyed me during the past seven years at UC Davis. I wanted to rediscover myself, feel free to express my thoughts, recommit to my values, show my contempt for demagogues and fanatics, and my abhorrence toward those who have the means to live well but feel entitled. I knew this transformation would be cruel to me and to those who love me, but it had to happen.

My cocoon—my chamber of anguish and rebirth—would be writing about the people I loved but lost, ignored but needed, and trusted but found to be dishonest. I needed strength to write about all my mistakes that I regret but cannot undo and the despair I feel but cannot turn into hope. I have to embrace my worm's body and grow wings to fly—fly away from those who hurt me and the places that remind me of their abuse. I have to write the book that could set me free.

*You need me to accomplish this,* I heard her voice again. *You cannot write this book without me.* She added with arrogance: *You need my critique. You need my inquisitive and intrusive attitude. You need my skepticism.*

Gabriel had been a constant voice of opposition ever since she entered my life, but also a voice of hope and redemption. I gave her the right to boast about all those times she saved me from trouble and bemoan all these times I fell short of her expectations. She was back again and eager to share every part of my life, even to become a coauthor.

Waiting to speak to a crowd of 2,000 people
a few days after the pepper spray incident.

## CHAPTER TWELVE

# THE PEPPER SPRAY

**November 15, 2011**

IT WAS DARK AND FOGGY outside the plane window. The tires bumped on the runway and were followed by the screeching sound of the brakes. My body was forced forward by the pressure of our sudden stop.

I was returning from a trip to France, where I had represented UC Davis at a United Nations conference on food technology. I was tired, sleepless, and anxious to come back, always thinking about the continuous student unrest. Student activism on the campus had intensified over those few days I was away. Protesters were moving from building to building and occupying classrooms and common spaces to oppose tuition increases and privatization.

The pushback I had received concerning the so-called 2020 Initiative, a plan I had proposed earlier that fall, came as a surprise. I had to find a way to get our community to understand the value of this plan. But most importantly, I needed to have the community trust my intentions and promises for the future. I knew how valuable a commodity trust had become in higher education. In most cases, administrators do not honor their promises, leading to many unfulfilled dreams. I had promised myself that I would not do the same.

Since I started as chancellor in August 2009, in order to encourage a climate of respect and trust, my office had honored all the promises the previous chancellor had made to the community: including a new museum and a new building for the school of music. I had to find the money for these two buildings. I made this decision knowing that I would have to work hard to honor the dream of someone else during a period of budgetary restrictions. I knew that this decision would push my own priorities further back. Yet, I took it as my responsibility to see that the Office of the Chancellor respected the promises it made, regardless of who was occupying the office.

The pushback to the 2020 Initiative came from two separate groups: staff in central administration, and faculty from the humanities and social sciences. When I joined UC Davis and asked about the demographics of the student body, to my astonishment only 1.5 percent of the 27,000 enrolled undergrads, or a total of 400 students, were from counties other than the United States. That meant that many Californian students were graduating from UC Davis without ever interacting with a student from another country. In the winter of 2010, we started a year-long study that involved learning from policies and best practices of a group of benchmark universities and how they integrated their international student population. Our study showed that to be internationally respected as an institution of higher education, you need to provide your students educational experiences that will make them leaders in a connected world. You could not achieve this without a measurable international student population (about 15 percent) and a vibrant international program. We developed a proposal to increase the international population on our campus from 1.5 percent to 15 percent, while retaining our own identity and, in parallel, also increasing the number of domestic students at a time when every other UC was going in the other direction. This intent formed the core of our 2020 Initiative.

There was only one catch: the success of this plan required tremendous discipline. There would not be space for political promises, uncontrolled spending, or the creation of projects of lesser importance.

The plan had two main goals: to increase the international diversity of the campus and improve the experience of all students by increasing the number of tenure-track faculty by 300. According to this initiative, starting in the fall of 2013, UC Davis could enroll an additional 5,000 students over a period of seven years to reach a total of 32,000 undergrads by 2020. From those additional students, we would aim for a maximum of 3,500 to be international and an additional 1,500 to be Californian students. This would bring the total number of international students to about 4,000 out of 32,000, or less than 15 percent of the total undergraduate population, aligning well with the top public universities in the country. In addition, we would be able to renovate several old buildings that had been left unoccupied due to lack of maintenance, replace temporary buildings from the early 1960s with permanent facilities, and even build a couple of new ones. These renovations would have been critical for a campus that suffered from historic highs of $1.4 billion in deferred maintenance, the highest among all UC campuses.

During the 2010–2011 academic year, the plan was vetted and shared with faculty and staff leadership groups, which supported it enthusiastically. It was then shared with President Yudof, who approved it and supported it when I presented it to the UC Regents. With their blessing, the plan was ready to go. Creating a more geographically and ethnically diverse student body would strengthen the interest of our Californian students in learning other languages, participating in transfer programs, and traveling around the world. This was a plan to create the citizens of the future.

The 2020 Initiative was announced as a preliminary plan during the convocation of September 2011. The pushback I experienced internally after this announcement took me by surprise. The same people who proudly held under their arm Tom Friedman's book *The World Is Flat* and who passionately advocated for new language programs, new courses on important world politics and cultures, and US international relations, came in droves to oppose the idea to bring to our campus those who live in these important countries, who have these different cultures, and who speak these interesting languages.

With the announcement of the 2020 Initiative, the faculty and students who proudly called me greedy and unethical and asked for my resignation in every protest on the campus quad, now added new words to their vocabulary: *neoliberal* and *privatization*. Together with the student and faculty protesters, several administrative staff expressed concern about the plan. They felt that it would be difficult to interact with international students because of their language impediments. Fearing that these new students would change our way of life, impact our culture, and modify the diversity demographic, these staff members became formidable opponents of the plan.

Despite sparking hope for an exciting future for the campus, the 2020 Initiative energized forces of opposition that soon called for more isolation. Faculty who scoffed at my "limited" understanding of American culture and history complained that this plan was a demonstration of my ignorance of the American reality. They insisted that this plan would only exploit the international students who would be left to fail, unprepared linguistically to understand the lectures. Little did they know that the new generation of international students have comprehension, reading, and writing skills at least as good as the domestic students, accents notwithstanding.

Such xenophobia surprised me. Never in my thirty years in the United States had I faced such an openly expressed American-centric and elitist point of view.

*How offensive can this be to our university members who are not American born?* I thought while the plane pulled up to the gate.

I picked up my belongings and anxiously awaited my turn to get out of my seat. Soon I was able to walk to the open door, which I did eagerly to rouse my feet from their numbness. I walked fast, almost running ahead of the others to get through passport control and then through customs to the airport lobby, where Spyros was waiting patiently. I was late.

"I won't ask how your flight was," he said, smiling. "Ten hours on a crowded plane isn't easy. What did you do? Did you sleep?"

"Not a bit," I admitted. "I sat there thinking."

"Thinking for ten hours!" he noted sarcastically.

"Yes, flying is the only time I can think without interruption."

Later, as Spyros drove us home, my chief of staff called. He had been with me in this role for less than a year, but I had developed a great sense of comfort and trust working with him. I believed he was someone I could rely on: smart, savvy, and trustworthy. In his previous role as a director of federal relations, he and I had made all the visits to DC together. My previous chief of staff, who had retired at the end of 2010 after many years of service, suggested him as a possible candidate. I liked the idea. He seemed personable, loyal, and straightforward. I was pleased we were able to attract him to this important role; it was a relief to finally feel that someone had my back.

"Hello?" I asked, trying to suppress a yawn.

"Linda!" His voice sounded apologetic. "I am sorry to bother you at this time," he continued. "I want to report to you that about fifty students and two faculty, those we all know well, have occupied the lobby of Mrak Building and plan to stay overnight."

"What do they want?" I asked, as if I could not guess.

"The usual," he responded. "They are asking you to resign for privatizing the university."

"Is there anyone in the building? We need to make sure that the students are safe," I asked, feeling for the staff who would have to stay there overnight.

"Yes," he responded. "Student affairs have things under control. But you may not be able to go to your office tomorrow morning. I will call you in the morning to let you know whether the back door from the basement of the building provides access to your office."

"What happens if it doesn't?" I asked curiously.

"If not, you could work from the residence. We can move all your meetings there. By the way, I was told that about thirty faculty from the humanities plan to write an open letter to you, complaining about the privatization of the university and the 2020 Initiative."

"This is not new," I responded.

"They fear that all the international students will be very rich and that they will create a class system on campus we have not seen before. As you can imagine, they are the same faculty who complain about your 'neoliberal ideas' on a campus known for its liberal views."

I wanted to laugh, but my lips only managed to make a grimace. "It is because the plan calls for the enrollment for more international students. Isn't it?" I continued without waiting for his response. "I do not know whether it is their hatred for me that forces them to act like this or their disdain toward people who are different."

"Hmm . . . maybe both," he responded.

The call was disrupted as our car entered the tunnel of the Bay Bridge through Treasure Island. I hung up the phone.

"The xenophobia of those who call themselves liberals irritates me," I said, causing Spyros to look at me in surprise. "Is it arrogance or control that forces people to express a view so hateful?"

"Fear of the unknown," Spyros said through gritted teeth. "Just that."

"Yes, but it is the role of the university to fight fear by embracing the unknown and make it familiar through hope and planning," I responded.

"How about the argument that rich international students will create a new bourgeoisie on the campus?" Spyros asked. "Did you think of us when we came to UCLA as bourgeois?"

We both laughed.

*What an irony, I thought. Most of our international students are not wealthy. They come from families who value a US education and who will do whatever it takes to give their children the opportunity to graduate from a US school. They will sell their home, work two jobs, and take no vacation; they will live with their aged parents in a small apartment to save money so they can send their son or daughter to UC Davis. They sacrifice because they believe that a UC Davis education will change their child's life for the better. They believe, like my mom did, that an education changes people for the better. They trust, like I did, that the United States recognizes merit, is blind to gender, race, ethnicity, and religion, and respects those who work hard.*

*They believe, like I did, that they will have an opportunity not just to live a better life but to create a new and better world here or back in their countries.*

I was not prepared to hear from the campus activists and the local newspapers that merit and wealth are bad words and belong to the vocabulary of racists and neoliberals. I've always believed that the answer to poverty is education. Education gives you the tools to change your destiny and reveals to you a better future for you, your family, and your communities. I also believed that those who transition successfully out of poverty because of hard work and commitment to their dream should serve as role models for others. In no previous institution before UC Davis did I have to defend students who were coming from hardworking families. Growing up poor and aspiring to live better, I never imagined that working hard and ethically to create wealth would be a crime. If wealth is dirty, no matter how you have created it, why then eradicate poverty?

I heard Spyros saying, "Try to relax and sleep well tonight. There is a new day tomorrow."

## November 16, 2011

I woke up in the morning confused about where I was. It took me some time to realize I was not in a hotel. Convinced for a few seconds that I was in our house in Indy, I felt rushed to wake up Helena to go to school. The morning light coming through the corner window made me realize that I was many years ahead of those moments. I jumped from the bed and ran to the shower. The hot water's power helped me put my thoughts in order.

Being out of the office for a few days meant a lot more work on projects that had been left unattended. I remembered a colleague administrator who told me once that she always took half a day off after every trip. I was envious of her ability to do so. Never in my whole professional life was I able to take time off after any trip. In fact, I managed to do the opposite because I always accumulated tons of work.

Since we had moved to Davis, waking up in the residence made me feel nostalgic for our house in Indianapolis. That was the house of my dreams. It had an Italian flare to it. Designed by a female architect well-known in Indy, there was visible attention given to the smallest details. My heart broke when we sold it. The residence in Davis was much bigger and more impressive, but it never felt like home. There were always people around. By 8:00 a.m., we had to be ready and out of the residence so that the two staff who were starting their work at that time could use the facilities for various university activities there. Many of the events would start right after work at 6:30 p.m. and end around 10:30 p.m. by the time the last visitor was seen out of the foyer.

Excluding weekends and holidays, on average, we had an event twice a week, requiring tremendous stamina on behalf of the residence staff. Those events were fundamental to the university and to me as chancellor. Four times a month, I had meetings with students, staff, and faculty. In addition, we had events for community members and leaders, events for fundraising, recognition of students, faculty or staff, and traditional celebrations. The number of visitors ranged from one or two to several hundred.

That morning, Spyros and I left the house around 7:45 a.m., each going to our separate offices. Many of the protesting students thought that Spyros was my bodyguard and were protesting spending their tuition to hire security. That made me laugh. I never thought then that something as amusing as this could become so serious later.

Poor Spyros. Since we moved to Davis, he had acquired many roles: he was a faculty member with full teaching responsibilities, a host for chancellor events, a personal driver everywhere I had to go, a personal chef, and a bodyguard whenever there was uncertainty about my safety. He was also the family financial advisor and secretary, the CEO of our house (as we used to tell the kids when they were young), in addition to being both father and mother to our children when I was not available. Nobody thanked him for that. At UC Davis, he was always criticized and mistreated by those who disliked me.

During that dreary November morning, we drove to the open parking lot next to the Mrak Building where my office was. Watching from afar, I could tell that there was a lot of activity in the lobby. Students were going in and out of the building peacefully, chanting and holding signs. I walked to the basement entrance of the building's west side, where a staff member waited by the locked door ready to open it to anyone who had business inside.

"Good morning," she said with a smile. I recognized her from my meetings with student affairs. "You should take the stairs up. Avoid the elevator. If you take the elevator, the protestors will see you and will make a scene. They control the elevator from the lobby. If they see you, they will get overly excited and will ask others to join them." She smiled. "We don't need this kind of excitement today."

I took the stairs five flights up, along with the rest of the staff trying to get to their offices. We all knew what to do. It was not the first time we had faced this situation. I was able to enter and exit my office during that day until later that afternoon without any problems. I was told that the students had left the building by 5:00 p.m. with the help of a few university police officers who went to lock the doors for the night. This time, the students agreed to leave without any objections.

"Why did they leave like this, without any effort from our side?" I asked a colleague who called to inform me that the lobby had been evacuated.

"One of the protestors told a staff member that they are planning something bigger and better," he said in his mild voice. "Never a dull day," he added.

"What does *that* mean? Did they say?"

"They will occupy the quad. They mentioned that they will organize the biggest camp ever." This was something of a relief, since the quad was an open area and they could stay and sleep there for as long as they wanted.

"That's great," I said. "This is good news."

"Not really," he responded. "They have invited all the tent occupants from Davis Park to join them, and are asking on Facebook for others from Sacramento, Berkeley, and Oakland to join as well. One thousand people have signed up to come."

"Are they students?"

"Not really."

"Who are they?"

"In Davis, many of them are homeless and among them people from Woodland who deal drugs." It sounded like someone was in the room with him, confirming what he said.

"From Berkeley and Oakland?" I asked anxiously.

"Well, that's another problem altogether," he confirmed. "We think that some were among those who instigated the Berkeley violence on Monday, and the Oakland mayhem last week. I am afraid to say that it will not be easy to deal with them."

I needed some time to think. *This didn't seem right. What if something goes wrong? What if a student gets hurt?*

"Hello," he said after some time. "Are you still there?"

"Yes, I'm here. Are you sure all this will happen? What if this is misinformation?"

"We don't know! We just follow the back and forth on their Facebook page."

"How do you get to their Facebook page?"

"We don't. Other students do and they give us this information."

"Do you trust them?"

"Yes, we do. They are against taking over the quad and have already expressed serious concerns. There are many students who oppose this takeover."

"Well, okay. There is nothing we can do today based only on assumptions. Let's talk about it tomorrow morning," I said, visualizing the scenes from Berkeley and Oakland.

I've always suffered from restless feet syndrome. That day, my feet were totally out of control. I could not stay put and almost jumped from my chair as if I were sitting on a volcano ready to erupt. I walked into the corridor looking for someone to talk to, but it was quiet. Everybody was gone for the day. I hurried down the stairs, letting the exit door close with a loud bang behind me, and rushed to the student affairs offices. There, I found the vice chancellor in a meeting with a few of his staff. He gave me a broad smile, and I felt a sense of comfort. He had served in this position for eight years and knew it well. I was confident he could help us manage this new situation, as he had managed so many others over the past two years.

"I came to say that we need to meet tomorrow," I said immediately, without having the mind to greet anyone.

"Of course!" he responded. "At this time, my staff and I feel that we need to send a letter to the students informing them of university policy. For example, they need to know that the occupation of the quad by non-students is illegal by university rules."

His staff nodded in agreement.

"We must explain the rules, and the penalties for violations. We also should mention that an encampment by non-students presents many safety issues and needs to be prevented."

"That sounds good," I responded.

"We also think," he continued in his calm voice, "that the letter should come from you, to attract the student's attention."

"It's fine with me. When are you drafting the letter?" I asked. I was beginning to wonder whether the letter would make things better or worse.

"Our staff will draft it tonight and you will see it tomorrow morning."

"Okay. Let's talk again in the morning. Good night to all of you, and thank you." I took one last look at their tired faces and returned to my office.

## November 17, 2011

The encampment on the quad continued to grow. Two different letters drafted by student affairs staff and signed by me had been distributed. We hoped the letters would deter more from coming, and that they would make the rules of the campus known to everyone.

On Thursday afternoon we held a meeting with the senior staff. Like every other safety meeting that semester, this one took place electronically. We had many commitments, some of them off campus, which interfered with our ability to participate in person.

"We have two issues to discuss today," I said after completing the roll call. "I will ask our vice chancellor for student affairs to give us a summary of the situation and introduce the issues."

After a brief summary, the vice chancellor introduced in a calm and steady voice the two issues: the growing number of tents and the demographics of the occupants.

"How many tents are there now?" I asked.

"About a hundred," the police chief answered.

There was some disagreement on this. The number of campers shifted from day to day, and while we didn't have an exact figure, we agreed that the quad could comfortably hold about two hundred small tents and we were not at that number yet.

"The second issue," the vice chancellor continued, "is that many of these individuals are non-students."

"How many?" I asked.

"Almost 75 percent, judging by age and appearance, are not students," the university police chief responded. "A few of them are known to the police in Davis as agitators. We have seen them before, and we know that they are not from here. Some are from the East Coast and have been seen at the Berkeley events."

This, too, came under debate. Staff from the Office of Student Affairs claimed that most, if not all, of the campers *were* students. Others in the meeting couldn't make an estimate at all.

"The difference between 75 percent and zero is huge," I observed.

"The demographic is changing during the day," another student affairs staff member added. "The number of students increases when they have a general assembly, and it tends to go down in the afternoon. It gets bigger again after dinner."

The police chief spoke. "If this encampment gets established, the effort to get the people out of the quad will become increasingly more difficult. We may end up with another Oakland crisis, or another Berkeley."

"How long could your staff provide oversight to the camp during the night?" I asked the vice chancellor of student affairs.

"We have very few trained staff, and they are exhausted from the protest activity. We've had almost two protests a week for a while now," he said.

"How about bringing other faculty or staff to help?"

"Both of these groups have shown great reluctance," he answered. "They are concerned that they will be labeled as the 'police squad' and they are afraid for their safety. Some of the protestors are aggressive."

"How about oversight by the police?"

The chief chimed in. "Our officer numbers are low because of the cuts, and most of the available officers have already been called in to support the campus police at Berkeley, UCLA, and UC Santa Cruz. I cannot ask them to do this in addition. Many of the officers have not seen their families for weeks."

The conference line grew quiet.

"So, what is the solution?" I asked, wanting to tease out what they were all thinking.

The one thing they could all agree on was that the tents needed to be peacefully removed. A growing camp without appropriate oversight would be problematic, especially considering the possible presence of guns, knives, and substance abuse. The numbers didn't *really* matter; it was lack of oversight that would put our students at risk. That having been established, I told them the tents had to be removed before the weekend. Taking any longer would make it more difficult to deal with the growing encampment. The university rules were clear: such activities were not permitted.

Dispersing an encampment carried risks. The chief of police suggested removing the tents on Friday night, but considering the problems in the past, when the university police was accused of brutality during night-time protests, I felt that such an operation after dark would be problematic. "The tents should be removed during the day," I stated, and I specifically asked that the police should help the students remove their tents, without use of force. Further, I insisted the police did not wear riot gear and refrained from arresting anyone.

"Is this doable?" I asked her.

"Yes," she replied confidently.

"Please make an assessment, and if it seems you can peacefully remove some tents then do so. If the occupants become aggressive and the situation becomes dangerous, then direct your officers to leave. Can you do this?"

"Yes," she said again.

Satisfied, I asked for regular updates in case something changed that would make the plan difficult. I also asked the senior legal counsel to inform the Office of the President about our decision and to let me know if they were any concerns.

No concerns were voiced. Yet, I had a growing sense of unease. My confidence faltered as I considered the violent potential of protests, especially when stoked by professional agitators. One example occupied my mind: when students had tried to take over Highway 80 at the south exit of campus a few months before. Many of the students ended up being beaten with batons by the California Highway Patrol. Some had ended up in the hospital. Something like that happening on our campus would be catastrophic. Yet, doing nothing and allowing the camp to grow was also dangerous. Empowering non-students, professional activists, and a small, aggressive core of UC Davis faculty to influence university policy through fear and intimidation was something we had to avoid.

At the time, our plan to peacefully remove the tents the next afternoon, with minimal physical conflict, seemed the best solution. The reassurances of the chief of police and the confidence of the two vice chancellors made me believe that the plan could be executed successfully. Little did I know that none of them were ready for such a task, despite their promises.

**November 18, 2011**

I was in my office making a list of questions for the two vice chancellors and my chief of staff. The provost was on travel for Thanksgiving. He had been in the position for less than a year and made travel plans and decisions with little consultation. His previous experience, as president of a small college for five years, gave him a sense of independence that was sometimes problematic.

I called the vice chancellor for student affairs on his cell phone. That was the best way to find him this early.

"Good morning, Linda. Did you sleep well last night?"

"No," I said candidly.

He sighed. "Neither did I. That makes at least two of us."

"I have a question for you," I said. "Do you think our chief of police understands what we want to do and can execute it?"

"If there is anyone who can pull this together, it's her. She is a tough cookie, trained in the Chicago police. Not too many women in the Chicago police could make it this far."

"This gives me confidence!" I said. "Please make sure that everything is clear to her. How about the comment from your staff member that all the people on the quad are our own students?"

"She is a great person," he said, "but she always takes the side of the students, and sometimes her observations are biased."

"Thank you," I said. "Can you think of any reason we should change our plans?"

"Not that I know of," he replied.

I hung up and placed a call to the vice chancellor for administration and facilities. He had direct oversight of the police, and I wanted to ask him the same questions. His cell rang twice, and he answered in his typically upbeat style. He tended to always be pleasant and funny, no matter the circumstances.

"Good morning," he said. "My guess is that you have many questions. Usually that happens when people don't sleep well."

"I have a few—not many!" I responded without much commentary. I was not in the mood. "What do you think about our chief? Can she do what we discussed?"

"Absolutely, she can," he responded with overwhelming confidence. "She is the best chief we have ever had."

"Can you please make sure that she understood what we discussed? Please let me know if there is anything that will make you worry. I do not want anything to go wrong."

"Do you still want the police to remove the tents in the afternoon? How about midnight tonight?" he asked.

"A lot of things can go wrong at night. Every time there is a night police operation people get hurt."

"Okay. If she couldn't do it, she would have told us. At least she would have told me."

"Please check with her again and keep me updated."

I hung up. The rest of the day was spent in meetings, but I could not get myself to focus. I wanted to go to the quad to look at the tents, but I was advised by student affairs not to do that. The previous two years on campus, I had been like the red cloth to a bull when it came to the core activist group. Seeing me would make them upset and they would ask more students to join, trying to create a scene. That was not needed that morning.

In the afternoon, I had a meeting with the Senate Executive Committee, where I gave them a summary of the situation and briefly discussed the decision to remove the tents that afternoon. I ensured them that our decision was to try to remove the tents without any force or arrests. It was during that faculty senate meeting when my chief of staff sent me a note that everything had gone well and that most of the tents were removed. For the first time in many days, I felt relieved. I asked him to wait for me by the building's main entrance. I met him there around five in the afternoon.

"Okay, what happened? Can you fill me in?" I asked.

"Well," he said reluctantly. "They removed the tents but pepper sprayed a few students."

"Pepper sprayed the students? Who did this? With what? With little spray cans my daughter carries in her purse?" I replied.

"No," he said gloomily. "The police pepper sprayed the students."

"Why? Where are the vice chancellors?"

"They are in the student affairs office trying to connect with the chief."

We entered the Office of Student Affairs, and I saw the two vice chancellors and some of the staff looking concerned and talking to each other in low voices. They jumped to their feet when they saw me coming. My heart was racing, and a voice was murmuring inside my head that something horrible had happened.

"What happened?" I demanded. "I thought things were going well, and now I hear that someone from the police pepper sprayed the students? Why?"

"We do not know what happened exactly, but it seems that at the end, after most of the tents were removed without incident, an officer pepper sprayed the students."

"With what?" I asked.

"With a canister."

"A canister!" I almost yelled. "Did you know that the police had pepper spray canisters?" I asked, looking around the room.

Nobody responded.

"No, we did not know," the vice chancellor responsible for the police said in a serious voice, one of those few times he had sounded cheerless. "There's a video that's already been put online," he continued.

This was terrible. "A video?" I repeated in disbelief.

My chief of staff spoke up. "We have also received multiple calls from people."

"Did anybody get hurt?" I asked, my temples throbbing painfully.

"No one as far as we know. Everybody is okay."

I wasn't sure who had spoken.

My voice continued to rise. "I need a report from the chief as soon as possible. I need to know the details, and I need to know what went wrong!" I turned and left the room, leaving my colleagues speechless.

I ran two flights upstairs and went directly to my computer. My email account was almost frozen with the number of incoming messages. I went to YouTube and entered "UC Davis." The seconds it took to download the information felt like ages. A video entitled "Pepper Spray UC Davis" showed up. It already had almost 120,000 views. It was 6:30 p.m. In less than two hours, this had become national news. I opened the video and watched as a police officer in riot gear pepper sprayed a group of students who were sitting defenselessly on the quad.

"Oh, my God," I cried hysterically. "What in the world is he doing?"

My chief of staff had followed me upstairs, and I went into his office where he was sitting quietly as if nothing had happened. *Maybe this is the way to deal with a crisis,* I thought, finding the possibility weird.

"Have you seen the video?" I asked him.

He nodded.

"What do you think?" I asked him aggressively.

"It is not good," he said, managing to sound composed.

My voice trembled, and I found it difficult to control. "Is that all? You call this not good? I call it horrible. I call it a disaster! They did *everything* I told them not to do. This goes against all the directions I gave. Was I speaking Greek when we were on the phone yesterday?"

"No," he said, as if I were expecting an answer.

Seething, I ran back downstairs to the office of the vice chancellors.

I went right into it. "Have you seen the video? It's a disaster! Who is this police officer?"

"We do not have confirmation yet. The chief claims they were surrounded and were afraid for their safety."

I was taken aback. "Excuse me? *Who* was afraid for their safety? The police?"

"The chief called us, saying that the police were surrounded by angry students and could not leave. That is why they used pepper spray. She said that this single video does not show the full story."

The director of communications walked in. "We are getting a lot of phone calls. We cannot stay quiet for too long. We need to send a message out from you, Linda. We have developed a draft you may want to look at."

## November 20, 2011

The last two days felt like a nightmare. I could not get a single report from the police or the vice chancellor to whom the police had been reporting. What became obvious was that something had gone wrong after the phone conversation where we discussed the conditions under which the tents could be removed. Neither party was willing to talk about it despite my multiple requests.

Early in the morning, I spoke with the University of California president, and I asked him to initiate an independent investigation. Professor Brown, one of the two faculty members well known for the campus protest activities, had already accused me of directing the officers to use pepper spray against the students. He had released a letter demanding my resignation for directing the use of pepper spray. This made it clear that I would become part of the investigation. Under these conditions, the only viable investigation was one that would have oversight from above me.

The day progressed, and I received no verbal or written response to any of my questions about the event. By late Saturday afternoon, the chief's unwillingness to speak with me and explain what happened made me believe that there was an issue she was reluctant to share. I made the decision to place the chief on leave, which I could not announce until checking with the UC president the following day.

At 5:00 p.m. that day, the director of communications suggested that I give an interview with media representatives as a group, instead of speaking with each one of them separately. Our campus was full of news trucks trying to interview students and others who witnessed the incident. By then, I had made a commitment to speak at the general assembly rally called by the Occupy UC Davis group on Monday of that week. Prof. Brown was the master of ceremonies.

The meeting with the media was scheduled to take place at the facilities of the communications group in one of the temporary buildings dating back to the 1960s, called Surge II. At 5:30 p.m., Spyros and I drove to Surge II and parked by the building. The director of communications opened the door for me, and we entered a room filled with conference equipment and chairs for the local media. As we tried to gather so we could start the conference, a staff member came by saying that a few students were by the front door and wanted to know what was happening. I decided to meet with the students then and there to explain.

I walked out of the room. "What are you doing here?" one student asked me, politely but aggressively, while others began recording the conversation.

"There are many TV stations and other media that have asked to speak with me. Instead of talking to them separately, we have decided to have a press conference," I responded.

"Why have you not called the students to this conference?" another student asked angrily.

"I promised to come to the students' general assembly on Monday, and I thought that was the best medium for me to speak with you," I answered.

"The *Sac Bee* put on their Facebook that you were going to hold a media conference, and they encouraged students to participate," another student mentioned, "but we're okay with your explanation."

The twenty or so students left, and I went inside to start the press conference. Around 6:15 p.m., I began to hear a noise growing from outside the building, and it felt that the building was shifting, like during an earthquake.

"What's happening?" I asked one of the staff members, who ran outside to see what the problem was. A few minutes later, he came back looking pale and panting.

"There are more than a hundred and fifty students pushing at the door and demanding to come in. They said—" he took a few breaths, "that they would either come in or break the doors down."

"Could you please go to the students and tell them that I will speak with them on Monday? Emphasize that this facility cannot handle so many people," I told him, all the while trying to keep my voice steady.

The staff member turned and went back to the entrance. The banging stopped a few moments later, and I thought my proposal had been accepted. But shortly after, the banging returned, louder than before. The staff member came rushing back.

"They do not plan to let us out tonight," he said. "They want to come in at any cost, even if they damage the building."

I started worrying that this would lead to even more ugliness. I was finally able to get the chief on the phone. She told me she was trying to keep the police away, but if the students broke the door down, it would be considered violence and she would have no choice but to call the Davis Police Department. I did not consider that an option, and I told her that I did not want the police to intervene whatsoever.

The banging and chanting grew more intense over the next two hours. At some point, the back door of the building gave in, and we saw several students running through a corridor. We moved to the conference room and locked the door. I heard staff crying, pleading for the students to leave peacefully. I personally did not feel threatened, but I knew that the students were out of control and that the situation needed to be defused.

I was in communication with the student affairs officer, through whom I told the students that if staff could leave, I would stay and meet with them in the building. They did not accept this offer and continued hitting the walls of the building and chanting slogans. The student affairs officer, Grizelda, suggested that we call a reverend in Davis who knew some of the students, and who could advise us accordingly. The reverend was kind enough to come to the facility immediately. By this point, media crews had formed a perimeter around the scene and were eagerly anticipating action.

The reverend's negotiations with the students led to an agreement, which I found acceptable. "The students have agreed to let the staff leave under only one condition," she paused to allow me focus on her words. "They demand that you stay behind by yourself to walk on a path the students will open for you. I was able to make them agree that they would not yell at you, insult you, or throw anything."

She paused again and looked at me to make sure that I was following. "They have insisted that you do not look down but look at each one of them and that you walk slowly." She looked at the staff, who were nodding positively. "I also think I should walk a few feet behind you."

I truly appreciated her offer.

At about 10:30 p.m., I walked through the silent students toward my car. The chanting of the crowd had reduced to barely a murmur, but their hatred had not lessened. It had turned into energy I could feel, building toward the catharsis of the flickering lights of hundreds of recording cell phones. The video later put up on YouTube they called, "The Walk of Shame."

During these two minutes, I did not feel fear, but I felt remorse. I was responsible for the mess our campus was in. I was the chancellor, and it was under my service the campus found itself in this turmoil. At the same time, I felt relief that the day was nearing its end. I would have felt the same relief if I were to be on the path toward ending my life.

**January 2012**

The pepper spray incident opened Pandora's Box. Like most such events, it aired out the pathologies, ailments, and inadequacies of leadership—both historic and present—on our campus and in our university system. In the months following the incident, I learned more about myself, my team, my colleagues, UC Davis, and the University of California system than I would have been able to in a lifetime. Like light in a dark cave, the incident exposed the power of personal benefit over ideology, and the true face of a public whose expressed interest in acting liberally oftentimes conflicted with personal biases or political aspirations.

Between November 2011 and March 2012, hundreds of articles and thousands of blog posts were written about me and the incident. Some featured the most amazing interpretations, twisted analyses, and conspiracy theories. Among these articles were calls for my resignation by the same people who had accused me in the past of being unethical and greedy. Now they had added to their list three more grievances: privatizing the university, cutting sports programs, and increasing the number of international students on campus. The pepper spray incident became, for them, the last nail in the coffin.

A letter from a student who was a member of one of the eliminated varsity teams—who claimed that he was among the pepper-sprayed students in the hospital—was published both in the *Sacramento Bee* and the *Davis Enterprise*.

In addition, the ringleader resurfaced with new articles, emails, and whistleblowers encouraging the community to "run me out of town." He further tried to get a few student senators from the UC Davis Student Association to file for a Senate resolution calling for my resignation. The articles and comments to the editor that followed the pepper spray incident changed their tone over time. They first expressed resentment for the incident and for my incompetence. This developed into frustration with selling the campus to the highest bidder (as they characterized fundraising) and forceful calls to the UC president and regents to fire me.

This mass hysteria included anonymous phone calls to the chancellor's residence asking for my resignation. Callers demanded that Spyros and I leave town and never come back again. Many of these calls were xenophobic and asked us to go back to Greece and take the rest of the family with us.

On a Saturday morning in the middle of January, I received an email from a friend. We were both faculty members and shared the same passion for teaching, learning, and respecting others' opinion. We relied on dialogue to resolve our differences.

"Linda, can we meet whenever we have some free time?" she wrote. "I need to share some information I came across that I believe you need to know."

*What now?* I thought.

"Do you want to come by? I have time now," I wrote back, anxious to find out what it was she needed to share with me. A wave of familiar nausea washed over me. Every day, something new!

A few minutes went by, and the doorbell rang twice. I opened the door to the smiling face of my friend. She was holding a small bouquet of white daisies. The fresh smell of flowers brought me a sense of relief, like a drop of water to the dry lips of a wanderer. At that moment, I would have given anything for a little more of the same feeling.

"This is to lighten your heart," she said, hugging me with a warmth I still remember.

"You came very fast!" I observed with a smile.

She chuckled. "I was on my way home from the farmer's market. That's where I picked up these flowers and called, hoping you would be at home."

We sat down at the kitchen table. I cut the long stems and arranged the flowers one by one in a vase. We spent some time watching silently, as if trying to decide how to start the conversation we meant to have.

"This is an amazing table," she said after some time, her fingers running softly along the cracks and knots of the recently treated wooden top.

"This table has been the center of activity for our family," I replied. "We brought it with us from our house in Indianapolis. It means so much to me. It is a big part of my past." I found myself remembering those family dinners, clinking our wine glasses and waiting for Spyros to cut the first piece of the roasted lamb he had made with great care.

"Linda," my friend started, "you know about the group that is working actively to force you out?"

"Yes, I know. They are not new to me. They started this effort before I even became chancellor."

She nodded. "You understand it's the same group that first called for a vote of no-confidence days after the pepper spray incident."

"Yes, I know that too," I replied. "Because of them we have two more votes of no-confidence hanging over me." I stood up nervously, cleaning the table of the daisy stems. I wandered over to the stove.

"How about some coffee?" I asked, trying to delay hearing the bad news. I filled the coffee maker with water, turned it on. Once the coffee was ready, I sat back down, ready to hear the rest.

"They are now propagating another story about you. They are saying that you brought the police to the Greek universities and that you were involved with the Greek junta." My friend's face was intense.

It took me some time to process the information. Suddenly, I broke into a hysterical laugh. She looked at me with surprise on her face.

"This is crazy to the point of being comical!" I managed to say between bouts of laughter. I felt relieved of the tension that had hijacked my body. "This is really funny," I added, trying to slow down and regain my posture.

My friend looked puzzled, clearly awaiting an explanation.

I started to explain. "Do you know how old I was when the colonels started the military dictatorship in 1967? I was thirteen years old! How many thirteen-year-old girls do you know who have conspired with the military against their country's democratic government?"

The absurdity of the accusation sank in, and she looked at me in amazement and visibly relaxed. "It sounds ridiculous, but that's what they are saying!"

Our moods had noticeably improved; sometimes outrageous accusations are so silly they can be immediately dismissed.

My friend continued. "What about bringing the police to the Greek universities last year?"

"You may want to know," I responded, "that since 1974 no one has brought the police to a Greek university campus for any reason."

She stayed quiet, wanting to hear more. "You might wonder why a newspaper like the *Davis Enterprise* would report something as crazy as this without evidence. This is what media hysteria results in: lies, speculation, and superstitions. The only thing interesting about such stories is that they manage to enjoy such long lives." I took a sip of coffee.

I had read the article in question already. In it, the *Davis Enterprise* claimed that as the chair of a committee that reviewed the state of higher education in Greece in the fall of 2010, I had suggested the dismantling of the university asylum and supported the use of police force on Greek campuses.

"It is true that I was asked to chair a committee. The other members were presidents from prestigious universities around the world, and our goal was to provide a high-level review of higher education in Greece. Our report, available both in Greek and English, has been on several websites. Nowhere in this report will you find anything close to the policies I am accused of promoting."

The committee had gone over the section on campus safety many times, in an attempt to incorporate language that was respectful of the constitution and the campus's asylum. The statement in the report read:

*Greek university campuses are not secure. While the Constitution allows University leaders to protect campuses against elements that seek political instability, Rectors have been reluctant to exercise their rights and responsibilities, and to make decisions needed in order to keep faculty, staff and students safe. As a result, University leaders and faculty have not been able to be good stewards of the facilities they have been entrusted with by the public.*

I told this to my friend. "That was the only statement about the safety of the university campuses in the report, and it led to no change whatsoever in the Greek constitution. A change in the constitution would require the overwhelming support of the parliament. I have no power in Greek politics.

"What should I do?" I asked, mentally exhausted. "I am really tired of fighting every ghost thrown at me."

"I suggest you do nothing for now. Just let the faculty senate chair know." She stood up and gave me another hug. "I have to go. I am glad we spoke. I will do whatever I can from my end."

I walked her to the kitchen door and kissed her goodbye. I noticed a KCRA news truck driving by. My friend noticed it too and shot me a glance.

"That's their regular route nowadays," I explained as she unlocked her car.

*They believe something is imminent,* I lamented.

**February 2012**

While accusations and conspiracy theories swarmed through social media, my office was submerged in a rigid silence. Everyone was instructed by the campus legal counsel not to speak to anyone, especially me, since I was under investigation. That left me totally in the dark about what had transpired between the counsel, the vice chancellors, and the police chief during the time that passed after our conference call in the afternoon of Thursday, November 16 and 3:30 p.m. on Friday, November 18 on the quad. When I shared my frustration with faculty, students, or staff who were searching for answers, stern faces told me they did not believe me.

"I still do not have the report I requested from the campus police or from the vice chancellors," I remarked with dismay to the senior legal counsel at our meeting in the last week of February.

"I need to remind you," he said in his legal way, "when independent investigations are initiated in the police department, the police union customarily forbids its members from speaking to anyone. The chief refused to be interviewed."

"Okay, I understand that. How about the vice chancellors?" I pressed, growing frustrated.

He sounded like he was reciting from a book. "Well, they cannot give you a report because you are being investigated as an individual, in your role as chancellor. They may be witnesses against you."

"Why are they going to be witnesses against me?"

I placed my notepad on the coffee table next to my chair and looked at the marks left on its pages from my sweating hands. I spoke my next words very carefully.

"You were on the conference call. You know what I said, so what else can they say about me?"

"I do not know," he responded with indifference. "You may have talked to the chief independently."

I remained silent as I tried to gauge his tone, then shifted the conversation.

"How many people have spoken with the investigative committee?" I asked.

"Many students and faculty who claim they were on the quad," he noted, "and members of the ad-hoc committee who were on the phone call."

"All the members?"

He looked at me with a surprise that he tried to suppress and paused as if trying to compose himself.

"My deputy and I did not speak with the investigative committee," he finally said.

"Why?"

I looked at him in disbelief while feeling a ray of hope. *This could lead to more information,* I thought calmly as I prioritized my next few questions. He mumbled an excuse that I do not remember. He looked subdued.

"I understand from my discussions with the interim chief that, per university rules, you and your deputy would have approved the police's execution plan. Is this true?" I asked pointedly.

"Yes," he said sternly after a noticeable pause.

"Did you then approve the execution plan for November 18, 2011?"

"Yes," he responded.

I pressed further. "Did you know that they were going to be in riot gear, against my order? And carry pepper spray?"

"I cannot speak about details in view of the investigation," he replied.

"Did you tell me what the execution plan was before the police went to remove the tents?"

"I do not think so," he replied.

"Okay. Why are you withholding critical information about what happened between the end of the conference call on Thursday and Friday on the quad?"

He shifted nervously in his chair.

"I was waived the privilege to speak with the investigative committee," he replied slowly while looking at his notes.

"By whom?"

"By the university's general counsel."

"Is it not true that I am the only one who can waive your privilege?" I asked aggressively.

"No," he said calmly. "You are not. I do not report to you. I only advise you. I report to the Office of General Counsel in the president's office. They tell me what to do."

"So, who holds my back?" I asked, without expecting an answer. "Are you my legal counsel to protect me with advice, or do you just use me as a shield?"

"You can speak with the president's office if you have a complaint related to my performance," he replied without emotion. He stood up, signaling he was ready to leave.

I stood up with him.

"Yes, I will, after all this is over! But for now, I want to know when I will find out what happened between the phone call and the incident. My orders seem to have been disobeyed, and I must know why and how that happened." The intensity in my voice surprised me.

"You will be able to read the internal police investigation report when it is submitted, if the president approves. I must let you know, however, that this report will never become public unless there is a lawsuit and an indictment."

He shook his head. "I am sorry for all this. I just do as they advise me. I know you don't deserve this. Excuse me for now. I have another meeting to go to." He turned reluctantly and walked out of my office.

The end of February concluded with many meetings with academic units, student groups, campus organizations, the Alumni Board, and the Foundation Board. These two boards, whose members were passionate about UC Davis, were disturbed by the impact of social media and our inability to connect with the students and alumni during this difficult time.

During the Foundation Board meeting in San Francisco in the middle of February, I was asked to give an update on the fallout from the pepper spray incident. One board member mentioned that he had tried to get on our website to look for information from one of the academic units, and a doctored picture popped up showing "me" pepper-spraying the students. His face was flushed, and his voice could hardly hold back his anger.

"Why do we allow hackers to get on our website?" he asked.

*I have been asking myself the same question,* I thought, *and every time there is a different answer.* I turned to the interim communications director. He had replaced the previous director, who had folded in the weeks following the incident.

"We have been able to stabilize our interactions with the local media," he said. He spoke with a confidence we all wished for.

"How about social media?" someone asked. "Many organizations do not give up when they face adversity."

"No university would allow hackers to replace official campus pictures with ones that ridicule the chancellor," another voice added. "Our inability to control the message in digital space is unacceptable and needs to be corrected."

They were talking to him, but they were messaging me. "Our weakness in communications has been a chronic problem," I whispered to the development officer who was standing next to me.

The communications group had proven difficult to transform. Most of the staff had strong relations with the local media and shared information, many times sensitive and most of the time unintentionally. Yet this information outflow kept hurting the campus and me personally. The communications group as I found it when I joined UC Davis reflected the media landscape of the nineteen-eighties. The group's leadership at that time was aggressive and divisive, and many good female staff members had left because of bad treatment. At the time of the pepper spray incident, the group was at its weakest point in terms of strength and was suffering from low morale and reduced funding. They were unprepared for a crisis of this magnitude. The repeated cuts across the university had left the group with only one person familiar with social media. Everyone else was struggling with the unexpected attacks and their limited understanding of social media.

Immediately after the pepper spray incident, our website went down, and our Facebook page was inundated with rude commentary and threatening messages. The staff became so overwhelmed by the barrage of uncivil discussion that they decided not to touch our social media outlets at all. This allowed hackers to attack our website and replace pictures, including mine, with offensive cartoons. Our staff had simply abandoned the task of keeping up with the troublemakers.

During that board meeting, anxious members directed me to address our weaknesses in social media, urging me to develop a branding campaign for the campus and to do whatever I could do to re-establish the campus's presence on the internet. Eventually, we decided to hire a company that would train our staff and clean up our Facebook and other websites.

At the time, I had no idea this would become a major problem years later.

## March 2012

Since December 2011, three independent investigations, two legislative hearings, and three calls for a vote of confidence had all played out in the public theater. In every act, I played the main character, whose actions were to be judged publicly. The spectacle was displayed all over the local newspapers and blog articles. The histrionics disguised hatred as passion, and the campus was at crossroads. The questions no one dared articulate were short but difficult: "Who are we? Where are we going?"

In my first two years as a chancellor, three possible paths had appeared before us. The first path was the most promising and inspiring, but also the most difficult. It was the "Path to the Future," an uphill battle that carried a promise for success in an uncertain future. Success required that we embrace our past with pride but move beyond what had come before. We would build on our strengths to create the global university of the future. The campus's proximity to local government institutions provided a unique opportunity to develop strong policy programs for the state and the nation. With a layer of policy laid over in the areas of food and health, sustainability, arts and culture, technology, and well-being, this journey would create a strong foundation on which to build a lasting university. A center of learning, inquiry, debate, and creativity, UC Davis would transition to a vibrant future while strengthening and supporting the cities around it.

The second path was what I considered the status quo. It was the "Path to the Present." This path would stay on a plateau and exploit every little corner of an already plowed field for an extra inch of advantage—but never aspire to explore new and higher grounds. It would celebrate who we are without challenging us to do more. It would aspire to different, but not necessarily new, initiatives. This approach would worry about failure and avoid high-risk plans. Along this path, everything exciting would be left merely to hope. This path would establish a culture where *doing* would become more important than *achieving*.

The third path advocated for a return to the school's roots. It was the "Path to the Past." It suggested that our best days were over and by going back to being an agricultural university, we would be fulfilled. This path promoted a university that reinvigorated its agricultural heritage, expanded its agricultural disciplinary reach, and cut any program that did not fit this model.

The two questions had remained dormant for years and erupted with the recession of 2009. They finally took center stage in the events following the pepper spray incident. In some interesting ways, the proponents of the paths to the present and the past found common ground and actively worked to fight against those who saw the future path as the destiny of our campus.

The three votes of confidence indicated that the campus faculty, by a large majority, had chosen the Path to the Future. How wrong was I to believe at that time that the questions had been answered once and for all? A few years later, I realized that the opposition had accepted only a temporary retreat.

Robert Arneson's *Yin and Yang* (two of the famous Eggheads scattered around campus) feature in a photo taken by one of my student assistants to remind me that "truth can be blind and ignored."

## Chapter Thirteen

# The Fear of Truth

**Spring 2014**

THE TWO YEARS AFTER THE pepper spray incident were probably the most successful in my career as chancellor, despite the rocky start. The 2020 Initiative was well under way and supported by the majority of those on campus, despite the controversy it raised early on. I had asked the provost to develop a budget process to provide a fair distribution of the new resources. The fundraising campaign had met its goal of $1 billion well ahead of time, and we were expecting to raise several hundred million more before it was done. For the past five years, the campus had been consistently placed in the top ten public universities in almost every ranking survey.

In April 2014, following a year-long effort that included many faculty and friends of the university from Davis, Sacramento, and the agricultural community, we announced the creation of the World Food Center. This was a campus-wide initiative recognizing that food drives a cross-cultural interest and permeates all intellectual boundaries. By June 2014, I truly felt that our ship had turned around and was heading toward the controversial Path to the Future.

My personal life had also undergone changes. In late 2013, our son,

Erik, decided to come to UC Davis to get a Masters in Epidemiology. He had previously been working at the Medical School of the University of Michigan as a microbiologist. Even if he chose to interact with us sparingly to maintain his independent lifestyle, the thought that he was nearby made me happy. Around the same time, our daughter, Helena, began practicing law in Los Angeles. After almost ten years of being separated from our children, we finally managed to all be in the same state, at least for a year.

One morning, Erik announced that he would be moving back to Ann Arbor in Michigan. "All good things must end," I whispered to myself.

During those days, I found it difficult to move quickly from one pleasant experience to the next. I was too busy to slow down and enjoy the happy moments that felt so short. I did not know how to immerse myself in a long-lasting experience of happiness. It almost felt that happiness was only touching me, never engulfing me.

## May 2014

As we entered the summer of 2014, my enthusiasm was tempered by larger university changes. The UC system's new president had been in office since September, and I had been trying to adjust to her style and align our campus to her goals. I found her management style to be unique, idiosyncratic, and self-centered. My efforts to connect with her and elevate UC Davis to her level of interest had not been successful. She was thirsty for power and self-promotion but rather uninterested in learning about the campuses. She was indifferent to anything she did not consider critical to her reputation. During her first year as president, I was concerned by decisions that were against the core mission of the university and had little benefit for UC Davis but carried a substantial financial burden for our campus.

In the beginning, we were told to interact with the new president only through her chief of staff, a young lawyer who aggressively filtered the information that she received. Eventually the president decided to keep the monthly meetings with the chancellors, an old tradition that every previous UC president had respected, but to limit her private meetings with each one of us to once a year. She also decided to keep the dinner with the chancellors the evening before her quarterly meetings with the Board of Regents. She expected us to send every piece of information to her through her chief of staff. At times, it became difficult to determine who was the decision maker: the president or her chief of staff. He would relate to us decisions without much explanation of the president's thinking.

Our monthly chancellor meetings shifted from a forum of meaningful exchange of information and informative discussions to her reading from prepared documents. The content was delivered word by word with brief breaks to make sure we understood the actions she intended to take. The few times we were allowed to speak seemed to me to be a ploy to identify nonconformists rather than a chance for the chancellors to honestly express their opinions.

Her actions were in direct conflict with what she expressed in the open—a strong commitment to use the chancellors' experience to help her run the system. As time went by, it became obvious that there was a fundamental misunderstanding between the chancellors and the president. When the previous UC presidents and chancellors spoke of the system, we all meant the union of ten unique campuses with shared values and philosophies but fundamentally different needs and opportunities. We always viewed our participation in decision-making as fundamental to the success of the system.

When this new president spoke about "the system," she meant one central command with ten physically separate campuses. That change in philosophy became evident at the beginning of her term. Even the staff who had served under many presidents before embraced the idea of one UC university, and they took a competitive stance against the chancellors—whom they characterized as parochial and narrow-minded. Any efforts to highlight our campuses' unique needs and opportunities were colored as provincial and unimaginative.

**June 2014**

It was an unseasonably warm and quiet Friday evening in early June. It was finals week, and the students had taken leave from afternoon sports, games, fundraisers, and parties. Everybody was busy, from faculty to academic advisors to counselors to students trying to finish the quarter without unpleasant surprises. Even the Occupy group at UC Davis had put aside their political agendas and were busy with school projects.

It was probably the only Friday of the year when I was not busy. It was a break before the graduation festivities of the year. With eyes shut, I let myself enjoy the soft rocking motion of my chair. I tried to relax, but I couldn't. My mom's voice on the phone earlier that day had sounded quite desperate.

"Mom, how are you?" I had asked, eager as always to hear her upbeat response.

"I am okay," she said in a voice that had a pronounced local accent, the one that reminded me of my grandmothers. I had not heard this accent in her voice since I was a child. "I worry about your father. He is not doing well. His condition is getting worse."

"I'm coming in two and a half weeks," I said. She did not respond. "You know that on June 28, I will receive an honorary degree from the American College in Athens, and I plan to come with Spyros and Erik on the twentieth." I paused for a few seconds to make sure she was listening to what I was saying. "You promised you would come to the event."

"I will come," she said slowly in a deep voice. "I just worry about your father. He cannot stay by himself anymore."

"How about your caretaker? Can she stay with him during the event?"

Mother hadn't gotten to see me graduate from any of the universities I had attended. She had no idea what a graduation ceremony was like. Coming to one where I would receive an honorary degree should have been a great experience for her, one that I owed her since I left Greece.

"Our caretaker does not work on Sundays," she said, "and I do not know what to do. I am afraid I will have to stay at home."

"Mom, don't be silly. I can find someone else to take care of Dad for a few hours."

"Are you sure you can do that?" Her voice had regained some of its usual hope.

"Of course, I can! You would think with a PhD I could at least do *that!*"

"Well, it's not just that. I don't feel well these days. I feel dizzy in the mornings. I went to the doctor, but he cannot find anything. He told me it was because of age."

"Mom, I think you have exhausted yourself caring for Dad since he was diagnosed with Alzheimer's. How many times have I told you that he needs to go to a hospice? You don't listen! Not only you do not help him by keeping him at home, you will kill yourself too!" I began to sob.

Her voice was soft. "Don't cry. I am so thrilled that I will see you in a few weeks! Just think about how happy we will be together again after so many months apart."

We said our goodbyes, and she told me she loved me. I held the phone to my ear long after she had hung up. Part of me hoped that the dial tone would change back to her voice. I felt hot tears running down my face as I recounted our discussion in my head. I raised the goblet mechanically and drank the rest of the wine, a mix of tears and alcohol.

The evening shadows turned into despicable ghosts that peered at me with piercing eyes and blew a cold draft through the room. I heard a young girl's voice ringing as an echo in my head: *My mom is dying. Somebody help!*

I dreamt of my mom sick on her deathbed, still young. Vigil oil burned in front of the Virgin Mary's icon. The young girl by her side had stopped crying and just looked at me watching her from the other side of the window with despair. I started banging on the window, trying to break the glass, but all I could see was the reflection of the dark sea behind me rising and pulling me to its cold depths. The young girl extended her hand as though asking for my help.

I jumped up from the rocking chair. I knew I had to go home.

**Summer 2014**

On June 20, 2014, I arrived in Greece. I had managed to participate in all the UC Davis commencement ceremonies, as scheduled, without receiving a single thank-you for the year's effort. In fact, there were a few students who even refused to shake my hand. "This is a thankless job," I remembered one of my mentors telling me about administrative positions. "If you want to be thanked, do the faculty job. I am sorry to tell you that administrators are hated."

We arrived at the airport in Athens in the evening and took a rental car to our flat. I left Spyros and Erik there with instructions to find something for their dinner and drove to my mom's home on the island. Since last speaking to her, Emma had come to take care of my parents full time. We had found her through a nonprofit organization that placed immigrant women in homes as full-time caretakers of elderly people. There was another woman, Maria, who had also been helping my parents with errands.

I parked in front of my mom's apartment building and rushed my way to the locked entrance. I rang the bell and waited anxiously for my mom's voice. Usually, her voice would come through the speaker near the door. My thoughts were scattered, as I knew that I was hoping for the impossible. This evening the voice on the speaker was different. "Who is there?"

"Mom! Is that you?" I asked, wondering if I had rung the wrong bell.

"Mrs. Linda?" I heard the same voice.

"Yes, it's me. Is my mom there?"

The door buzzed, and I pushed open the glass door to the building lobby. The lights of the small lobby went on automatically, and I noticed that the elevator was patiently waiting for my arrival. I walked to the elevator, dragging my rolling bag behind me, and waited for its door to close. I looked in its mirrored walls and saw someone I barely recognized. My hair was a mess, and the highlights made it look like a clown's wig. My face looked tired and much older, and my eyes were red from the tears that had started flowing down my face. The elevator slowly moved up and stopped on the first level.

I got off in the dark hallway and turned immediately toward the apartment, where a short black figure was already waiting at the door.

"Are you Emma?" I asked.

"Yes, Mrs. Linda, and happy you are here," she responded in broken Greek. "Mamma wants you every day and cries."

I walked through the living room toward my parents' bedroom, leaving my bag in the hallway and throwing a quick thank you to Emma. Their bedroom door was ajar, and a soft light was escaping into the small corridor that separated their room from the rest of the apartment. I pushed the door open and saw Mom sitting on her bed fixing her hair. Such a familiar gesture.

"Mom! Are you okay?" I whispered. My father was sleeping quietly in his bed across from hers. I rushed to her side to hug her, then placed my head on her neck to take in her familiar scent, something I did as a child whenever I felt insecure.

She ran her fingers through my hair. "I am okay now that you are here. Are you hungry? Emma has prepared something for you. She is a great cook, you know!"

She slowly got up out of bed.

"We should sit on the veranda," she said. "Help me put on my robe. The weather has been so nice this summer. We haven't had any mosquitoes." She held my hand as we walked onto the veranda, and for a moment I saw her again with the eyes of my childhood: strong, supportive, and beautiful. She steered me steadily to the veranda while Emma looked on with a smile.

Once we sat, Emma asked me if I wanted to eat.

"Yes," Mom said.

"Not much," I was able to add quickly. "I need a drink, maybe some ouzo with ice."

The veranda looked nice, even in the dark. Mom showed me to a comfortable chair next to hers, and we sat holding hands and looking at each other.

"You look tired. It must have been a long trip from California."

"I'm fine, and I'm more concerned about you."

"I feel exhausted," she simply said. "Dad is not doing well, though Emma has been very helpful. I wish I had decided to bring her sooner."

"What did the doctor say about your exams?" I asked.

"Why don't you eat something first, and then we can talk?"

Emma walked back onto the veranda and set a tray on the table between my mother and me. She lit a candle and glanced at Mom.

"Thank you, Emma," Mom said, "this is all we need."

The tray was filled with foods I like: feta cheese, olives, spinach pie, two slices of bread and a narrow glass with ouzo and ice.

"Her spinach pie is very good," Mom said. "I gave her the recipe, and she does it as well as I do."

"I doubt that," I said as I sipped some ouzo out of the glass. The burning sensation was welcome.

"Do not just drink," Mom said in her soft voice. "Eat some food to help you digest the ouzo. Otherwise it is going to hit you hard."

*That's what I need*, I thought, *to become unconscious and wake up with this bad dream over.*

"Drinking does not solve any problems," she added as if she had read my thoughts. She looked at me calmly, but her eyes flickered in the candlelight with a noticeable uneasiness.

"What did the doctor say about your exams?" I repeated my question.

She waved her hand dismissively. "Nothing to worry about, that's what he said. I have a decreased count of red cells in my blood, and he prescribed some iron pills." She looked at me intensely. "But this is not what I worry about. Your dad's health has turned for the worse."

"Mom, he has been suffering from Alzheimer's for the past five years, and he is ninety-five years old. Dad will not get better, only worse. At some point you have to accept that."

"I will never let your father go into assisted living. I will take care of him until his last breath."

I could feel myself getting upset. "Yes, but this will kill you first! You gave him everything, and he took everything! Do you want to give him your last breath as well? If you die before him, because of him, I am telling you right now that I will send him to an assisted living facility."

"You are very hard on your father," she said slowly. "I forgave him."

"Oh really? Why? For all the good deeds he did for you?" At this point I was almost yelling as anger took over.

"Your father was a good man, but he was trapped by his own demons," she responded calmly.

I sniffed. "He was trapped by his demons only when we needed him. We would have been dead from starvation without the help we received from Grandma and your sisters. Do you remember how hungry we were all those months we spent in Crete? He was always gone, and now that he is here, he wants to take you from me."

Mom grew quiet. Her eyes were wet with tears. I fell to my knees and grabbed both her hands. "I am so sorry Mom, but I cannot lose you—not for him!" She cradled my hands, and I felt her warm presence soothe me.

"You should forgive him. You owe it to yourself. How will you live with this anger inside you?" she asked calmly.

My anger turned to despair, and I started crying quietly. She continued to hold me. We stayed like that for a long time. Eventually she gripped my arms and moved to pull me to my feet.

"We can make you a bed to sleep here tonight, unless you want to go to Ritsa's house. She is expecting you. It will be quieter there. We get very busy here early in the morning."

As much as I wanted to stay with my mother, that evening had proven emotionally taxing, and I needed to get out. She stood up and walked me to the door. "Sleep well and come any time you want. Dad does better in the morning. He would like to see you," she added.

"Does he even remember me?" I asked.

She smiled. "He remembers your voice, but not your face. We will help him put the two together."

I took my bag, loaded it into the car, and drove to Ritsa's flat on the other side of St. Lavrentios Hill. I was exhausted. The only thing I wanted to do was to go into a deep sleep. Nothing else.

It was late in the morning, almost midday, when I found myself lying on a sofa covered by a lightly scented white sheet. I was wearing pajamas, and my head rested on a couple of fluffy white pillows. It took me some time to realize that I was sleeping in Ritsa's living room.

"Good morning!"

I looked around until my eyes found my cousin Ritsa. She looked wonderful for her age in a pair of white summer slim pants and a light blue blouse that made a stunning contrast to her reddish hair pulled back in a French bow.

Ritsa, being eleven years my senior, had been my idol since I was a preschooler. With an attractive smile and a pair of almond-shaped brown eyes, she had always been beautiful. Before I went to school, Mom and I visited Ritsa's mom almost daily. She and my mother were not just sisters but really close friends. In those days, when there was very little to eat at our home, Ritsa's mom would generously share their meal with us. Most of the time Ritsa was not at home. She was either at school or with her high school friends doing homework or working on projects. She was older and fashionable, and I was so impressed as a young girl with her lipstick, clothes, and particularly her confidence.

"You were very tired last night," Ritsa said as she carried in a tray with French coffee and cookies for both of us and placed it on the table next to the sofa.

"I slept well and without nightmares," I said as I tried to pull myself off the sofa and fold the sheets.

"Don't," she said, while she dragged a chair over to the table. "We will leave the sofa like this so you can rest anytime you want. In any case, there are just the two of us in the flat, and I do not expect any visitors."

I let the sofa be and went over to the table.

"Your dad's health has deteriorated," she commented while dipping a cookie into her coffee. "Did you see him last night?"

"Dad was asleep when I got to their flat last night. I spoke with Mom. She will die before she lets him go. What am I going to do?"

"Your mom will refuse to place him in assisted living," she said, shaking her head in disbelief. "You do not know how many times I tried to have this discussion. She rejects me every time. Have some coffee."

"For now, I need to take a shower, get dressed, and go to mom's. Thank you for letting me stay." She looked at me with a warm smile. "Are you coming for the event at the American College this Sunday?" I added while downing the last sip of the strong coffee she had prepared for me.

She nodded. "Of course, I will. I would never miss this celebration. What an honor for you!"

"Yes, I agree." I said shyly. "It is a gift to my mom. After all these years, this will be the first time she will have seen me in university regalia. First time at a graduation ceremony. I just hope she is healthy enough to make it."

We hugged, then I grabbed my bag and left.

It was almost 1:00 p.m. when I rang the bell in my mom's flat. This time, my mother answered, in the upbeat voice I remembered.

"Welcome, come upstairs!"

*God, please help me*, I thought. *Keep her healthy. I still need her, maybe more now than ever.* I took the stairs one flight up and found myself in front of the apartment's door, where Mom stood, smiling like old times.

"Mom," I said as I embraced her. "Is there anyone here?"

"Just your dad sitting outside. Both Emma and Maria went to run errands. They will be back later." She closed the door behind me. "Your father is sitting on the veranda. You should join him. He will be happy to see you. I will make a plate for you. We have made octopus in red sauce and French fries, exactly the way you like it."

Dad sat on a comfortable chair with his back to the glass door that connected the veranda to the dining room. His back was straight, and his head was full of white hair, which was nicely combed back. He looked younger than his ninety-five years. He had been handsome when he was young, even though I never thought of him that way as a child. For many years, I found him repulsive, arrogant, and insensitive. I was convinced he did not love us and that if he felt anything for us, it was a sense of ownership and power. He drove me away and kept me away for many years. Yet, when our children, Erik and Helena, were born, his heart melted for them. My father became to my children the father I never had. My children changed him, softened him, made him feel that he could still love.

It was too late for me, though. Our relationship remained polite but cold. To this day, I wonder whether he truly loved me. If he did love me, he was unable to show it or express it. Maybe he was afraid to accept it. In the past he had lost everything he had loved with passion. He knew that I was distant and that my love for Mom was undivided, but he never confronted me. He knew that there were many times when I hated him, but he never complained. In front of me he remained silent, reserved, and dignified. I tried to respect him, and he did the same for me. Our discussions were short and polite . . . with a weird twist. Our discussions were short and polite and always ended in a war story.

I drew back the glass door and entered the veranda. The sound of the door did not attract his attention. I went and sat across from him. He looked at me with surprise but said nothing.

"Dad," I said, "it's me, Linda. I came from America to see you and Mom."

"Good morning," he responded with a smile. "Is Georgia inside?"

*He has no idea, who I am*, I thought. *He has a way of pretending he knows people. I am sure he will ask Mom who I am when he finds the opportunity.*

"How are you?" I asked him, trying to get a conversation going.

"Thank God," he said, looking away. "I am not complaining."

I remained silent for some time and just looked at him. He avoided my stare, like a shy little kid.

"Dad, do you know who I am?"

He looked at me with a smile and shrugged his shoulders.

"I'm your daughter."

His eyes flickered. "Do I have a daughter?" he asked with genuine surprise.

"Yes, you're married, and you have a daughter," I said calmly. "I'm

Linda, remember?"

"But I never got married!" he objected with an animated voice. "I went back too late."

I remained silent, trying to figure out where his mind was.

"Was it before the war, or after?" I asked calmly. He looked so vulnerable. I could hear Gabriel's voice in my head: *Why are you doing this to him? You are such a monster.*

"I was engaged and . . ." his voice tapered off into a whisper.

"And then what happened?" I prompted.

He appeared to concentrate. "They . . . they . . . took her away."

"They did not take her away," I said, smiling. "Mom is inside preparing a plate for me to eat."

"They took her away," he repeated with a sobbing sound as if he could not hear me. "I was not there to save her. They took her and killed her. I promised her that I was going to save her, but I did not get there in time. Sarah died, and I never loved another woman." He wiped his eyes with a pale blue handkerchief that had his initials monogrammed on it—a gift from my mom for his ninetieth birthday.

It was not the first time he had spoken about Sarah.

"How about Georgia? The woman who is inside and who takes care of you."

"I love her too. She is my sister. Thank God, who spared her life and left her with me," he said, shaking his head in awe.

"I will be back," I said as I stood up to go inside.

He smiled and then turned away to join his thoughts in a space where time had collapsed into only a few moments.

I walked into the kitchen where Mom was working on the final touches of a plate for me.

"Ah, there you are," she said, "I thought you would eat outside."

"No, I'll eat here. Dad seems to prefer some quiet time."

We sat, and I started eating mom's delicious octopus dish, but my mind was occupied by the question that had been nagging me all this time. "You're coming to the event this weekend, aren't you?"

"Of course, I am. I have been waiting for this my whole life."

The octopus was delicious. "What if we go shopping for a new dress for you, new shoes, and a new handbag?" I asked. "This is a gift from me. We'll have fun shopping together."

Her eyes sparkled the way they used to, when such outings were more common. "I would love to!"

"How about tomorrow?"

"Tomorrow . . . ahh . . . okay," she said reluctantly. "We could ask Emma to be here with Dad."

Something about that moment felt like the final act. There was something in the air that told me this might be our last chance to be together. I started crying.

"Why are you crying?" she said with concern. "Come, we must enjoy every minute being together. Moments do not last long, but memories do, and these memories are important for both of us, especially for you."

I did not tell her of my conversation with Dad about Sarah. I first heard her name in the mid-nineties, before Alzheimer's began fogging his mind, when Mom and Dad had visited us in Michigan. We had been sitting on the porch one day when he brought up Sarah. We had been talking about something else, and he stopped in the middle of his sentence to look at me wistfully. His head bent as though under a great weight.

"I was engaged once," he said in a mournful voice.

"You were?" I said in surprise. "And?"

"They killed her . . ." he said bitterly.

I was shocked and confused. "How? Who?"

He gripped the arms of his chair. "They . . . the monsters . . . the SS took her and her father, Sior Giacomo. They took them away and they never came back. I was not there to save them." He began to sob.

I was frozen in my seat. Questions swirled in my head like falling leaves, though I could not make myself ask one. I looked at him in disbelief as he took out a cigarette, lit it with a match, and took a deep breath of smoke. Words stuck in my mouth, and I felt like I had never known him.

I was afraid to ask for more. I was afraid to learn the truth. I was afraid to carry the weight of the horror he lived in his life. I was afraid to feel sympathy and pity for him.

I was afraid to love him.

**June 29, 2014**

I jumped from the sofa, breathless, my heart pounding like a striking clock. I saw Ritsa standing over me. She was patting my arm.

"Linda," she said in a low voice, "your mom just called. Your father had difficulty breathing, so they took him to the hospital in an ambulance."

"Where is Mom?" I asked in a hoarse voice. I groped for my phone under the pillow.

"She is at home."

I looked at the time. It was two-thirty in the morning.

"What do you want to do?" she asked.

"I'm going to my mom's first, and then to the hospital."

Ritsa nodded. "I am coming with you," she said, and ran to her room to grab a few things.

Over the course of the next two days, Dad's condition stabilized. He had early signs of pneumonia that they were able to treat with antibiotics. Yet his overall situation had deteriorated substantially. The change in his environment made him even more confused, and he could hardly acknowledge anyone. I continued to sleep at Ritsa's, and during the day, I went back and forth between Mom's flat and Dad's room in the hospital.

"He is still fighting pneumonia," the nurse told me. She knew my parents, as she had lived in their neighborhood.

"He refuses to eat and drink," she went on.

"What are we going to do?" I asked, longing for answers. "Can somebody feed him?"

"We tried everything, but he is not responding." Her face and voice implied the future was unchangeable.

"My father never liked hospital food. He can be very stubborn," I said.

The nurse nodded. "I don't think it just that, though. Maria brought food from home. She cooked his favorite dish and he still didn't respond." She was listening to his pulse. "He does not have many days to live. In his mid-nineties, Alzheimer's only accelerates the unavoidable." She walked slowly to the side of Dad's bed where I sat on a small chair, white like the rest of the room, and she touched me on the shoulder.

"Linda, my advice to you is to start preparing for his passing. You should bring the priest to give your dad his final communion." Her eyes met mine.

"You're talking about my father?" I said and started laughing so hard that it brought tears to my eyes.

The nurse was taken aback. "Does he not believe in God?"

"He believes in God for sure," I rushed to respond. "It is . . ." My voice hung in the air, and I could think of no explanation that would make sense. I cleared my throat. "My dad is not on good terms with the Church. It is a long story."

"Yes, but without communion his soul will be in limbo. God will not accept him," she insisted.

"The suffering my dad went through in his life would canonize anybody as a saint," I responded in anger. "He does not need communion. He needs to go in peace."

My eyes turned to him. He was staring at me with a smile on his face. I reached out and squeezed his hand softly.

"Dad, I love you," I whispered, surprised by the words that came out of my mouth, light as a breath.

"I know," he said, and his unfocused eyes sparkled as they filled with tears.

I stood up and lowered my face to touch his warm forehead with my lips. My heart thumped so fast that I thought it was going to break out of my chest. My ears started humming. By the time I sat back on the chair, his eyes had focused elsewhere. He was in a place between the worlds of the living and the dead. That was the last time I spoke with him.

That night, Mom felt sick. After waking up from her afternoon nap, she could not speak or move her right hand. I was convinced she had suffered a stroke. We called an ambulance to take her to the emergency room in the Sygrou Hospital in Pireous. I asked Emma to stay with Dad at the hospital, and I called my cousin Eleni to ask her to meet me at the hospital. It was about ten o'clock that evening when Mom was admitted to the ER. At about 4:30 a.m., while Eleni and I were waiting for the test results to come back, a nurse called out my name.

"The doctor is ready to see you," she said in a neutral voice.

I walked behind her through corridors filled with people on trollies. Some moaned, others slept, others waited anxiously. The stench—a mix of blood, urine, and medication—made me nauseated. We moved quickly to a row of small offices where the anxious families of patients were sitting quietly in small groups waiting for news. Anxiety was evident on their faces and in their voices.

The nurse knocked on a door that stood ajar and slowly opened it. On the other side was a small and dark office, in complete contrast to the bright white of the corridor. The doctor, small and balding, sat behind a mountain of papers. He stood up to greet me and sat down with a folder in his hands.

"Do you speak Greek?" he asked in an accented voice.

"Yes, very well," I replied in Greek.

His voice was friendly. "Well, this makes it easier for us to discuss your mom's condition. She did not have a stroke."

"This is good news, isn't it?"

"I will let you assess that," he said seriously. "Your mom has a metastasis in three places in her brain." He waited for me to respond.

"Excuse me?" I said and laughed nervously. "Mom was never diagnosed with cancer. How can she have a metastasis? Are you sure?" I was sure he was making a mistake.

"Ms. Katehi, Greece may not have the equipment you have in America, our hospitals may look poor and dirty compared to yours, but our doctors are equally good, if not better."

I went numb and my thoughts ran wild. "I apologize," I manage to mumble. "I am just stunned."

"She has to be admitted to an appropriate unit where they can begin therapy." He presented a stack of papers prepared for my signature. "We will keep her tonight, but tomorrow the choice is yours. She can stay here, or you can move her to a cancer treatment center."

I signed the papers mechanically, still trying to get over my initial shock. He gathered them up, stood, and politely walked me to the door. I almost bolted out of his office. I do not remember whether I thanked him or just closed the door behind me. I started running through the corridors as if I could leave the bad news behind me. I saw Eleni waiting for me at the same bench where I had left her.

"My mom is dying," was all I managed to say before bursting into tears.

A couple of weeks later, on July 20, 2014, Dad passed away. I was in Davis when it happened.

I had come back to the office for a couple of weeks while he was in hospice care and Mom was going through intensive chemo and radiation therapy. Emma and Maria had split the burden, one of them staying with Mom and the other with Dad at all times. Eleni and Ritsa and her younger brother, George, had offered to help while I was in the United States.

The next day, I traveled back to Greece for Dad's funeral. In the weeks after Dad's death, Mom's condition deteriorated despite the efforts to contain the cancer. The most prominent oncologist in Greece was treating her in a private hospital with its most advanced therapy program, but four weeks later, the doctor suggested that we take her home. In her eighty-ninth year, she was too weak to manage the intensity of the treatment. The cancer had metastasized to her bones and its progress was uncontainable.

The oncologist suggested that we take her home for as long as she could manage the pain, but when it became too much, we were to move her to a hospice facility where they could administer the appropriate medication.

We managed to keep her home only for a couple of days. The pain was so severe that we had to move her to the hospice clinic where Dad had been less than a month before then. Every morning I went to her side and stayed until late into the night. The medication kept her in an almost continuous hallucinatory state, which she would occasionally come out of and briefly recognize me and ask about Spyros and the children. Most of the time, she spoke with an intensity I had not seen before, about people and events that had happened long ago. Other times she lamented Dad's absence from her life when she was young, or my separation from her for all those years I was in the United States. Her delirium lasted for many days until she eventually fell into a coma.

It was a Friday morning, August 29, when my cell phone rang at 4:30 a.m. in our flat in Athens. It was my assistant Lisa's voice, soft and apologetic for the early call.

"I am calling about your planned trip to China next week. I know it has been planned for several months, but I told the organizers that your mom is very sick and that you need to be with her." She paused to make sure I had time to think.

"And?" I asked with agitation.

"They do understand the situation, but they say that a last-minute change will upset the Chinese hosts."

"So, what should I do?"

"They asked whether there is any chance you could go to China, even for a few days, and then go back to Greece." She remained silent for some time as if she wanted to decide what to say next. "Do you know—"

"Do I know what? When my mom will die?" I asked, bitterly cutting her off.

We both remained silent, trying to decide where to go from there.

I calmed my voice as best I could. "Listen . . . I will see what I can do. Please tell them that I will try to accommodate them. My original ticket would bring me back to the office tomorrow, so I will stay with that plan unless something happens. Then we will go from there."

I turned to Spyros, who had woken when the phone rang. He had been following the conversation. "Do as you find appropriate. It is your decision," he said.

It took me less than two hours to get ready and drive to the hospice clinic.

I grabbed a few sweets and a coffee for Emma, who had spent the night next to Mom's bed. Emma liked sweets, especially the ones that were dipped in chocolate.

"How is she?" I asked while I handed her the coffee and the chocolate covered buns.

"She was good all night," she said.

Maria was there as well, and she came to kiss me. They had both spent the night. Now that Dad was gone, they were both dedicating their time to keeping her company.

"Your mom was quiet last night," Maria said. "At some point her breathing was so quiet that I thought her heart had stopped. She has been calm."

I sat next to Mom on my usual chair and I took her hands in mine— those hands that I loved so much, that I held so dearly when happy and clutched when anxious, those hands that gave me so much warmth, hope, and stability.

We stayed like this for hours.

It was getting dark. Shadows began to layer over the familiar hills, the towns, and the beaches of the island I called home. With the darkness fell a veil of silence over the birds and cicadas that during the day flitted about the hospice windows. The room slowly turned dark too, only lit by the two vigil oil lamps Maria had brought and placed on each nightstand in front of the icons Mom had brought with her from home. Emma, Maria, and I, all dressed in black, sat silently looking at Mom's chest as it moved up and down in a quiet rhythm.

Emotion overtook me.

"I cannot believe she is dying!"

I heard myself saying angrily, frustration flooding every neuron of my brain. My hands had begun to shake.

"I told her to put Dad in hospice care when his disease incapacitated him. I told her that trying to take care of him by herself would kill her too! But no, she insisted on being his servant. For what? For his negligence when we were young, vulnerable, and in need of his support? He took everything from her and gave her nothing in return. I cannot believe she's leaving me like this. What am I going to do?"

I looked at Emma and Maria, almost lost in the darkness, trying to wipe their tears. I covered my face with my hands and began to cry. Morning came as a storm that bends the trees' branches to their roots, forcing them to face their beginnings.

For a moment, complete silence wrapped its arms around us. The whole room felt serene, and the scent of the burning wax became mixed with a familiar incense. I heard the soft ruffling of feathers, as though a bird had entered from the window. I turned my head to look at the window, but it was closed. The ruffling continued its soft, periodic sound. It came from all directions. I tried to adjust my eyes to the dark as I started looking carefully in the corners, holding my breath, and trying to focus. My eyes searched frantically until they stopped on my mother's face, calm, youthful, and benevolent.

And then as I moved my eyes to the side, I saw *her* as I had never seen her before, serious, silent, and prideful. She stared at me so intensely that I forced my eyes away. *You're here*, I managed to say in my mind as I reached out to hold Mom's hand. *Don't take her. I need her.*

*Not anymore.* Her familiar voice sounded calm and imbued me with intense fear as I remembered how I had pleaded with her—without success—not to take my friend Georgina.

*She needs me*, I tried to counter.

*She is on her way*, she responded with an uncharacteristic softness. *But I did not come for her. I came for you because you need me now more than ever before.*

I said nothing, only kept caressing Mom's hand and trying to engrave this moment in my memory. That was the last time I saw Mom alive. On Saturday morning, I left for Davis, planning to come back immediately after my trip to China the coming week. On Monday morning, hours after I had arrived in Davis, Eleni called me at 3:00 a.m. (California time) to tell me that Mom had passed away. I bought a ticket to Greece and made it on time for her funeral. The day after her funeral, I boarded a plane to China.

That night in the shadowed hospice room by mother's deathbed, in the flickering lights of the candles, Gabriel and I made amends. That night was my passage from one life to another. This new life that started with my mom's death and would lead me into a storm the likes of which I had never seen before—the biggest that I had yet endured.

At the height of the controversy, the area outside
my office was often a mob scene.

## Chapter Fourteen

# The Final Meeting

## Fall 2015

A YEAR AFTER I BURIED both my parents, Erik married his
fiance Emily and Helena got engaged to her partner of many years. A
year of double loss was followed by a year of double engagements and
a wedding, all too late for Mom to see; one of her wishes that never
came true.

The excitement of the summer of 2015 was short-lived. In early fall,
the UC president announced her plan for a retreat with the regents to
discuss the plans of the university. Under the gentle encouragement of
the chancellors, she agreed to add one more day for a pre-retreat meeting
with us and the other members of her leadership team. The chancellors
saw this retreat as an opportunity to meet with her and talk about issues
that had become roadblocks in our ability to effectively run our campuses. A few of those issues were sensitive and needed to be discussed
with tact. We needed time and a safe environment in which to hold
these discussions.

At the forefront was the issue of the high number of presidential initiatives that we were expected to execute without additional funding and
which directly competed with the academic programs on our campuses

for resources. In addition, we hoped to discuss the implications of: the high-conflict tone of interaction between the president, the governor, and legislators; the uncontrollable budget run-offs of UC Path; the payroll consolidation program across the ten campuses; and the substantial increase of the president's staff both in Oakland and in Washington, D.C. Chancellor Nick Dirks at UC Berkeley and I agreed to speak with the other chancellors and collect topics for that day's discussion.

After a conference call and an in-person meeting with our colleagues, we created a list of important issues, with one coming consistently at the top: our participation in decision-making.

We submitted the list to the president's chief of staff. Within a few hours, we heard from the president's office that she wanted to have a conference call with Nick and me as soon as possible. The urgency of the request indicated a problem.

"Thank you for your report," she said in an anxious tone after her assistant connected her to the line. "I read it and decided that you have totally missed the point. No one asked you to look at the past. I asked you to look *forward* and identify topics of interest."

"We spoke with every chancellor," Nick interjected, "both in writing and in person, and this is exactly what they submitted."

"Well, if that is the case, they missed the point too," she continued. "Are there no ideas about the future? I mean the future of the UC, not of your campuses."

"But our campuses *are* the UC," I managed to say.

"I am not interested in grievances," she said, cutting me off. "I am interested in the future. Why is it so difficult to speak about the future?"

"There are many topics on our list that focus on the future," I said, "and we have made a list of about a dozen of them."

She lashed out. "None of these are exciting. They are boring. Our retreat will not become a therapy session. We should spend our time making a new list of the topics we will discuss with the regents. I think it will be best if I set the agenda. I'll send information soon."

With that, she hung up. Nick and I stayed on the line quietly trying to absorb the essence of the discussion. After a few seconds of deafening silence, we said goodbye to each other and hung up too.

The retreat with the chancellors simply reinforced the status quo. It included typical interactions such as repetitive presentations about each campus, interspersed with short comments. No new information was given to assist our understanding of the other campuses or help us design or discuss possible new collaborations. The president seemed disinterested and asked very few questions but wrote feverishly on a yellow notepad.

I knew she was just trying to stay awake and had no intention of revisiting those notes. In her time as president, it had become clear that she was the type to make up her mind alone and then have others make the arguments for her. This was characteristic of those with limited knowledge but an endless capacity for arrogance. It was a deadly combination.

My misgivings were justified a few months later. By the end of 2015, the political stresses in the UC system had begun to grow. A state representative, Kevin McCarty, who was the chair of the statewide educational budget committee, started accusing the university of mismanaging its resources. He initiated a legislative hearing on the UC budget and asked the president to submit a list of answers to his questions. Those in the UC budget office suggested a financial model that expensed the work of the faculty, including the number of teaching hours, office hours, research hours, and service hours, comparing expenses against staff's wages and benefits. Immediately after this announcement, the president's office started putting pressure on UC Davis to take responsibility for the development of this model and to defend it at the legislative hearing in place of the UC Office of the President.

*She is trying to use us as a shield*, I thought bitterly.

In a conversation with the UC Davis provost, I put forth some of my concerns.

"Many institutions have tried in the past to parametrize how faculty think and innovate, and to develop financial models based on that. They have all failed," I said to him. "Unfortunately, you promised that UC

Davis would develop such a model despite my objections and the objections of our budget office." He became defensive, seemingly uninterested in my arguments, as if he could not comprehend the difficulties and risks involved.

I tried to explain. "Do you not understand that you cannot develop billable hours for a mathematician who is trying to solve for the first time a hundred-year-old theorem, for an artist who is trying new tools for a different type of art, for an engineer who is developing the first intelligent system, or an author who is working on an award-winning book of poems?"

His response was an email back to the president's office claiming that he had been pressured not to do it. I only know because, by accident, he copied me on this email. The president's office insisted that it be done, labeling me as the source of their problems. They did not care that the formula they wanted to use would probably conclude that Socrates was unproductive and Cicero a talker but not doer. Luckily, the formula never came about because the people in our business office declared that they could not create it without distorting the facts.

The president's office, bitter about this turn of events, arranged for the budget hearing to focus on UC Davis's budget practices and to take place on the UC Davis campus. Rep. McCarty, with his critical eyes on me, gladly accepted the offer.

The hearing was scheduled on the same day the Office of the President had asked me to participate in a regent's meeting at UCLA. I chose to participate in the regent's event and, as a result, I missed the hearing in front of an infuriated legislator who had hoped to humiliate me. McCarty had publicly expressed dismay at the idea of bringing more international students to the UC Davis campus and came prepared to interrogate me about the 2020 Initiative. His isolationist approach, which had led him to call the 2020 Initiative a "threat to Californians," came in direct conflict with our effort to internationalize the UC Davis campus. Losing his opportunity to use the hearing as a platform to get his name in the local newspapers and promote his fear-mongering message enraged him. The only comment he was able to pass in my absence was to characterize the 2020 Initiative as the "chancellor's ludicrous and insidious plan."

## Winter 2016

In January 2016, I was asked by DeVry University to join its board. The school was interested in my experience in public institutions. It was not the first time I had been on the board of an organization. Almost all of them were unpaid positions in nonprofit organizations.

There is a difference between being on the board of a nonprofit and a for-profit organization. Participating on the board of a nonprofit is generally an honorific position, and your input is advisory. It is considered to be service to the public and the profession. Paying boards of for-profit organizations have different requirements: you need time to prepare for meetings, and you are expected to use vacation days or non-paid days for activities related to these boards. In recognition, you are paid a stipend and given stocks which vest after a maturation period. They also pay for all travel-related activities. According to university policy, these activities must be reported twice a year. When I joined UC Davis, the policy allowed for maximum participation on three such boards simultaneously. In 2016, I was one of thirty-nine administrators who had been members of such boards.

Every organization typically wants its leaders to participate on boards relevant to their experience because they offer exposure to different forms of leadership. Being on boards provided an opportunity for me to learn how other organizations run and to get ideas about new models. A lot of this knowledge I found invaluable in my work as a faculty member and as an administrator.

DeVry was a for-profit school that was part of a model that had been encroaching badly on public education. The UC Davis School of Engineering had a graduation rate of less than 50 percent, while DeVry's engineering programs had shown graduation rates above 90 percent. What accounted for that difference? Some have claimed that the numbers are not true; others that they are accurate. In my mind, the idea that it was all a big lie was reprehensible. Not all the difference could be attributed to business fraud. What was it then, that made the for-profit educational industry so successful and growing, and what could we learn from some of their practices and successes that might be translated into programs at our own professional schools?

After speaking with my chief of staff and legal counsel and receiving their approval, I decided to conditionally accept the invitation to DeVry's board and submitted the required paperwork to the Office of the President. Some weeks later, my assistant, Lisa came into my office while I was going through emails to give me an update.

"I just called the Office of the President. They said that it will take five to six months for your request to be approved officially, but since there is no conflict and you are not on another paid board at this time, they do not see a problem in accepting the invitation and participating in the DeVry meetings. Many others in the UC are doing the same. They said that official approval will come later."

There was something about the DeVry board invitation that made me anxious. Having no reply from the president directly after sending multiple messages threw up warning signs. Now in my office, standing idle in front of the glass window but seeing nothing other than my confused reflection, I lacked confidence.

It was not only the silence about the DeVry board that concerned me. There had been a similar silence from the president's office concerning our request to proceed with plans for a Sacramento campus. This initiative had been in development for three years. The plan was to create a new UC campus satellite in Sacramento that would focus on food, nutrition, and policy. Such a project in the center of Sacramento could change the face of the town and strengthen the university's connection with the city. It would also become the bridge between the Davis campus and the Sacramento Health Center, two important parts of UC Davis that I was trying to keep together and not let drift away, something that had already begun when I first came on as chancellor. Sacramento was excited about the plan, but it appeared that the president had no interest.

By the end of 2015, I felt stonewalled in nearly every direction by the office of the UC president.

**March 20, 2016**

It had been a hard month and a half. I was sitting at my desk and could hear the commotion in the lobby, a heated exchange between the students occupying the space and the staff who were trying to reach their offices and execute their administrative activities. It was hard to believe that we failed to secure the fifth floor from a student takeover, something we had agreed on the day before. This was not the first time students had occupied space demanding my resignation, yet we had a process in place on how to prevent an occupation of the chancellor's lobby. We would normally close the lobby before students could claim the space. Yet, it seemed that this time we had failed badly.

"Everyone is on the phone," Lisa's voice sounded loud from her office. "Do you want me to connect you?"

"Yes, please!" I responded as I finished writing the questions I wanted to ask during the call.

The group I had invited on this call was a small one, according to advice I received from the officers at student affairs. It was just me, two officers from student affairs, the chief of university police (a person who had replaced the previous chief and in whom I had tremendous confidence), and a safety officer, all of whom I trusted completely.

"Chancellor," said one of the student affairs officers, "we have information from some students that is very sensitive."

"Please go ahead," I responded, anxious to hear.

"The students say that there is someone high up in the provost's office who has been giving the Fire-Katehi group a lot of information." He paused to let me understand the weight of his statement.

"How do you know that this information is correct?" I asked.

"I trust the students who told me. They know many of the protesters who openly talk about it. These students know things that have only been discussed in our safety council and with your leadership team. In my opinion, we are discussing too many details in this safety council and the leaks make us unsafe."

There was silence on the phone.

"What do you suggest?" I asked, hoping that this wasn't true. If I had not known this person and had not developed the trust I had in him, I would be sure he was lying.

"My advice is to stop discussing details in council and instead speak about strategies without dates or times. We can discuss those in a smaller meeting. You may want to practice the same with your leadership team."

"Do we know who is leaking the information?" The question flew off my lips, leaving a strong burning sensation behind.

"I am not sure," he admitted. "The students insist that this person is high up in the organization because of the accuracy of the information provided to them. They also mentioned that this person is supportive of the protesting students and their cause. This person hopes that you will resign if the students keep up with the pressure and is encouraging them to continue." He paused. "The same students said that the *Bee* and legislator Kevin McCarty have reached out to the Fire-Katehi group, encouraging them to stay strong and providing them with advice and ideas. This has made these activist students feel empowered."

"The last piece of information does not surprise me," I said wryly. "Legislator McCarty is no friend for reasons I do not understand. He is pushing his colleagues to ask for my resignation. He wants me out at any cost. About the students, let them stay in the lobby until they are tired and ready to go home. We do not want arrests or any other incidents. We have bigger issues to address."

They all agreed, and we hung up.

I sat back in my chair, trying to comprehend what I had just heard. There was much to think about, and a little voice inside me said the solution would not be easy. I anticipated that whoever had been leaking information would want to lie low when things began to heat up. This made me suspect the provost himself, who was the only one asking to go on vacation in the middle of this crisis. In addition, the *Sac Bee* had taken responsibility for seeing me ousted. They had been publishing two or three articles a day since mid-February supporting the Fire-Katehi students, calling me a failure and asking the president to fire me. In one meeting with the president's communications staff, her director of communications mentioned that one of the *Sac Bee* editors had been calling her office daily to ask whether the president would fire me or penalize me any time soon. In addition, over a two-month period, the newspaper had filed 190 requests under the Freedom of Information Act that covered every possible action in my office and in the residence. They were looking for dirt they were convinced they would find.

## April 11, 2016

I was on my way to meet my colleagues at the medical school. My steps had brought me to their floor, but my mind was already distracted and tired. Conversations with my colleagues were always welcome and stimulating, but I was emotionally drained. It had been almost three months since the issue with the boards had erupted. This issue had turned into a personal crisis for me and had set off ugly sentiments of hatred, jealousy, and regret—highlighted almost every day on the front pages of the local newspapers. Every one of their comment was flawed, rude, and made to cause pain to me and my family. Kevin McCarty used this crisis as a political platform and kept asking for my firing for being on the Wiley board between 2011 and 2014, something the UC President's Office had approved annually. For my participation on the Wiley, the *Bee* started calling me unethical, greedy, and incapable of the role I was holding. During those moments, I saw the horrible side of human nature: ungrateful, vindictive, unjust, and insolent. I had seen it all.

The elevator's door opened, waiting for me to come out. I hesitated, though I did not want to be late for this meeting. I opened the door to a room full of happy people sitting around a long conference table and chatting with each other. For an instant, I wished I were one of them. The big clock on the wall showed 10:00 a.m. exactly.

It felt as I if I had entered another world, one more promising and exciting than the one I had been living in for the past three months. The air in the room was light and upbeat.

*Thank God for the change*, I thought, and sat in the chair designated for me at the head of the table.

We began our meeting by going around the table for introductions, a standard way to open a discussion with such a big group. A few minutes in, my phone began to ring. It was buried in my purse, which lay by my feet. I bent downward and put it on silent, trying to focus on the opening comments of the chair in pediatrics, but my mind was on the call. A few minutes later, I heard my phone buzzing again. This time I let it buzz, though it was very distracting. There was something that made me anxious about these calls. My mind started wondering what else had happened since that morning, but I tried very hard to suppress any thoughts and participate in the discussion.

A few minutes later the door opened and the assistant who had led me to the conference room came in and bent down to my ear.

"The president is looking for you," she whispered in an anxious voice. "She needs to speak with you immediately, in three minutes to be precise. She will call you on your cell phone." I grabbed the phone from my purse and nodded to her reluctantly. I asked the group to continue, and I followed the assistant, who quietly led me out the conference room.

She showed me to a small room with an empty desk and a phone. She closed the door and left. I felt nauseated again. My anxiety the last few days had given me a stomach sickness I could not control and had made my hands sweat constantly, something I had only experienced when I was under serious distress. I could not write on a pad without leaving visible wet marks.

My phone rang.

"Hello?" I said quietly.

"What in the world are you doing?" Janet's voice raged like a thunderstorm. "You are doomed! Do you understand that? The whole world is talking about you!"

"Excuse me?" I managed to respond, totally clueless about what she was referring to.

"You are going to destroy our state budget negotiations. Why did you double your communications group?"

I was confused. "I apologize, but I do not know what you are referring to," I responded, trying to compose myself. "First of all, I have not doubled the communications group, if anything I reduced it substantially from the size it was before I joined UC Davis."

"Why did you release material to the newspaper? My office specifically instructed you and your staff not to release anything."

"I am not sure what you are referring to. If my office released anything to the newspaper, it was without my consent. I am not in my office now, but when I go back, I will find out what happened and will contact you with an answer to your question."

"The *Bee* is writing articles about you, one after another, they say you tried to remove material from the web about the pepper spray," her voice sounded hoarse and angry.

"No one can remove anything from the web," I responded calmly. "I am an engineer and I can tell you this much; no one can scratch the internet. The *Bee* is speaking nonsense. Technically, no one can erase anyone else's articles or blogs."

She hung up as abruptly as she had called. I was not sure she was able to hear a word of what I said. I walked back to the meeting, but my mind was already gone. I have no recollection of what we discussed afterwards.

An hour later, I walked into my office to find my chief of staff quietly speaking with my assistant.

"What happened?" I asked them.

"Well, the *Bee* misconstrued information, and they claim you spent an enormous amount of money boosting our communications group and trying to wipe the web of the pepper spray incident to improve your image," my chief of staff replied with an ease I found out of place.

"Where did they find this information?" I asked, holding my temper.

"Our office released some documents yesterday. The documents included the budget for the communications office and a couple of contracts with consulting companies." His otherwise relaxed face had begun to look uneasy.

"Did you submit any explanations about the material you released? Did we not agree that no material would go out without explanations and without the approval from the Office of the President?" I asked. "I just spoke with the president. Apparently, there is a rumor going around claiming that the communications department, which is under you, has doubled in size. Is this true?"

We both knew the answer, but I wanted to find out what his thoughts were.

"Well, they misinterpreted the increase in benefits and salary for the existing staff as funds to increase the size."

"I see. Why then is there no explanation?" I asked him pointedly.

He thought for a moment. "I did not know the documents were released," he finally said in a low voice.

"Who knew, then?"

"The legal counsel did."

"The legal counsel just told me that your office gave them the okay. In fact, the director of communications did that," I responded with rage in my voice.

He looked decidedly uncomfortable at this point. "Well, the communications director has been tired and busy and didn't read the email when she gave them the okay." The words spilled out of his mouth, as if I was responsible for all this.

"And what about scratching the web?" I continued. "What is this all about? Is this about the contracts we had years ago in 2012 to help the staff learn how to manage social media when people were posting all kinds of fake pictures?"

He just kept looking at me.

"In one of these contracts, you wrote to have the firm do a review of the communications office," I added. "At least submit an explanation to the president as soon as possible. Can you do this?" I asked.

He was very upset at his mistakes having been brought to light. "It does not matter what we tell the *Bee*," he answered. "They will twist everything we say and will present it any way they want. They want you to leave. We are all very tired with all this business."

And with that, he turned and stormed from the room. I collapsed in my chair and heard Gabriel's voice in my head. *Did you hear his last comment?* she said. *He has given up. Maybe he wants this to end sooner rather than later.*

I tried to ignore her.

*He worries about his job, not yours. He has already turned against you,* she continued.

I rubbed my temples. "Please stop. I am not going to fall for this."

*Probably, he knows that the newspaper will not let go and he is thinking about himself and his life after you leave,* she continued. *Very few are so idealistic as to remain loyal under these circumstances, and he is not one of them. Can you blame him for that? The Bee is out there to get you. They represent the collective outcry against a woman they do not like and cannot trust.*

She did not sound sarcastic or triumphant in her statements, she only sounded reasonable, and I was listening carefully for the first time in a while.

She went on. *You represent something they cannot see in themselves. Something they cannot imitate or reproduce, and for that reason you present them with a singular challenge. They abhor you for who you are and the changes you want to introduce.*

I tried walking around the room, but my mind continued to race.

*Your failure will transform this challenge to a hope. A hope for maintaining what brings comfort and security. You brought them change and discomfort and you have to pay for that,* she concluded.

### April 22, 2016

Living for months under a barrage of accusations from the newspaper, the calls for resignation by Kevin McCarty, and the outrageous blogs by "Fire Katehi" had trapped me in a space of continuous anxiety. I was torn between work that needed to be done, the stress from the continuous criticism, and uncertainty for the future. The Sacramento *Bee*'s ferocious accusations had turned the ambivalent feelings of the town of Davis into a perspicuous contempt toward everything they believed I was responsible for. I reached out to the board of the *Davis Enterprise* for a meeting, and they expressed an interest in speaking with me. The group included the editor and two journalists. It was led by the owner of the paper, who never in the previous seven years had shown an interest in meeting with me—despite my office's invitations for an introduction. I met with the group in the conference room next to my office.

"For all your years here," the owner of the Davis newspaper said in an accusatory voice, "you have not been able to understand our culture."

He was sitting comfortably a few chairs away from me in the conference room and peering at me intensely.

"You make too much money for this town, and you do not seem to understand how much more you are making compared to everybody else. Your greed led you to accept these board positions. What were you thinking?"

His statement sounded perverted and pretentious, considering he was speaking about a town known for the high cost of real estate and its highly educated, eclectic, wealthy, and exclusive community.

"You have made this university a corporation," the sportswriter for the newspaper threw at me with an ardent voice. "Before you, the people of this town could go to the football games with their families, bringing their sandwiches and their drinks, and they would lie on the grass to enjoy the games. You decided to stop all this and force the families to buy tickets and spend a fortune on junk food from the stadium kiosk so that you can make money on the backs of the people."

"You do not pay attention to our city," the editor chimed in with a sobbing voice. "You try to move the university to Sacramento. Why do you not value our community?"

"I feel so sorry I failed you," I managed to say, trying to suppress my own tears of regret.

The meeting continued in that vein, and afterwards I returned to my office.

"Your call with the president has now changed to an in-person meeting on Monday afternoon," I heard Lisa's voice as I entered the office later that day.

I nodded in acknowledgment.

"That was a surprising meeting," I noted to my chief of staff, who sat quietly by the door, referring to the Davis press meeting we'd just had. "Did you know that they've had these grievances?"

"No," he replied, looking down. "I thought this would have been a productive meeting."

"By the way, why did we stop allowing the people to bring their own food to the stadium?" I asked, ignoring his comment.

"I do not know but I will find out," he replied and abruptly left the room.

I had to bite my tongue to keep from making any comments about his office's inability to gauge the feelings of our surrounding communities, despite overseeing public and community relations. It would have been pointless.

"Lisa, could you please call Janet's office to find out what the topic of the in-person meeting is?" I stood up from my desk and tried to arrange my scattered thoughts. After spending some time going through emails that had piled up, my chief of staff reentered the room.

"I found that the change at the football stadium," he said, "started almost ten years ago as an agreement between the university and the union of the food service workers, under the previous chancellor."

"This is interesting! I wonder why they took me to be responsible for that," I noted in anger. The conversation moved on to my meeting with the president scheduled for the following Monday. After some arguing, my chief of staff promised to find out the nature of the meeting and provide me with an agenda. Eventually he made an excuse and left the office. The weekend went by and I did not hear from him. I left a message on his phone, but he did not respond.

**April 24, 2016**

It was a beautiful Monday morning in Davis. I stood in the residence's courtyard. My meeting was at 2:30 p.m., and I wanted to have plenty of time in case there was traffic. I asked Spyros to once more play the role of driver and give me a ride so I could go over the pack of documents that were waiting for my signature. He agreed without a complaint. The events of the last two months had been weighing heavily on him, but he was trying not to show it. On the contrary, he was going out of his way to act relaxed, funny, and flexible. Yet the extra lines on his forehead repudiated his words.

My watch, a gift from Spyros a few years back for my birthday, showed 2:15 p.m. We parked in the covered garage next to the University of California office of the president building and walked through the entrance toward the security guard post that doubled as a receptionist desk. I suggested to Spyros that he go wait in a coffee shop across the street and try to be back by 3:15 p.m. Using my university card, I went through the security gate and took the elevator to the twelfth floor.

*Something tells me that this may be the last time I will walk on the twelfth floor*, I thought. I was alone in the elevator going up, and I was relieved that no one else was there. I did not feel capable of pretending to be nice and relaxed. It would have been hard to sustain small talk with my stomach upset and my nerves stressed. I greeted the receptionist on the twelfth floor, who responded with a Southern politeness that you cannot easily find in California. She asked me whether I wanted to use an office until the time of the meeting, and I accepted her offer.

She showed me the way to an empty office, painted gray like all the other offices in the building, with a table in the middle. The typical UC posters of campuses were on the walls in frames. The chairs were arranged around the table as if a group had left in a hurry, causing disarray.

I sat across from the window and looked out over San Francisco and Oakland, the twin wonders of the state of California, with their extreme wealth and extreme poverty side by side. The sister cities are like the daughters of a dysfunctional family. One city, wealthy beyond belief, projects a sense of unique beauty, superiority, and generosity like no other. The other is poor and plagued by unemployment, drugs, and juvenile incarceration. It is rarely talked about in the news unless there is a demonstration or a crime.

My mind went back to the previous few months. Since February 2016, I had spoken with the president in person only once, on March 25, after our campus budget meeting. It was the only time when the two of us had met to discuss the DeVry issue. Our discussion had focused on the student protests and the need for better support in my office. She mentioned that I had to make some changes in my office and bring people around me who could help me avoid mistakes. She made the point that I needed someone to support me who could be more intuitive and firmer, using the failure with DeVry Board issue as an example. I had agreed.

"You need someone you can trust who would do everything to protect you and prevent mistakes. Not just a 'yes' person," she had said, smiling as she stood up to indicate the end of our meeting. "You can call me any time you want," she had added, but I did not feel she meant it. There had been uneasiness in the air.

Back in the present, my watch showed 2:27 p.m. I pushed my thoughts away and walked to Janet's office. The hallway was dim and quiet. I could only hear the clicking of the computer keys coming from the executive assistant's office. I stopped by her door and knocked hard enough for her to hear me.

"I am here for a meeting with Janet," I said plainly.

"Janet is on the phone," she replied with a friendly smile. "She will be with you in a few minutes."

I sat on the chair in the hallway in front of the assistant's office with my eyes on a row of thick and heavy-looking oversized books printed proudly by the UC Press. *Fiat Lux* was printed with gold letters on the front hardcover.

"Let there be light," I whispered.

The sun's rays flowing through the window blinds reflected off the books, and for a moment, the letters were engulfed in a bright sparkle that made me shiver.

*How much I loved my alma matter for the light it had brought to my life,* I thought. *A love that at times made me a forceful, relentless, and unforgiving guard of the UC quality and values, sometimes to my detriment.*

My thoughts were interrupted by Seth, Janet's chief of staff. Wearing a black suit, as always, he walked past me quickly with an unusually friendly smile and disappeared into the assistant's office. It felt peculiar seeing him smiling. Since we had a difference of opinion on some issues, he rarely looked friendly to me. A young lawyer brought quickly to a position of power, he was totally committed to Janet and disrespectful to everyone else, including the chancellors. His only value was his extreme loyalty to his boss in return for the power he was allowed to collect and visibly exercise.

As I was waiting in front of the assistant's office, I noticed that Seth was quietly waiting by her desk. I stood up to see out of curiosity what he was doing when the assistant announced that Janet was ready to see me. That's when I saw Seth stepping behind me into her office.

Janet stood by her wooden desk, serious in a dark suit with a raised collar and holding a dark blue folder. Her head was turned away from me, as if she were engaged in a discussion with an invisible friend. She asked me to come in and have a seat while her eyes moved from the invisible friend to the sofa in her office. Her office had hardly changed from the time of the previous president, despite its new and distinctly different aura. The only difference I remembered from before was a big picture hanging on the wall over the sofa, showing Janet fully dressed as a cowboy riding a horse, leading a long line of other riders. This picture is so distinctive that it attracted my attention the first time I had gone to her office.

She sat on the armchair across from me, and Seth took his place on a chair. She looked morose and moody, but he looked happy. I managed to keep my eyes on Janet's face, but hers were fixed somewhere away with a visible nervousness. She seemed anxious to be done with this business.

"I am a blunt person, and I will speak as such," she said in her deep voice, following a brief silence of a few seconds. "This whole issue that has been going on for the past few months has not allowed you to focus on running the university. Also, we have heard from a whistleblower familiar with your family who has accused you of nepotism."

She stopped to take a breath.

"We have heard from yet another whistleblower who claims that you have misused student fees." Another breath. "And finally, you spoke with the *Chronicle for Higher Education* without telling me. I want you to resign from the university immediately." She continued to avoid meeting my eyes.

My mind grew numb for a second, and I lost my voice, something that had not happened to me in quite a while.

*Why won't she look at me?* I thought. *She wants me to resign from the university now because of two whistleblowers. How does she know I have committed an impropriety?*

*She does not know and does not care,* I heard Gabriel whispering nervously. *So much for due process. They convinced her that if she supports you any further, they will prove that she flies along with you on a broom. She is scared, and she wants you gone.*

"What do you mean 'resign from the university'?" I managed to say in a voice that was plain and steady, while my eyes had not moved an inch away from hers. I wanted to meet her eyes to learn the truth, but she managed to keep them away. "I am a tenured, distinguished faculty member," I managed to continue.

A surprised look came over her face tinged with annoyance. She moved uncomfortably on her chair and remained silent for a few seconds.

*Unbelievable!* I thought. *She did not remember that I am a tenured faculty member!*

"Well, you have a choice," Janet interrupted my thoughts with a voice projecting power and determination. "Either you resign from the university or you resign as a chancellor only. It's your choice. But, if you choose to only resign as a chancellor, I will have to investigate you and your family publicly."

My heart sank.

*What choice does she give you?* I heard her voice as an echo in my head. *Either you leave as a cowardly thief or stay at the university and let your family suffer.*

"What are you accusing me of?" I asked with a trembling voice.

Without looking at me, Janet opened her folder, exposing a page full of highlights. She paused for a second to look them over and then said, "I do not have the details here. I only have my notes." She waited for a few seconds as if she were looking for the right word. "But, if you want, I can prepare a letter for you," she added.

*She cannot even articulate what you have done wrong!* Gabriel murmured next to my ear with a horrified voice.

While I tried to process this information despite Gabriel's continuous rumbling, I observed Janet; her face was gray and serious, her eyes still avoiding mine, and her position showed strength but not confidence. She kept looking at her chief of staff, as if she were mentally practicing her speech with him. Her eyes always focused away, forcing me to look in that direction and see Seth's smile drawn on an otherwise scornful face.

"I understand that you are asking me to leave," I finally said. "I need to go home, take everything in, and I promise I will call you tomorrow morning to continue this discussion."

"No," she said, "there is nothing to continue. I expect you to resign now, before you leave this office."

"I cannot resign without knowing what you are accusing me of," I responded back, "and I need to discuss this with my family, as your accusations now involve them. I cannot tell them that I resigned, charged with something that you could not explain to me."

She paused for few seconds, then twisted in her chair before continuing to press. "If you do not resign from the university now," she said anxiously, "I will place you on leave, and I will publicly investigate you and your family. And, if you only resign as a chancellor, I will still have to investigate you publicly, because of the whistleblowers and the importance of your position."

My eyes filled with tears. I felt anxious at the prospect of losing my temper. I was afraid that I was going to cry and humiliate myself in front of her.

*She's threatening me*, I thought.

"I need to speak with my husband," I said, trembling. "He is my partner in life, and I owe it to him to discuss this issue before I make any decisions."

Janet was clearly growing unsure of herself. She first looked at her chief and then at her desk.

"You can use my phone to talk with your husband, and then you resign before you leave," she said.

Blood boiled in my veins.

I felt like I was losing my mind. Then, amid my mental anguish, I stumbled into a moment of clarity. My head cleared. It became obvious that Janet was not interested in the truth. That being the case, there was no reason to continue to engage her. The discussion was not going anywhere, and I was not planning to leave the university under the shadow of unjust and vilifying accusations. If Mom were alive, she would have never supported a cowardly exit under threats and intimidation. She would have asked me to fight for my innocence.

"I will *not* resign, not here, not now," I heard myself telling Janet in a steady voice. "I will go home to speak with my husband, and I will call you tomorrow to continue the discussion."

I stood up, grabbed my purse, and started walking toward the door. Both Janet and Seth stood up but did not move from their places. They looked frozen. As I left, closing the door behind me, I heard Janet's voice: "I expect you to bring your resignation tomorrow morning by 8:00 a.m., here, in person."

I did not respond. I stepped out of her office, as in a dream. Walking to the elevator, I saw for the last time the heavy UC books that lined the hallway, like sorry, forgotten guards.

I found myself in front of the elevator where the chief of staff to the previous president, and a friend of mine, was waiting. She smiled sadly at me, knowing that something was wrong. She said something I do not remember, and I responded with a few words that probably made no sense. She was always friendly with me, but that day she looked embarrassed. She exited two floors below, and I felt relieved.

I walked out of the elevator, went through the security doors, and said goodbye to the guards I had known for almost seven years, convinced I would never see them again. I looked at my watch. Its hands were fixed at 2:45 p.m., as if time had stopped, petrified by the events of the last fifteen minutes. I saw Spyros waiting for me, sitting on a bench a few steps away from the security desk. I looked at him and smiled wryly. He did the same. He stood up and came next to me. He took my hand in his and squeezed it with compassion. His youthful trust reminded why I had loved him so much. A love that had kept me in the light and away from the shadows of evil.

"She asked me to resign," I whispered.

He gripped my hand more firmly and softly said, "Let us discuss in the car."

I grabbed him by his arm, my stomach was hurting. We were quiet until we got to the car. Once we were inside, I felt I could not breathe, as if I had locked the air out.

"What are we going to do? God save me, what are we going to do?" I kept repeating. "She asked me to resign from the university, and if I don't, she is going to publicly investigate all of us."

He didn't say anything right away, as the weight of my statement settled onto his shoulders. Instead, he decided that the car was in fact not the best place for this.

"Let's go someplace to discuss it," he said in a calm voice.

My phone rang. It was Suad, a colleague and friend. Her voice sounded uneasy.

"Linda," she said, "a colleague of mine called from Berkeley a few minutes ago saying word has been going around that the president asked you to resign. Is this true?"

"When did they learn about it?" I managed to ask her through stifled sobs.

"Sometime in the morning, they said. This rumor has been going around Berkeley the whole day."

"It is not a rumor," I said, with a calmness that surprised me. "I guess they found out before I did. In fact, she threatened me into resigning, but I left her office without responding."

"Good for you," she said. "So, are you going to be at the residence today?"

"Yes," I said mechanically.

"Okay, then. I will come by around 6:00 p.m.," she said, and hung up.

We ended up driving aimlessly around the streets of Oakland for almost half an hour. Eventually, we ended up at a bar. It was still the early afternoon, and we were the only customers. The waitress came by to bring us the menus, and we asked for a beer for Spyros and a martini for me. We stayed quiet for a few minutes, just looking at each other.

"Tell me how it happened," Spyros said, his eyes a sea of green specked with tiny yellow spots. In a low, sad voice, I recounted the events of the meeting. Spoken aloud, it all somehow seemed more surreal.

When I had finished, he said, "Love, you did the right thing."

"I am so sorry that I've failed you," I whispered.

"You have not failed me," he said in a strong voice. "It is Janet who has failed the university. She has failed everyone, not just you."

Around 4:00 p.m., I stepped away from the table to place a few quick calls. I started with Andre, the chair of the senate. I had always known him to be a straightforward, an honorable person, principled in ways I have not seen in others and with an integrity that commanded respect. I told him about my meeting with Janet.

He listened until I was through, then asked if someone was driving me. He was concerned at how upset I was. I told him that yes, Spyros was driving me. Satisfied, he asked if he might come by the residence later that day to discuss in person. I told him he would be most welcome and thanked him. Next came the call to our children. I told them that Dad and I needed to meet them that night.

"What's going on, Mom?" Erik sounded worried. "Are you okay?"

"If you mean healthy, yes we are," I responded drily. "We will be at home around five. Please, come by."

The last call I made was to Viva, who, over the years, had been not only a great friend but also an amazing supporter and counsel. She advised me that I would need a lawyer, and she told me she knew an excellent one. We spoke for no more than a few minutes, and like the rest of my wonderful supporters, she made plans to get in contact later that day to earnestly discuss my options and plans.

I decided to avoid speaking with anyone else that day. I felt exhausted, detested, and angry. I went back to our table and ordered another martini, my first time ever having two in a row, and managed to calm down. We made our way back home. We both remained silent, lost in our thoughts.

After getting home, we did not exchange a word until the bell on the front door rang. Spyros opened the door to Andre Knoesen, Linda Bisson, and Bob Powel. Linda and Bob, previous chairs of the academic senate, had been informed by Andre and had come to talk to me and understand what happened.

We clustered in the kitchen. Linda was the first to speak. "We were told this afternoon by some colleagues at UC Berkeley that the president forced you to resign. It would seem the news was leaked out of her office before she even spoke with you," she said.

I nodded. "She has put a lot of effort into forcing me out, and the wheels have been in motion for some time. I want your advice," I said, looking at each one.

They all, Spyros included, thought that I should fight against Janet's accusations. It was part of my contract as a chancellor that I served at the pleasure of the president. She could ask me to leave at any time, but nowhere was it written that she had to incriminate me to obtain my resignation.

"It is one thing to resign because she does not want to work with you anymore," Andre said emphatically. "It is something else entirely to leave the university for something you have not done."

The rest of them nodded in agreement. "Besides, most of the faculty are with you, and they will do everything it takes to keep you," he finished. I appreciated his confidence, but I had begun to worry about the faculty angle to this. I had relied on the faculty for support many times over the years and was afraid that they would grow tired of going out of their way to support me. I voiced this to the group gathered in our kitchen. No one had an immediate answer, and a stressful silence settled on our conversation. Shortly after, the doorbell rang again.

It was Suad, my faculty advisor of over two years, and a true friend. She had been an exceptional intellect on issues of social justice, particularly those related to women. Her work was driven by strong values rooted in principles of shared governance, academic freedom, and freedom of speech. She and I had met under difficult circumstances that had arisen from the pepper spray incident. She had begun as a strong critic of mine, since she was deeply concerned for the safety of students and the integrity of the university, but in time she had become a respected and loved friend. She was always ready to speak the truth.

"Faculty have started writing letters to the president and local papers supporting you. More than four hundred have signed in only a few hours."

Finally, some encouraging news. Whether it would be enough to accomplish anything had yet to be seen, but knowing I had support did much to alleviate the anxiety that gripped me. Soon after Suad arrived, we were joined by Erik and Emily. My son and his wife were young, proud, hardworking, and principled. They were in the prime of their lives and careers, and it would be awful to see them engulfed in a mess like this because of the hatred, jealously, and vengeance of others and the uninformed and mindless action of the UC president.

My daughter-in-law was defiant. "Let them investigate us. There is nothing they can find," she said with confidence. "Erik and I have done nothing to violate university policies." She spoke with a determination and toughness in her voice I had not heard before.

Everyone I spoke with that day told me not to resign without knowing the charges and without being provided evidence of wrongdoing. They advised me to get a lawyer, considering that the threat of a public investigation was real and imminent. It was close to midnight when Viva called to tell me that she had arranged for me to have a meeting the next morning with a lawyer. That was the instant I truly realized that this was not a movie I was watching, not a nightmare that would disappear the moment I woke up and opened my eyes. This was a reality that no one had prepared me for.

The early signs of the Fall.

## CHAPTER FIFTEEN

# THE INVESTIGATION

**April 26, 2016**

I DO NOT REMEMBER MUCH of the rest of the discussion that Monday night. As soon as the last person left, a sense of loneliness took hold of my heart and anxiety overwhelmed me. My head hurt, and the wine wasn't helping. I finally set the glass down next to the empty bottle.

I let my weary feet lead me to the bedroom, knowing I would be too restless to sleep. I found two pills left from a pain prescription for an operation years before. I took them, put my head on the pillow, and a few minutes later I descended into a deep sleep with no feelings, no worries, no dreams. A sense of falling slowly into a dark well came over me, but I was not afraid. I did not feel regret, only absolute peace. The last thought I had was, *Maybe this is what death is: an easy way to run away.*

The tranquility seemed to last but a moment, and soon I was awake. Spyros was already up—his spot on our bed was empty. The old white clock next to my bed showed 2:30 a.m. I checked my phone to see that Viva had already left a text reminding me of the morning meeting with the lawyer.

"Girlfriend, please call me as soon as you wake up," she wrote.

It was the middle of the night, and I was terrified. My lungs felt like they could not take in enough air, and I thought I was suffocating. I jumped out of bed, feeling dizzy, and stumbled my way into the family room to find Spyros sitting on the sofa, his eyes open but focused on nothing. I curled up next to him and started to cry.

"What are we going to do?" I mumbled as my body began to shake. He covered me with a blanket and started softly stroking my back.

"You have lost a lot of weight, and I worry about you," he said calmly. "You need to pull yourself together. You must be strong and move on." There on the couch, with his soothing voice in my ear, I fell back to sleep wondering how I could ever move on.

The true morning finally came. At 8:30 a.m., Spyros and I met Melinda, the lawyer Viva had found, for the first time in her office in Sacramento. We drove there without carrying any documents with us. We had just my story. For over an hour and a half, I went over everything that had happened during the previous week. I described in detail my discussion with the president and my decision to not resign in her office despite the pressure and accusations. I also told Melinda that I had a deadline set by the president to present my resignation in person at 8:00 a.m. that day, which I had already violated.

"The best thing you did," Melinda said in her strong determined voice, "was not resign on the spot. We have democracy in this country and a constitution under which everyone is considered innocent until proven guilty. I will call today and tell them that I represent you and that you are not ready to resign without knowing the charges and without having a further discussion."

At 10:00 a.m., Melinda called the Office the President. After leaving messages on three different phones, someone called back saying that the president was not interested in having a discussion and that the deadline for my unconditional resignation had been extended to 2:30 p.m. that afternoon.

I had lived under a dictatorship in Greece between 1967 and 1974, during which people lost their jobs, were arrested and thrown in jail, were interrogated after being accused of defying laws or for being enemies of the government, and were killed or let go. Even during that dictatorship, the accused were told what the accusations were. When I asked the president what the specific allegations were, she could not even articulate them. She had only assured me that if I pressed for that information, she would provide a letter.

*How is it possible this is happening in the United States in 2016?* I thought.

Melinda told us she would continue working to schedule a meeting with the president and suggested Spyros and I head home. We left Melinda's office in distress, hoping to have an opportunity to speak with the president and, at the very least, have the chance to exit in a way that would protect my family and my professional integrity. We would need at least that much to start the next chapter of our lives.

In the meantime, the news had gone around the world and back. In every case, the leaks were traced back to the Office of the President. Media trucks paraded in front of Mrak and around the chancellor's residence, with reporters knocking on every door they thought I might be hiding behind. My office staff called to tell me I should not go to my office because of the media presence, and because my chief of staff had been directed by the Office of the President to prevent me from going there. He offered to bring to the residence anything I wanted but suggested that I stay away.

The UC Davis communications office was not returning calls, but someone was giving my personal number freely to reporters, according to those who were calling me on my cell phone. A journalist from a TV station in San Francisco called me while I was driving home from Melinda's office and wanted to confirm that the UC president had asked me to resign. When I asked how he had found out, he said from faculty at Berkeley the day before.

"This is my personal cell phone," I told him, trying to control my anger, "and I am so disappointed that you used it."

Later that day, a colleague informed me that he had heard a discussion about the incident on a local NPR station. Around noon, Melinda called to tell me that after a lot of back-and-forth with the Office of the President, she had been able to arrange for a meeting on Thursday morning (almost two days later). She suggested that the two of us negotiate for several things in exchange for my resignation as chancellor—my return to the faculty, and control of the timing and content of the announcement.

In the meantime, the campus was left in a disarray. The provost was nowhere to be found, and my chief of staff would not return my calls, blaming his busy schedule without me in the office. Nobody knew what was going on. The media were reporting that I had been asked to resign, and some stations claimed that I had left for Greece to flee the investigation. Individuals with connections in the capitol shared with Melinda that Janet had called the governor on Monday morning to tell him that she would have an important announcement to make on Monday afternoon. The same individuals mentioned that her vice president for government relations was going to various legislative offices announcing that the UC Davis chancellor had been fired for ethics violations. When they asked what the violations were, he responded that these were personnel issues and he could not discuss them.

"The negative PR campaign from the Office of the President has already started," Melinda told me over the phone. "We need to meet this afternoon and develop some strategies. Janet has committed to a course of action, so you must think about how you want to proceed. Let's meet at 2:00 p.m. in my office." She hung up.

It seemed Janet had told people I had been fired for ethics violations before she had even called me into her office. She had been lying the whole time in her office when she claimed she wanted this quiet, with no publicity, assuming that I would leave the university. I had, however, foiled her plan by not playing along. She assumed that I would resign from the university in fear of public exposure when she had already unleashed her smear campaign.

I spent the afternoon that Tuesday in Melinda's office planning for our discussion with the president. We tried to figure out who would be there and how we would ask for a dignified exit for me from the campus.

We arrived at the residence around 3:30 p.m., exhausted. The place was surrounded by media trucks. We drove into the garage with a host of reporters running after our car. I had to duck forward in my seat to hide from them. They hesitated, but when they got a glimpse of me coming out of the car, they rushed, pushed the garage door back up, and approached me with their mics on.

"You're trespassing," Spyros managed to tell them in an angry voice.

"Fuck you!" one of them yelled. "This is public property. We have the right to come in. This space is not yours. It belongs to the public."

I ran for the door that separated the garage from the kitchen, while Spyros managed to keep them away from me until I was in the house.

It was Wednesday afternoon, and I was in the residence preparing for the meeting at the president's office scheduled for the following day. I had been told that Janet would not be there but would be represented by her chief of staff. That showed either how high she had elevated him within the organization, or how low she now considered this chancellor. Melinda would be there to support me.

You'd think that in times like these the clock would slow down, forcing you to experience the pain of the agony for a lot longer. Yet, that day I felt totally numb, as if I existed in a space where time had no meaning and feelings were nonexistent. Suad came in the morning to bring me a list of almost 450 faculty who had signed a letter to the president in support of me.

"There would have been more," she mentioned, "if the Fire-Katehi students had not hacked the account and corrupted the faculty signatures. We sent the letter to the president and as many newspapers as we could. There is one problem—faculty are beginning to wonder where you are and why the provost and chancellors' offices are silent. Faculty want to know, at least, whether you are here or in Greece."

I nodded. "Should I email people to tell them that I am on campus? I cannot tell them anything about resignation without having a discussion with the president, but I can tell everyone I have not fled."

"Yes," she replied, "just a simple email saying that you are here will help."

Around noon, I sent an email to the leadership team telling them that I was on campus, that I planned to keep my appointments, and that I was completely committed to the university. Many of them thanked me for the update. A few hours later, I received an email from a colleague with a screenshot of an article published in the *Bee*, timestamped at 2:45 a.m. that day. It announced that I had been placed on leave and was being investigated. I called Melinda.

"Have you received a letter?" Her voice was difficult to hear over the noise of her car.

"No. How about you?" I responded.

"No. It seems that the *Bee* got the letter first. Very early this morning."

"I know. I got a message with a screenshot of their article. They should have had the letter since 2:45 a.m." I felt like I was in the middle of a dust storm, disoriented, uncertain, and almost lost.

"Call me when you get the real letter," she said, and hung up with her usual energy.

Around 6:00 p.m., the faculty started coming to the residence for the reception and the dinner meeting that had been scheduled weeks in advance. Among them the elusive provost. He kept away from me, obviously trying to avoid a discussion. We all tried to keep a smile on our lips and talked about the campus as if nothing had happened. It was an act that made me extremely tired.

I felt my phone vibrating in my pocket. It was Melinda. I walked discretely to the hallway and answered.

"Hi, Melinda," I said.

"The president's office faxed me a letter, and they claim to have sent it to you. I think it is what they gave the *Bee* early this morning. Have you received it?"

"No, not yet. What does it say?"

"They said the letter will be released to the media soon. Janet is placing you on leave and plans to investigate you for three improprieties. First, nepotism in relation to your husband, son, and daughter-in-law. Second, for lying to her, and third, for the misuse of student fees. We will have time to discuss these, but for now you need to get back to your meeting as I have more to do on my end. Please call me after your dinner to discuss."

I listened to the ringtone after she hung up with an apathy that surprised me and walked back to the reception area, where I found the provost. He had been sitting on one of the two wooden chairs we had brought from Indianapolis. The chair across from him was empty. I sat in it and looked at him. His face was riddled with anxiety.

"Have you seen Janet's letter?" I asked him plainly.

"Yes," he said. I remained silent. I decided not to ask him how.

"Please help me run the campus," he said after a short silence. "The faculty will hate me."

I looked at him speechless, stood up, and left. I felt exhausted. It was 6:30 p.m.

## May 8, 2016

Days had come and gone, leaving behind a trail of more questions than I could answer. I was not able to keep track of either time or events unless I recorded them carefully. That morning, I found myself at the bar of the Southwest terminal in Los Angeles International Airport trying to catch up on my writing, an effort to make accurate records of events as Melinda had suggested. I was waiting for the flight to take me back to Sacramento. The days had been packed with thoughts, mixed with memories, emotions, and lengthy debates with myself, leaving me very little time for doing productive work.

Three days ago, I felt the need to see my daughter, Helena. I missed her as much as I had missed my mom, and the comfort she provided with her presence, her words, her love. I felt ashamed to ask my daughter to perform a role that belonged to me only, placing so much weight on the her. My desire to see her was so strong that my sense of humiliation did not stop me. I made the reservations on Thursday, and Friday morning I boarded a plane to LA.

A young, impressive, fashionable, beautiful, and smart woman, Helena had always remained the baby in my heart. When I think of her, what comes to mind is the face of an innocent two-year-old with wide blue eyes, a broad smile on her pink lips, and an abundance of energy and capacity for love. When we decorated her bedroom in the first house we ever owned, in Farmington Hills, Michigan, the beauty of the white lace drapes on her bedroom windows, the white-painted bamboo dresser, and her pink, flowery blanket made me cry.

When Helena was young, I prayed I would live long enough to see her blossom, educated, and a bride—desires deeply rooted in my culture. My wish came true twenty-seven years later, when the exuberant two-year-old transformed into a beautiful woman, to be married in a white lace dress in San Francisco in July 2016. I was determined to not let my own misfortune spoil this dream, which was only a few months away.

When I decided to visit her, I knew she was going to be traveling. I wanted to get out of town, and I did not care whether I had to be in her condo by myself for a day. That Friday morning, after an hour-long flight, I unlocked the door of her condo. I put my pajamas on, filled a glass of wine, and made a phone call to a friend. I was so tired and upset.

I felt deeply depressed, despite the two different types of medication I was getting. I acted between two extremes: short periods of intense enthusiasm and elation, followed by distress and desolation interspersed with panic attacks.

When Helena returned, she was nervous about my condition and anxious to see me. We had both missed each other terribly for almost half a year. We had so much to talk about that it was difficult to know where to start. We sat next to each other on her large, beige sofa and wrapped ourselves in a soft, red blanket. Our discussion became stormy very quickly. Being a lawyer, she kept asking me questions with typical intensity. She was asking about events and probabilities, while I was focusing on emotions.

We talked over each other for some time, until we both became upset and decided to slow down and change the discussion. We picked a movie to watch on Netflix, but my mind was away most of the time. She noticed it and made no comment. I caught her multiple times glancing at me with visible concern.

Saturday morning, the two of us went to a spa in Hollywood to do our nails. It was a gift from her and her brother for Mother's Day. I felt so sad. How much did I wish that day were different! Not only did I not know what my future was going to be, but the accusations reverberating through the media had shattered my confidence.

"How can I ever repair my reputation?" I asked while we waited for our nails to dry.

She sighed. "Your obsession with your reputation is forcing you to make wrong decisions," she said with her usual intensity. "Your definition of reputation is old and outdated. It does not fit the present culture of social media, which thrives on drama."

I looked at her, and she smiled at me sadly. "You have to let go and move on," she said.

*How can I do this?* I thought. *Reputation and dignity were the only things my family was left with after a war that took everything they had away— their husbands, their fathers, their brothers, their sons. It took away their hopes, their sense of security, their confidence. What they were left with was a good reputation and a deep sense of honesty.*

"It feels so impossible," I grumbled.

That afternoon we spent our time writing the invitations for her wedding in July. How much I had wished to do this under different circumstances! My heart hurt as I wrote addresses on the envelopes. The quiet, almost ceremonially coordinated motion of our hands working together side by side in the flickering light of a few candles relaxed me completely, and for a short time I felt total peace. I suddenly realized that what I was doing with my daughter right then mattered more to me than anything else. I had wished for and dreamed of that moment in ways I had wished for nothing else—not for my career, not for titles or money, not even what I called my reputation.

Living these moments felt exhilarating, as if I had regained my soul, my sense of being, and purpose in life. We spent almost five hours working on the invitations. Every card carried an interesting story attached to the recipient. Despite the heavy mood, we laughed and gossiped and talked about pretty much everyone.

When the invitations were finally ready to be mailed and our wine glasses were empty, Helena turned to me, her face serious.

"Mom, this job has been like cancer to you and Dad. It has changed both of you. You have not been the same people I knew before you joined UC Davis. Now this is your opportunity to recognize it and get rid of this disease."

Her words made me listen. She was right—this job had been eating away at me for a long time. Like a cancer, it had to be gotten rid of if I wanted to survive. Yet, the thought was always heavy with questions about me and my future.

"If I survive this, I will have to rebuild my life," I said, while she nodded in agreement. "At this point, though, I do not know what that means," I added anxiously.

She rested her hand on mine. "Don't worry; it will all come to you when you are ready." My heart swelled at her words, and I felt a glimmer of hope for the future.

As the month progressed, I started preparing for the investigation. The Office of the President advertised broadly that Janet had contracted two very well-known Californian prosecutors from Orrick, Herrington & Sutcliffe to investigate me on the three accusations she had listed in her letter. In a strange way, I was thankful for the work I had to do in preparation for this investigation. Every day for almost two months I woke up early to begin working and toiled well into the night.

I did extensive research by checking through all my emails. I organized every single folder and catalogued every document I had drafted, authorized, and signed since February 2009 when I was approached for the chancellor position at UC Davis. I collected evidence that overwhelmingly contradicted every single one of the allegations, which grew and evolved as time went by from three to five to seven.

*Thursday, May 12, 2016*

Sheryl Vacca
SENIOR VICE PRESIDENT
CHIEF COMPLIANCE AND AUDIT OFFICER
May 12, 2016

Re: Independent Investigation

Dear Chancellor Katehi:

I am providing this notice to you in my capacity as Director of Investigations with the Office of Ethics, Compliance & Audit Services at UCOP.

Following up on Sheryl Vacca's letter to you dated April 29, 2016, this letter is to provide you with **additional information** about the investigation that has been initiated into allegations regarding your conduct.

In summary, the following allegations will be investigated:

1. *Whether certain actions related to the employment of your son and daughter-in-law may have violated University conflict-of-interest and human resources policies, and policies related to the appropriate use of student fees, and whether you accu-*

rately represented to the President her knowledge about and/or involvement in these issues;

2. Whether certain actions related to the certain social media and strategic communications contracts were appropriate and consistent with policy, including whether you accurately represented your role in, and the scope of, these contracts;

3. Whether certain student fee revenues were misused by the campus specifically by being used for unapproved instructional purposes;

(and in addition)

4. Whether you violated University policies related to travel reimbursement in connection with your board service with John Wiley & Sons, and your trips to Greece;

5. Whether you violated University policies by retaliating or threatening to retaliate against employees for their participation in or cooperation with the Office of the President related to these matters.

. . .

You have a right to consult on this matter with persons of your choice. This may include representation **that you engage, including legal representation.**

The University **has retained Melinda Haag of Orrick, Herrington & Sutcliffe LLP** as an independent fact finder to conduct the investigation, under my general supervision.

On June 19, they added one more charge.

| *Sunday, June 19, 2016*

Sheryl Vacca
SENIOR VICE PRESIDENT
CHIEF COMPLIANCE AND AUDIT OFFICER
June 19, 2016

Re: Independent Investigation

Dear Chancellor Katehi:

On May 12, 2016, I sent you a notification letter regarding an independent investigation related to your employment with the University of California. That letter identified allegations for investigation. . . .

This letter is to update you that, *in addition to the previously identified allegations, the investigator will conduct factfinding* related to the following topic:

*What, if any, representations you made regarding intentions to donate certain compensation received for board service with John Wiley & Sons, and the circumstances and actions related to those representations.*

And on June 22, 2016, one more.

*Wednesday, June 22, 2016*

Sheryl Vacca
SENIOR VICE PRESIDENT
CHIEF COMPLIANCE AND AUDIT OFFICER
June 19, 2016

Re: Independent Investigation

Dear Chancellor Katehi:

... On June 13, 2016, I sent you another letter to update you that the investigator will conduct fact finding <on an additional topic>.

This letter is to update you that, *in addition to the previously identified allegations*, the investigator will conduct fact finding related to the following topic:

6. *Your management, judgment and candor regarding service on boards of directors, including but not limited to DeVry University.*

## July 2, 2016

The new allegations were a desperate attempt to find something that would stick. After engaging the most expensive firm in the state of California and a very visible media campaign, it was imperative that something be found. During these two months, I became convinced that completing the investigation and publishing the findings was the only way forward for me and the campus, despite the pressure from the president and the *Bee*. There was so much said from the beginning that needed to be clarified and corrected: the accusations, the multiple allegations, and the rumors about my family. The whole campus had been thrown into a spin that brought shame and uncertainty by these attacks, so we all deserved an answer. The only way to get it was from the findings of the investigation, even if it was initiated by the accuser.

My days spent collecting evidence gave me confidence. Stacks of paper covered the floor of my small office in the residence where we stayed during the investigation. The documents were grouped by allegation, with numerous attachments and appendices. For each of the allegations, I created a timeline and a historic description of events supported by emails, documented decisions, policies, and letters. I checked every travel expenditure and reimbursement, all vacation days and sick days, and any other cost incurred in the office or in the residence while I was chancellor. I had to demonstrate that not a single penny had been expended to benefit me or my family or anyone else.

Some of our UC Davis travel policies were more restrictive than those of the main university, especially those that involved honoraria or reimbursement from outside agencies. Specifically, as it applied to me, all honoraria and reimbursements were made to the university's name directly, so no one could accuse me of getting reimbursements from places without reporting them.

These months, productive though they might have been, were a sort of purgatory. While trying to prove my innocence, I had to grapple with many questions about myself and my future. I had to remember that the truth was my defense and my savior and that I needed to bring it all into the light.

The day of my deposition came before I knew it. I was ready for it both mentally and emotionally. Gabriel had promised to be with me, observing quietly but not interrupting with commentary unless there was a serious reason. I gave my defense as best I could and felt confident about the results.

In early August, several weeks later, Melinda called to tell me that the report was out and that I should take my time to review it carefully. From a collection of 2,669,217 emails and electronic documents, the investigation team reviewed approximately 67,796 of them and interviewed in-depth over fifty individuals on every aspect of my character and my actions as chancellor. Three of those who offered to speak with the investigators were previous directors of the communications group who had been asked by their supervisors to leave the institution for various well-documented reasons. They all were anxious to avenge.

One of them had publicly humiliated me and yelled at me, as he did with other female employees both in his group and in my office. He was a rude, dismissive, and vindictive individual. They all left with a grievance, and they all found an opportunity to pay me back.

"The deputy campus council was going around with a notepad trying to sign up people to speak with the investigators, as if he was trying to register people to vote," a friend told me, sounding disgusted when we talked a few weeks earlier.

The report was full of low-level gossip and unverifiable rumor by those who did everything they could to expose and hurt me. I never anticipated any better from them, so their statements did not surprise me. Everything else that I considered to be a serious allegation was found false. The report brought me a sense of relief that I had not felt in many years.

I welcomed that moment of truth; the moment when I would be able to do what I had wished since late April and move away from the evil that surrounded me, denounce my heinous relationships, and remove the loathsome mask that had been forced upon me since I had come to campus. It was my time to reject those who meant to harm me and my family, to expose the acts of those who hated me for what I believed, to move out of the darkness I was subjected to, to get out of a space where I did not belong.

In that singular moment I felt free—a feeling that I had almost lost in the darkness that surrounded me. With a sense of relief, I started drafting my resignation letter. This letter was intended as a thank-you note to the numerous faculty, staff, students, alums, and community members who believed in me and supported me during my tenure as chancellor and whose voices were dismissed by the UC regents and president. After I signed the letter, I opened a window to let the sun in. I felt its warmth touching my heart. It was Tuesday, August 9, 2016.

Sunset in Tinos, as seen from our house; an eternal beauty that can only be found in nature—signaling the past, the present, and the future.

## Epilogue

# With Eyes on the Future

**September 2019**

IT IS LATE AFTERNOON ON the veranda of our home in Tinos that clings to the cliffside like a bird's nest facing west over the Aegean. The hot fall day has given way to a calm and warm evening. Not a speck of a cloud hangs in the air. They have all departed, leaving the sun to its serene dominance as it travels toward its night's rest. Spyros and I are sitting in our chairs under the stone arches, watching the sun meet the sea at a place far away, where air and water seem to meld into a fine mist. Every afternoon we wait here to watch this breathtaking exodus of the king, an extravagant passage repeated every day with great solemnity.

It has been three and a half years since I left the chancellor's office at UC Davis and never looked back. Some days the elapsed time feels like an eternity; other days like the flicker of candlelight. Yet, when I look at my reflection in the mirror and search deep inside my soul, I find nothing that reminds me of the person who served as chancellor. She has become a mere memory of a shadow that had been given shape and life by the hatred, contempt, fear, and vengeance of those who later voted to punish her for her wickedness. I am free of the cries of her violated soul, the pain of her burned legs tied to the stake, the suffering from the bleeding stone wounds on her face. I put a dagger in her straw heart and buried her in the cocoon I left behind when I turned into a butterfly.

For the past two years, I have rejoiced with the girl who ran giggling and laughing in the tall wheat fields, the young woman who went to the United States to meet her destiny, the engineer who was amazed at every new glance at the night's clear sky. I met again the mother who gave her heart to her family, the administrator who saw her service as a way to make a difference, the woman who wanted to erase discrimination, the person who was not afraid to speak her mind and accept her faults. I found her again in soul and body, and I embraced her. I rediscovered myself in the space I had left behind years ago and regained my power to dream again of a new world.

For the first time in many years, I feel free to choose what makes me happy and proud of who I am and what I have accomplished. I reached my cloud tower but found how anxious I am to leave it behind. Being there helped me realize how much more there is to see beyond it; a view that had been obscured by my obsession with reaching it. Now, I feel eager to start a new journey, one free of a need to prove myself to me or anyone else—free to make a difference in education and unbound by a destination. I feel empowered to enjoy the pleasures that life has given me, including two wonderful children and their spouses, three smart and beautiful granddaughters, a new university campus to thrive in, stimulating research projects, and the glorious sunsets in the waters of the Aegean. I hear Spyros's voice next to me: "It's time." We are sitting in our veranda facing west, looking at the sun as it dives slowly into the water and its deep red color turns into an explosion of gold, magenta, and purple—leaving behind a dazzling, flickering path in the water. For a moment, every sound stops, every animal looks up, and every bird grabs a branch to watch and pay their respects to this violent fire that has sustained life on Earth for an eternity, running the same path from east to west—day after day, without a miss. I am surprised to realize that I do not feel saddened by the end of a glorious day but hopeful and excited for the beginning of the next one. My heart feels light as the brilliant red of the sunset fills the sky. This daily ritual has amazed thousands of generations and reminds me how small and, at the same time, how important we are. We are a spectacle of God's design, as Gabriel keeps reminding me in her warm voice, which rings softly in my head. "Yes, God's design," I repeat in agreement, feeling Spyros's warm hand grip mine.

# ACKNOWLEDGMENTS

I started writing parts of this book almost six and a half years ago while trying to record details about meetings, events, discussions, and decisions. It was a tedious and painful effort I had to go through trying to prove my innocence against politically motivated attacks by a group that had turned into a mob. This effort triggered an outflow of deeply embedded memories and feelings that overwhelmed me and almost crushed me. It opened wounds I had pretended never existed. It also unleashed happy memories hidden under my dusty climb on my ambitious career path. Writing this book connected me with my past in a way that liberated me from my ego and made me the person I always was.

My life blessed me with two people who loved me unconditionally and never doubted me or saw me as something I was not: my mother and husband. They did not try to make me the person they imagined but gave me the freedom to become myself. They empowered me to make decisions, fail, succeed, and learn. They encouraged me to feel unique and stay humble. They critiqued my actions without criticizing me and made me stay strong even when, internally, I was collapsing. They have been the reason for whom I am, and for this, I love them eternally. My mother's memory and my husband gave me the strength to survive and thrive.

I would not have published this book if it were not for my loving children, their wonderful spouses, and my beautiful grandchildren, to whom I hope our family story gives a sense of pride and resolve. This book expresses my love for my cousins, who have loved and supported me since I was born. I am indebted to my dear friend and colleague, Suad Joseph, who guided my writing with honesty and care. I am thankful to my many friends and colleagues, who supported and critiqued me with honesty and respect, and to my students, who have made me proud of their achievements. I sincerely thank the hundreds of faculty and staff at UC Davis who publicly thanked me for my services when I resigned from the chancellor's position. Last but not least, I thank my publisher, Naren Aryal, and the staff of Amplify Publishing and Mascot Books for their support during the past six years of this effort.